THE THEATRE OF HAROLD PINTER

Mark Taylor-Batty

Series Editors: Patrick Lonergan and Erin Hurley

B L O O M S B U R Y

LONDON • NEW DELHI • NEW YORK • SYDNEY

Bloomsbury Methuen Drama
An imprint of Bloomsbury Publishing Plc

50 Bedford Square	1385 Broadway
London	New York
WC1B 3DP	NY 10018
UK	USA

www.bloomsbury.com

Bloomsbury is a registered trademark of Bloomsbury Publishing Plc

First published 2014

© Mark Taylor-Batty, 2014

British Library Cataloguing-in-Publication Data
A catalogue record for this book is available from the British Library.

ISBN: HB: 978-1-4081-7531-6
PB: 978-1-4081-7530-9
ePDF: 978-1-4081-7533-0
ePub: 978-1-4081-7532-3

Library of Congress Cataloging-in-Publication Data
A catalog record for this book is available from the Library of Congress.

Typeset by Fakenham Prepress Solutions, Fakenham, Norfolk NR21 8NN
Printed and bound in Great Britain

For Anna, Gabriel and Samuel

CONTENTS

Contents

ACKNOWLEDGEMENTS

I am grateful to those who have provided supportive contexts for me to pursue my study of and transmit my passion for Pinter's works in recent years: Mareia Aragay, Francis Gillen, Tali Itzhaki, Tomaž Onič, Craig N. Owens, Avraham Oz, Sandra Paternostro, Enric Monforte Rabascall, Linda Renton and, importantly, Mark Dudgeon at Bloomsbury Methuen Drama. My work with Basil Chiasson and James Hudson kept an intellectual engagement with this body of work alive over particularly difficult periods. Basil contributes a chapter to the final section of this book, and I'm grateful to him and my other contributors – Harry Burton, Ann C. Hall and Chris Megson – for adding depth to this work. Thanks go to Ewan Jeffrey for his excavation of family structures in Pinter's writing; the intellectual genesis of the chapter on family in this volume is owed to him. I also want to acknowledge all the students on my 'Theatricalities' module over the years, who continue to shine fresh lights into the corners of these dramas. I am particularly grateful to Patrick Lonergan, whose generous and helpful comments on the draft manuscript were invaluable. Many thanks to all the Facebook friends who responded online to my general queries over cultural and political history, especially Sara Allkins, Clementina Angelina, Alex Chisholm, Paul Kleiman, Caitrin O'Seaghdha and David Whitaker. I remain grateful for the trust that Harold Pinter demonstrated, and for the support of Antonia Fraser. Thanks especially go to Juliette Taylor-Batty, for her comments on drafts, and for all her strength and care.

Quotations from the work of Harold Pinter are reproduced with the kind permission of Faber and Faber and Grove Press.

INTRODUCTION

In announcing the recipient of the 2005 Nobel Prize for Literature on 13 October of that year, Horace Engdahl, the Permanent Secretary of the Swedish Academy, came through a gilded white door to meet the gathered media and announced first in Swedish, then in English, French and German:

> The Nobel Prize in Literature for 2005 is awarded to the English writer Harold Pinter, who in his plays uncovers the precipice under everyday prattle and forces entry into oppression's closed rooms.[1]

This brief justification for giving the award to Pinter that year focussed on his dramatic writing, and made reference to his reputation for artistic representation of everyday casual language, the threat of some hollow, ominous space that such language obscures or avoids,[2] his frequent use of enclosed spaces, and his foregrounding of repressive interpersonal or state behaviours. This book will examine some of those precipices, that prattle and oppression, and will consider other important aspects of Pinter's work, including his aesthetic interest in the fragility of memory, the concerns over trust and betrayal, male companionship, the complications in friendships and sexual relationships, representations of family, and the abuse of language to territorial, emotional or political ends. As such, one of the purposes of a volume such as this is to clarify what is distinctive or important about the writing style of the author whose work it is surveying and offer some appreciation of the contours of the legacy he leaves behind. In the case of Harold Pinter, we are examining an author who has been perceived to have influenced the art of the playwright itself. David Hare admired his 'alarming range', adding that he 'can play great, big major chords made up only of anger, indignation and contempt'.[3] Edward Albee articulated his admiration for Pinter's 'active aggression against the status quo' and lauded his 'extraordinary ear', describing him as 'a composer'.[4] David Mamet noted that, as a young man, Pinter was his hero and 'really was responsible to a large extent for me starting to write'.[5] Patrick Marber recalls being mesmerised by the 1980 National Theatre production of *The Caretaker* and spoke of how it 'was one of the things that inspired me to work in the theatre'.[6] Ariel Dorfman pointed out how he 'showed me how dramatic art can be lyrical without versifying, can be poetic merely by delving into the buried rhythms of everyday speech'.[7] Sarah Kane cited Pinter, alongside Howard Barker and Edward Bond, as writers she was particularly keen to learn from,[8] and Barker and Bond had, in their turn, acknowledged the importance of the older writer, while maintaining their own distinctive approaches. Even Arthur Miller, Pinter's senior, acknowledged that he 'could not have been exposed to Harold Pinter's work and not learned anything from it'.[9] Pinter's achievements as a writer are integral to any appreciation of late twentieth-century British theatre.

Harold Pinter was born in October 1930 in Hackney, the much-loved only son of Jack and Frances Pinter. His home on Thistlethwaite Road narrowly escaped the bombs of the London Blitz ten years later, and he was evacuated to Cornwall, then to Reading and, briefly, to Yorkshire, where his life-long and well-known passion for cricket was first ignited. In the aftermath of the war, a Labour government sought to establish new, egalitarian ideals for the nation's welfare, health and education and, for example, the 1944 Education Act brought new opportunities to a whole generation of children, and eased access to Grammar Schools for young working-class scholars. Pinter's cohort benefited from these new opportunities and, alongside a number of his local friends, he gained a high-school education at the Hackney Downs Grammar School.

As a teenager, he developed a perhaps offbeat passion for modernist literature and European cinema, wrote poetry with enthusiasm, and was one of a close community of male friends frequenting the Hackney Boys' Club who shared their reading discoveries and enthusiasms with auto-didactic fervour. At a debating society in his sixth-form years, Pinter voted in favour of a motion that declared 'Film is more promising as an art form than theatre', and once held forth publicly on the subject of 'Realism and Post-Realism in the French Cinema'.[10] In the Hackney Public Library, he discovered the works of Ernest Hemingway, James Joyce, D. H. Lawrence, Virginia Woolf, W. B. Yeats and foreign literature such as Fyodor Dostoevsky's novels or the verse of *poète maudit* Arthur Rimbaud. In Pinter's 1973 short drama *Monologue*, a man reminisces about times spent with an old pal with whom he has lost contact. Locating their shared past in Hackney (he mentions the Balls Pond Road), he talks as if confronting or challenging his friend, reminding him: 'who got you going on Tristan Tzara, Breton, Giacometti and all that lot? Not to mention Louis-Ferdinand Céline, now out of favour. And John Dos',[11] evoking the rich cultural diet of Pinter's youth. In his novel *The Dwarfs* (1990), Pinter writes scenes in which three young men engage in intellectual discussions about the values and qualities of music and literature, and these debates over Bach, Shakespeare or the function of art are likely recreations of real conversations between Pinter and his teenage friends, Michael Goldstein and Ron Percival. Pinter's early appetite for literature went as far as a form of fandom; in 1946 he wrote an enthused essay on James Joyce's *Ulysses* that he saw published in the school magazine; over the winter of 1949 to 1950 he wrote letters to Henry Miller, presuming to discuss D. H. Lawrence with him, and received encouraging replies containing copies of the writer's publications. He later discovered Samuel Beckett in the form of a fragment of the novel *Watt*, published in *Poetry Ireland* in 1952, and subsequently stole a Beckett novel (*Murphy*) from a library on the spurious but logical justification that the stamp inside the front cover indicated that nobody had taken it out for over a decade. He was so taken with Beckett's writing that in 1955 he wrote a letter to Mick Goldstein defending *Waiting for Godot* without ever having read the text or seen a performance of it: 'is it Beckett's business to answer questions he himself poses?'[12] he puts to Goldstein, who clearly had not been impressed. In that bold reply we see the germ of an artistic stance yet to express itself creatively.

At school, Pinter had been encouraged in his extra-curricular literary interests by an inspirational and influential schoolmaster, Joe Brearley, whom Michael Billington describes as Pinter's 'counsellor, intellectual mentor and lifelong friend'.[13] Brearley had fostered an appreciation of Renaissance drama in his students, taking them to see productions of Shakespeare and Webster plays, and even initiated them into the craft of acting: under his tutelage, Pinter played the leads in school productions of *Macbeth* in 1947 and *Romeo and Juliet* in 1948. The teenage Pinter found the rich language of the Jacobean plays that Brearley exposed him to truly intoxicating, and would enjoy speaking Webster's concise verse on long walks he would share with his schoolmaster from Clapton Pond to Finsbury Park.[14] This passion for declaimed, styled language was perhaps one inspiration for seeking employment as an actor, and Pinter went to study briefly at RADA in 1948. With other students there, he performed T. S. Eliot's *The Rock* in London churches. He left after two terms, impatient with what he perceived to be the atrophied methods and attitudes of that establishment and some of the people he met in its student body, but he was to return to actor training at the Central School of Speech and Drama in 1951 after having secured some voice work on BBC radio. He auditioned for Anew McMaster's repertory troupe later that year and got a job on their tour of Ireland. He would later join Donald Wolfit's repertory company, and played mostly Shakespearean roles for the best part of three years. He would witness some memorable examples of traditional stagecraft from those two classical actors, whose working methods had their genesis in the actor-manager systems of the mid-nineteenth century. Speaking of Sir Donald Wolfit, Pinter recalled his performance as Oedipus in a production of *Oedipus at Colonus* (at the King's Theatre, Hammersmith, in 1953) in which the actor demonstrated impeccable timing and manipulation of audience expectation:

> he stood with his back to the audience with a cloak around him and there came a moment when the man downstage

finished his speech and we all knew, the play demanded it, the audience knew, that Wolfit or Oedipus was going to speak, was going to turn and speak. He held the moment until one's stomach was truly trembling and the cloak came round; a tremendous swish that no one else has been able to achieve I think. And the savagery and power that emerged from such a moment was extraordinary.[15]

Writing about Anew McMaster in 1968, he similarly recalled 'the rare tension and release within him, the arrest, the swoop, the savagery, the majesty and repose'.[16] In both instances, Pinter seems to have relished and appreciated the meticulous engagement of the audience in the grip of drama, and the crucial value of image, positioning and the pregnant pause.

As a jobbing actor, having adopted the alias David Baron, Pinter was exposed to an intense period of learning script after script, performing night after night, rehearsing during the days, and moving from town to town. In 1954 he played leading and supporting roles in Whitby and Huddersfield, and toured as an assistant stage manager in a play in which his chief task was to manipulate the mouth of a talking stage horse. He spent much of 1955 in Colchester rep in lead male roles, or was cast as villainous types, and in 1956 he acted lead and support roles in thirty plays for the Barry O'Brian Company in Bournemouth and Philip Barrett's New Malvern Company in Torquay. He had met his first wife, Vivien Merchant, during his stint with the Donald Wolfit company and they played opposite one another as Rochester and Jayne Eyre in March 1956. They married that September. Pinter continued the season in Torquay into 1957, before touring in a production of the farce *Doctor in the House*. He then got work first at the Alexandra Theatre in Birmingham before returning to London to work for Fred Tripp's Company at the Intimate Theatre in Palmers Green in the winter months bridging 1957 and 1958. Vivien gave birth to their only child, Daniel, in January 1958. Pinter would continue to act in rep until 1959 and overall, during the 1950s, he acted in just short of a hundred plays. He noted of his early relationship with the stage that 'I saw very few plays, in fact, before I was twenty. Then I acted in too many'.[17] Most of the plays he acted in, other than the rich seam of Shakespeare with Wolfit and McMaster, were the typical fare of light comedies, farces and thrillers that were the bread and butter of the post-war repertory theatre: he acted in seven Agatha Christie plays, three by Noel Coward, two by J. B. Priestley and one each by Terrence Rattigan and Graham Greene.

Pinter's early dramatic writing might be considered in the context of the kind of theatre, cinema and literature he was exposed to as a young man and as a jobbing actor in repertory theatre. Like any artist, he absorbed the influence of work he admired, and reacted against forms of expression that were not to his taste or which he actively derided. As his early work as a repertoire actor took him on the road, he snatched moments to write in dressing rooms and boarding houses. His only novel, *The Dwarfs*, was composed little by little between 1952 and 1956. It was to be re-imagined and re-worked by him as a radio play in 1960, a stage play in 1963 and finally edited and published in 1990. A full television (later staged) adaptation by Kerry Lee Crabbe was also published in 2003, forming something of a closing frame around his career as a dramatist with material from its very beginning. That early novel contains in developed or germ form many of the themes that were later to underpin Pinter's plays: the sparring between friends or rivals, the risk of betrayal through failure properly to know oneself and one another, the miscommunication of needs between men and women, and the nature of emotional territory and its relationship with the real spaces, rooms, in which it is staked out.

In early 1957, responding to a request from his Hackney chum Henry Woolf for a play that Woolf might direct at the University of Bristol, where he was studying for an MA, Pinter wrote his first dramatic text, *The Room*, the opening image of which was inspired by Pinter having met and witnessed Quentin Crisp serve food to a silent male partner. It was first performed in a converted shed on the University campus in May that year. Over the spring and summer, while on tour in a farce, Pinter wrote *The Birthday Party* (the circumstances of which were inspired by meeting an indolent gentleman staying in lodgings in Eastbourne in the summer of 1954) and later *The Dumb Waiter* (placed in Birmingham, where Pinter worked between July and October in the year of its composition). Set in naturalistic spaces, rooms with their fourth wall removed, and featuring recognisable characters, these first plays from Pinter's pen were, on the surface, both traditional in terms of their scenic realism and contemporary in their display of working-class people and environments. Such characters in such environments were very much characteristic of the new drama that was finding favour on the London stage of the late 1950s in the aftermath of the success of John Osborne's *Look Back in Anger* at the Royal Court Theatre in 1956, during what has often been characterised as a period of renewal and radicalisation for British theatre. Pinter quickly came to be considered as both at odds with his writing peers of the time and also typical of that period of new writing, most particularly for the manner in which his plays were constructed from the seemingly realistic dialogue of the man and woman on the street: Ronald Searle captured the playwright in a cartoon, published in *Punch*, as a dog jotting down overheard conversations.[18]

The Birthday Party was taken on by the young theatre producer Michael Codron in 1958 and became Pinter's first professional production of any of his plays, staged at the Lyric Opera House, Hammersmith, after a debut at the Arts theatre in Cambridge in April. The play was to suffer debilitating put-downs from the London critics, which effectively resulted in the production being dropped by the theatre's management after only a week of performances before dwindling audiences. Pinter's career as a playwright was by no means determined at this stage, and he needed to continue his work as a jobbing actor well into the following year. He was nevertheless able to pursue his writing with some support from the BBC Third Programme, which commissioned the radio plays *A Slight Ache* and *A Night Out* for broadcast in 1958 and 1960 respectively. He also saw a collection of his sketches performed in 1959 in two reviews by comic actors including Kenneth Williams, Peter Cook, Sheila Hancock and Beryl Reid. In this way, Pinter was able to maintain a modest profile until his fortunes were to change radically and quickly with the success of *The Caretaker* in 1960, which was to run for over a year. When Methuen took the bold step of deciding to publish contemporary plays in 1959, Pinter's work appeared in their second catalogue, and he saw two plays published in 1960.

He produced a string of acclaimed TV dramas in the early 1960s which contributed to his becoming something of a household name, and his reputation was quite firmly consolidated with *The Homecoming* in 1965 and *Old Times* in 1971, both directed by Peter Hall and premièred by the Royal Shakespeare Company. In the 1970s he became an associate director of the National Theatre and his integration into the British theatrical establishment was thereby complete, though his reputation as a writer of significance was still in the process of being evaluated: in 1973, Simon Trussler stated that he was 'not quite so confident that Pinter's work will survive to "classic" status as Osborne's or Arden's'[19] and by the 1980s Martin Esslin argued that 'he has now undoubtedly attained the status of a contemporary "classic"'.[20] On the back of this confident public persona, Pinter in the 1980s and 1990s adopted the role of political commentator while turning to more overt political situations in his plays *One for the Road*, *Mountain Language* and *Party Time*. His later plays – *Moonlight*, *Ashes to Ashes* and *Celebration* – manifested characteristics of much of his earlier writing while merging the kinds of theatricality that distinctly different previous works had achieved. *Ashes to Ashes*, for example, is structured around a husband and wife conversation in a domestic environment that was reminiscent of much of his 1960s writing but manages to articulate a suffocating shadow of the Holocaust and a desperate attempt to recognise and negotiate personal responsibility in the face of atrocity. His international reach as an artist had been consolidated and built upon by his impact as a writer of political plays and his outspokenness on political issues so that, for example, in post-dictatorship Spain, Portugal or Greece, across South America or in difficult political environments such as Belarus, he came to represent an ideal of art speaking to political situations and against repression. Whereas in Germany and in France, for example, his name was forever allied in arts journalism to that of Beckett, elsewhere he was more likely to be named as synonymous with the pursuit of liberty, democracy and humanism.

Harold Pinter died on 24 December 2008, succumbing to cancer at the age of 78. He left a legacy of twenty-nine dramatic works, numerous sketches, twenty-two screenplays and a significant body of poetry and prose writings, in addition to his one novel. In response to his death, the Broadway theatres in New York dimmed their lights the day before his funeral. The theatres of the Ambassador Group in London did the same the following week and one among them, The Comedy Theatre, changed its century-old name to The Harold Pinter Theatre in 2011. One of the ambitions of this book is to participate in the ongoing appraisal of the legacy of a writer who made such a remarkable impact on world drama.

What set Pinter's very first plays apart from much of the drama that preceded and surrounded them, as shall be explored in the first chapter of this book, is the manner in which they exploited and subverted established theatrical discourses in their treatment of audiences. They represent the experiments of a talented young writer, composing drama at first with no reason to believe that his work could be guaranteed professional performance, capturing the rigid discipline of the well-made plays that he was saturated in as an actor, but applying a modernist perspective from his wide reading, a perspective that would not, or could not, permit or acknowledge a consistent, reliable and commonly experienced world. Latching onto this aspect of Pinter's work, the critic and producer Martin Esslin equated the approach with the artistic visions of contemporary European writers of existentialist dramas and saw 'Pinter's characters in the process of their essential adjustment to the world'.[21] For better or for worse, Pinter was to be thereafter considered a key practitioner of Esslin's artificial category, the 'Theatre of the Absurd', and that label has been attached to his name or work whenever such shorthand categorisations might prove unthinkingly convenient. The contrasts and comparisons that Esslin draws in his important and perennially successful volume are enlightening, but the distinctiveness of Pinter's voice does not escape from the survey. If we consider Ionesco's contemporary plays such as *The Bald Prima*

Donna (1948), *The Lesson* (1950), *Jack (or Obedience)* (1950) and *The Chairs* (1952), these were all set in recognisable middle-class homes, but characters were sketched figures who behaved impulsively or in grotesque manners and seemed always at the mercy of a cliché-ridden language. With none of Pinter's rooted realism, theirs is a world where logic is awry (a pair of seeming strangers with the same surname must trace their steps to deduce that, by living in the same home and sleeping in the same bed, they must be married) and where conventional norms are turned upside-down (women with three noses are more attractive than those with only two). Language is the tragic victim of these plays, and the human condition is displayed as being at the mercy of its ineffectual fragility. Ionesco's critique is one also of the lazy misuse of language, of its inefficiency as a vehicle of communication, and while some of this latter treatment is evident in Pinter's writing, his focus was more keenly on how articulacy and the use of language were allied to the major and minor struggles for controlling authority within given situations.

Esslin later published a monograph on Pinter entitled *The Peopled Wound* in which he went some way to correct and contextualise the earlier placement of the writer in his constructed category of the absurd,[22] but persisted in seeing a predominantly 'lyrical vision which builds up a communication of an individual's otherwise inaccessible and inexpressible experience of living'.[23] Other early critics of Pinter's writing emphasised the inaccessible aspects of his work, and his name became something of a by-word for unexplained mysteries in the theatre. The tools of critical analysis were employed to unravel or chart these mysteries, and, for example, Lois Gordon applied Freudian analysis in 1969 and Katherine Burkman pursued the metaphors and structures of myth detected in Pinter's plays. Austin Quigley in 1975 characterised this critical demystification programme as the 'Pinter Problem' and proposed (perhaps ungenerously) that any obscurity in the author's work was of the critics' making, and that understanding might not be found in the literary unpacking of the semantics of Pinter's language. He argued that the generation of meaning in and by Pinter's dramas might be approached by appreciating how that language is wielded to create impact, between characters and across the stage threshold, into the audience. Guido Almansi and Simon Henderson took this further, promoting critical methods for considering the 'strategic use of language' in the plays under scrutiny.[24] This focus in turn attracted varied critical apparatus such as discourse analysis and theories of performance and reception, and of gender and identity.[25] Marc Silverstein expanded the approach to 'language' in 1993 to encompass all behaviour and expression that might be 'read' in Pinter's works. He developed a foundational reading of the oeuvre that positions Pinter's political expression within the confrontation of a character's presentation of self and the language of their circumstances that dictate their ability to claim or sustain that state of identity. Charles Grimes later furnished something of a definitive survey of the author's politics in 2005, the year of Pinter's award of the Nobel Prize for Literature.

My own approach in this book is to consider Pinter's plays as imagined in their theatrical contexts, to understand them as dramatic expression that is only alive, meaningful and meaning-generating in the moment of performance. This necessitates a sustained critical conceit, as clearly any two performances (let alone any two productions) of any one play will be very different, and to try to imagine a 'faithful' performance is, in itself, to open up a theoretical can of worms about the authority of the text and its relationship with its writer. Of course, these plays exist as unchanging literary artefacts within their Faber bindings, and literary readings are therefore easier to pin down through close readings and analyses of their textualities. These are seductive in that they offer the critic the pleasure of a forensic chase, and present themselves as 'evidence' of sorts. In maintaining a performance perspective in the pages that follow, though, a healthy balance is attempted between an appreciation of, for example, the kinds of intertextual material that Pinter triggers and of how such material might operate within the cumulative set of responses we make in an audience over the course of an evening in a darkened room. Those responses are subject to change once we leave that room, and can be guided, stifled or embellished by further such trips to the theatre, by returning to the printed text, or by opening the covers of books such as this. They are, of course, dictated by what we take into that room with us and our understandings are inevitably inflected by a set of cultural assumptions and contexts that are often barely definable themselves. Starting from such unsteady intellectual premises, then, this book aims to trace a set of paths that I detect through Pinter's work. By considering the fascination with the bond between male friends that permeates his work, and the implications this has for male/female relationships, I examine how Pinter shifts his scrutiny from focussing on the pressures that such human interaction incurs (and their value for comedy), to the risk of damage that jealousy, lack of trust and betrayal bring to potential or healthy relationships. As the structures of family enter his work to foreground the fault-lines caused by such behaviours, the theme of betrayal (of the self and of one another) becomes more pronounced, before becoming more explicit in the form of moral corruption in his political works. The incursions made by strangers into domestic environments in his early plays, and the threat to secure or indolent stability that these represent, are the chief engines of those dramas, and I intend to chart how that territorial intrusion transforms through Pinter's work into more sophisticated forms of infringement of comfortable discourses (gendered expectations, for example) and into asserted ownership of narratives of identity and of the shared past. In approaching these thematic traits, a consideration of how Pinter wields and constructs dramatic form as part of his mode of expression will be supported by some of his work as director and his writing for media other than the stage, including his substantial body of work as a screenwriter.

This volume is rounded off with contributions from four people who have different investments in Pinter's writing. Harry Burton first stepped on stage in a Pinter play in 1991, as Jimmy in *Party Time*, directed by the author himself. He offers a view on Pinter's writing from the perspective of someone who has confronted that material numerous times in rehearsal rooms, and trodden it across the boards in various theatres. Chris Megson is a London-based theatre academic and actor who, in his chapter, considers issues of identity construction in Pinter's 1970s plays, offering an approach to understanding these least political of plays that positions them against the emerging identity politics of that era. Based at the Ohio Dominican University, Ann C. Hall is presently the President of the international Harold Pinter Society. She offers a set of reflections on how Pinter mobilises the language of misogyny in his three political plays. Finally, the Canadian scholar Basil Chiasson looks back over Pinter's political expression and considers how it broadcasts the traces of a neo-liberal agenda that came to dominate Western political structures and expression over the period of Pinter's committed writing. These contributions offer depth and density to this book in concentrating on a handful of Pinter plays, and the experiences that they might engender for us on stage.

CHAPTER 1
INVASIONS AND OPPRESSIONS

Awkward Investments in Enclosed Spaces
The Room, The Birthday Party, The Dumb Waiter,
The Hothouse

Engaging with any work of art, we first subconsciously gather information about the frame through which we might 'read' that art before digesting it. Opening a novel, for example, we might instantaneously recognise the indicators of genre that guide our appreciation and expectations of how the narrative will be told and how it might unfold. Once that frame has been recognised, the aesthetic experience falls easily into place. All cultural objects engage us in these ways, and many straightforwardly fulfil the expectations that have been ascribed to them culturally: a painted portrait tends to look like and even flatter its subject; a fairy story might playfully transgress 'safe' narrative subjects and end with a morally sound outcome; a romantic comedy film will end with the overcoming of some difficulty that has separated two people, and their happy union is celebrated in a communal scene. Part of our enjoyment of such cultural objects can often be precisely because they follow the 'rules' set for them, but we also enjoy the variations on a generic theme that the artists involved have constructed. Such traditional cultural discourses, however, might be considered to imply a stable, recognisable and even reliable world, and such an implication does not chime always with all artistic temperaments. What we call 'realism' in these contexts might not be altogether 'realistic': our world is not reliable, not always stable, and certainly not so predictable.

Theatrical discourses tend to declare themselves early. We begin to form a sense of our frame for appreciating the play from the poster that advertises it and get further information from any programme we buy and any arrangement of the stage as we enter the auditorium, if it is not concealed behind a curtain. That curtain itself reveals a certain set of traditions and expectations of course, and such a performance will begin with a 'reveal' that suggests a world deliberately and craft-fully separated from our own. Once a performance begins, we usually very quickly settle on an understanding of the discourses that are activated for us to 'read' what follows: realism or figurative playing and design, contemporary or historic setting, comedy or tragedy. When we have a sense of this semantic frame, we begin to enjoy first by investing in key characters: 'meaning' in the theatre is constructed through a chain of cumulative and inter-related emotional connections made across the divide between audience and characters. Traditional drama, throughout the centuries, has functioned by promoting audience investment in key characters, and using early scenes to establish those investments. Such investment is the chief point of contact between the play and its audience; it provides a context for understanding what is being presented, what is significant or trivial within the drama, and for creating expectations of how the difficulties that are established in the play might be resolved. Most traditional plays soon establish some conflict that is to be resolved, and we often invest in specific characters who might clarify the background to that conflict through expositionary dialogue. The investment is a quickly negotiated attachment that we make: 'this person will explain the background here', 'this person is morally upstanding, I care what happens to her'. There might be a lead character who seems emotionally driven to take a specific course of action which involves great personal risk, and we invest our hope in them that the outcome will be a positive one, and our pity is invoked when things do not go their way. There might be a secondary 'reasonable' character who tries to persuade the first to take or avoid certain actions, and we invest in that character a hope they may be able to influence the first with their sensible advice, and therefore feel a frustration if that does not succeed.

In his early plays, and frequently throughout his playwriting career, Pinter seemed intent on re-writing this experience of investment, and manipulating the Aristotelian contract of cathartic reward via pity and fear in the process. If you invest hope that any one character in a Pinter play will clarify his or her objectives, or give you a clear understanding of their context or history, then your investment will be quickly frustrated. If you invest in a hope that a reason why conflict has arisen between two individuals will be clearly expressed in their dialogue, then that investment will be soon undermined. When one character begins to demand a clarification from another as to why they are behaving a certain way, you might desire that this character will succeed in bringing forth a straightforward response that will clarify which way the drama might proceed, but you will soon be disappointed. Pinter's plays simply do not function in these ways, and were even constructed deliberately to frustrate those very usual expectations of how a piece of theatre might declare its frame for being read. In this way, the audience's near-instinctive pursuit of 'meaning', of what a play is 'about', is immediately set out of kilter – the expected frame for 'reading' the material is deliberately incomplete. In effect, Pinter often provides the drama without a reliable key by which to read it. Recalling the first ever performance of a Pinter play, *The Room*, in May 1957, its director Henry Woolf described how, confronted with this deliberately dislocated frame 'the audience woke up from its polite cultural stupor and burst into unexpected life, laughing, listening, taking part in the story unfolding onstage'.[1] Pinter himself tangentially addressed the bewildering experience his plays might engender in a speech made to the National Student Drama Festival in 1962:

> A character on the stage who can present no convincing argument or information as to his past experience, his present behaviour or his aspirations, nor give a comprehensive analysis of his motives is as legitimate and as worthy of attention as one who, alarmingly, can do all these things. The more acute the experience the less articulate its expression.[2]

The 'alarmingly' here is a satirical nod towards conventional stage realism, where such altogether unrealistic human behaviour is expected of traditional characters. The last sentence, though, is most telling as it hints at an artistic credo, one that recognises a complex relationship between human experience and the artistic expression, the communication of that experience.

When Pinter wrote *The Room* in early 1957, he was aware that he was writing for the actors and audience within a university arts faculty; the first (and then only) department of drama in the country at the University of Bristol. He may have felt that this context would have been tolerant of a more experimental mode of writing than he might then have conceived of providing for a more commercial context. He also knew he was writing a play to be delivered into the hands of a friend with whom he had shared a passion for certain modernist authors, and so someone who would be sympathetic to the ambition of the non-realist tone of the piece. This was a comfortable set of circumstances for a first attempt at writing drama; he was provided with a context within which his work would be rehearsed, conceived and performed and which had space for experiment and failure with no other consequences than, at worst, that he might simply regard the venture as work in progress. With *The Room*, he could expand into a dramatic space the ideas he had pursued in his youthful prose and poetry, most notably the metaphoric possibilities of a symbiosis between a person and the environment they inhabit and the consequent potency of invasion into that environment from outside. *Kullus* (written in 1949 and first published in 1968) is structured around the premise of one character assuming control of another's room, and this concept was later expanded, adapted and developed in other works such as *The Examination* (1955, published 1959), *The Compartment* (unpublished, 1963) and *The Basement* (1967). The notion of one character entering a seemingly stable scenario and disturbing or upturning the familial or social arrange-ments he or she finds there is to become a staple element of what became described as the 'pinteresque' in critical reviews.

In *The Room*, Pinter takes the domestic chamber of the title and makes it a precarious location. He does this by taking two routes: one operating on his characters, as any playwright might, and another operating on his audience, which was altogether less usual in the 1950s. Whereas a dramatic tension is most often achieved by having the audience made aware of crucial details before the characters on stage discover them, Pinter constructed his first drama with his audience kept at an equal level of ignorance as his key protagonist, Rose, a woman of sixty. The play opens with her serving bacon and eggs to a silent man, Bert, in a basic bedsitting room. This room contains a bed, a stove, a rocking chair and a table and chairs. We note a humble household environment and assume a domestic relationship, a husband and wife. The relationship is presented in an almost stereotypical, comedic frame: a wife wittering away inanely around her husband, while he remains stoically silent, reading a simple magazine and eating his uncomplicated evening meal. We learn from Rose's seemingly inconsequential chatter that Bert is planning to go out, that it is a bitter winter day outside and that she has a seemingly nosey concern for whoever has moved into the basement flat below. Bert's silence and Rose's nattering allow an audience to settle into what seems to be a domestic comedy or light drama, and we would tune our early investment into the character of Rose. That investment might be expected to develop into a sympathy and care for her, but also – given the comic potential of the housewife stereotype in mid-twentieth-century popular comedy genres – a possibility that she is being set up for an entertaining fall.

A knock at the door reveals Mr Kidd who, claiming to be checking on the pipes and asking after the furniture, comes across straightforwardly as the landlord of the building. Our usual tuning to theatrical discourse might cause us to expect him to offer something that would move the plot forward, indicate some crisis or demand upon Rose and Bert, but instead he comes and goes, providing only an opportunity for a comic dialogue that establishes his ownership of the house, but in terms that render the building in indefinable terms. He claims not to know how many floors it has, for example, and makes statements that subtly undermine Rose's claim to the room as a stable site of home. He recalls the rocking chair, which she indicates she brought with her on moving in, but does not remember the armchair in which he sits, though Rose tells him it was there when she arrived. By telling us that the room used to be his bedroom, and stating he can 'take his pick' of any room now, he establishes for us a sense of the potentially temporary nature of Rose's tenancy. Expecting information from a new character that will impel the play forward, the audience are left bemused and amused by the bumbling Mr Kidd, and Rose's immediate response to her husband upon the landlord's exit, 'I don't believe he had a sister, ever',[3] adds to a sense of him as an unreliable testimony in the play. This folds our investment back into Rose: it is she who must deliver for us a sense of where this play is heading, especially as she now sees her ever silent husband off out into the cold.

A husband who has said nothing and a landlord that brings no message, offers no dramatic dilemma or development; traditional male authority figures are presented as vacuous, seemingly without purpose in the early scenes of *The Room*, and this undermines any sense that the key female character is there simply to entertain us as a comic foil. The next scene begins to present her as a potential victim: two people looking for lodgings intimate that her room is to be let. Mr and Mrs Sands are disclosed standing in her doorway as Rose goes to it to take out her bin. She offers them warmth by her stove, and they come in and converse. They claim to be looking for the landlord but do not recognise the name of Kidd that Rose offers, and this partially unsettles the world on stage that has been established for us. Rose's insistence that Mr Kidd is the landlord and the Sands' brusque certainty that he is not might cause doubt in us about who is in charge in this world without a reliable authority figure, until the Sands inadvertently offer a sinister alternative in the form of someone who lives in the dark in the basement. Pinter protested once that 'I wouldn't know a symbol if I saw one'[4] but it is difficult not to consider the mysterious figure, comfortably residing in an unlit, damp basement, as symbolically diabolical in some fashion, or as representing something repressed and unwelcome. Mrs Sands offers a lengthy speech on her and her husband's encounter with the man in the cellar who had informed them that a room was vacant, and the room number given is indeed that of Rose's humble abode. The threat of eviction is tied to this character below, and the dramatic tension that might drive the play is now established.

A couple of themes have become noticeable by this point, consolidated in niggling between the Sands; the repeated reference to parentage and the infantilisation of husbands by their wives suggest this play has some concern to displace or upset traditional male social roles. If the play establishes these disturbances in male presence, though, it is not to serve to address gender in any direct way, but perhaps does so to prepare the ground for the re-assertion of male authority that takes place in the play's second half. No sooner that the Sands have left, Mr Kidd returns, now with a credible story, and a clarification for why he provided no information when first he appeared: he could not mention his given task while Rose's husband was still present. All of a sudden, some of the play's mysteries are being set straight and a sense of momentum consequently builds. The presence in the basement with whom the Sands had engaged is drawn more clearly by Mr Kidd, who explains that he has been waiting to let Rose know that the man downstairs wants to see her. He tells of how this man lies in the dark in the damp basement, just waiting for his audience with her. This implacable, insistent patience has all the qualities of a guilty secret, a skeleton in the cupboard, and Rose's responses of denial affirm this, as she seemingly protests too much that she has no connection with the mystery figure, declaring 'I don't know him' four times (104–5). She only finally concedes to meet the stranger when Mr Kidd suggests that if she does not do so immediately, the man might come up to confront her when her husband is at home. This reasoning, the need to keep whatever this man's business with Rose is outside of her marriage, adds to the sense that she has some clear notion of who this man is or what he might represent, and that any intervention he might make could unsettle her contented, staid existence.

No sooner does she agree to meet the man, than we find him momentarily at her threshold. He is a blind black man, walking with the aid of a cane. His blindness puts paid to any of the abstract interpretations that might be applied to his penchant for staying in the dark (why would he need light?) but is also a clear signifier of his otherness, allied here to his ethnicity. His given name, Riley, both supports and troubles this otherness, as the name is ethnically

Irish in origin. To be both black and Irish, while not improbable, was so unlikely in 1957 as to indicate to a London audience a deliberate clash of ethnicities, both of which, black and Irish, were subject to suspicion and hostility in certain social environments in the wake of the immigration surge on the back of the 1948 British Nationalities Act. Black characters (and indeed actors) on the British stage were relatively scarce in the late 1950s, so that Pinter's decision here seems purposeful. When black characters were present on stage in new plays of the time, the social issues surrounding their ethnicity and treatment were to the fore.[5] Even if we consider that determinism to have been nothing more than 'othering' Riley, the social signifier of a black character in relation to issues of tenancy (and, as we learn, familial or sexual relationship to a white woman) would have been so potent on the British stage in 1957 that its resonances cannot be ignored in appreciating the structure of this play, though these matters resonate differently on the stage today. What Pinter finally does, then, is not only clear up mysteries that might encourage allegorical readings of the play in performance, he injects a very clear stamp of social realism which, nonetheless, serves no clear ideological purpose other than to rush the real world rudely into this womb-like theatrical room on the back of a meaning-resistant metaphor. The play's resolution is not straightforwardly understandable, or we are not encouraged to read it in social terms, but early audiences to the play would very quickly have experienced a shift in register, recognising social realism was being signalled, and that shift in register at the very least augments expectations to indicate that this scene is very serious in its implications. Riley makes demands upon Rose that suggest social or familial obligations. Speaking on behalf of (and, seemingly, as) Rose's father, he implores her to 'come home' and addresses her as 'Sal' (108), implying a previous existence that Rose seeks to deny or resist. As a truncated form of Sally (which is itself an amicable form of the name Sarah), 'Sal' suggests a homely familiarity, but also an incompleteness. As with his own name, it fails to accord properly with its putative owner and this signals a crisis of identity that contributes to Rose's instability. Where elsewhere on the British stage in the late

1950s, black characters addressed or signalled contemporary social tensions associated with their emigration from Caribbean islands to British mainland contexts, here Pinter inverts that theme of the trauma of re-location, and suggests that Rose should return home with Riley as her guide, that it is she who has sought exile, escape, opportunity, but that she holds responsibilities to the place and people she has left behind, represented hauntingly by the patriarchy, the father figure.

It is at this point that the play reaches its dramatic crisis. Rose's husband returns home to find his wife in semi-erotic contact with this stranger as 'she touches his eyes, the back of his head and his temples with her hands' (109). He delivers a brief speech in which he explains his domination of the road and his van in notably gendered terms: 'She was good. She went with me. She don't mix it with me. I use my hand. Like that. I get hold of her. I go where I go. She took me there. She brought me back' (110). This quasi-sexual possession of machinery indicates a final, implacable masculine assertion of power, and is completed by Bert knocking Riley from his chair and kicking his head against the iron stove, and Rose declares that she has gone blind.

The killing of a black man on stage in 1957 evoked the racially motivated abuse and violence that was all too evident in British society at the time, but it is contextualised here as the elimination of a sexual rival, or of a wife's personal history that might reclaim her identity. Rose's blinding bonds her all the more to Riley, but its instantaneous coincidence with his beating suggests punishment or sacrifice by association. The sexualised behaviour and language render all this as primal display. All these associations linger after the curtain falls, but in the moment of Bert's assault on Riley, we as audience have no recourse to such thoughts as we experience a vital, visceral shock and revulsion at the violence before us. In the moment of performance, the climactic ending resists interpretation. Pinter delivers this first challenge to an audience not through narrative, plot or character, but through a sudden, immediate contact with unsettling action.

Pinter was to return to and develop a number of the preoccupations of *The Room* later in 1957 when he wrote his first full-length play, *The Birthday Party*. Both plays contain central characters who have settled in a tenancy that suits their unchallenging and unambitious existences, and both experience the demand to return to face unnamed obligations. The threat of expulsion, the association of power with sexuality, infantilisation and blindness feature in both plays, and, structurally, their innovative treatment of narrative expectation is similar. With *The Room*, Pinter had written a play that refuses to permit an audience an easy immediate connection with any of the characters, and used comedic stereotypes (nattering housewife, dotty landlord, reluctantly submissive husband) and seeming mysteries or unclarified absurd behaviour (a man who lives in the dark) to resist a narrative that might explain character motivation or situate the inevitable crisis within social realism. With *The Birthday Party*, he would capitalise upon and systematically formalise those dramatic instincts.

The Birthday Party centres around former concert pianist Stanley Webber being sought out at his adopted home in a seaside boarding house by Goldberg and McCann, two agents of some gang-like community who interrogate him, overcome him and abduct him. His family-like connections with mother and father figures Meg and Petey, and his failed romantic connection with neighbour Lulu, position him as a withdrawn individual, regressing to a pre-adult state, and this deliberately complicates audience association with him, making him something of an anti-hero. The play opens on a mundane breakfast scene, with Meg serving her husband Petey cornflakes and then fried bread and wittering away at him, much as Rose did when feeding Bert in *The Room*. Here, Meg asks questions to which she already knows the answer or which serve simply to sustain a chain of responses: 'Are you back?', 'Are they nice?', 'Is it good?', 'Is it warm out?'.[6] Unlike Bert, Petey responds, but with the bare minimum to sustain the banal chatter that seems to satisfy Meg. In this way we are introduced to simple, friendly, inoffensive folk in their own domestic environment, which we understand doubles as a proudly run business, a boarding house by the sea. Pinter unfolds the play at first with traditional expositionary manoeuvres: we learn that two men are going to come and seek lodgings there, and that there is already a lodger upstairs called Stanley who is a piano player by trade, whose indolence is mockingly tolerated in a loving, maternal way by Meg. Any usual development upon the exposition, though, is put on hold, and instead there is a lengthy section where Meg and Stanley's ambiguous relationship, part flirtatious, part mother/son, is presented. There is something disturbing about this quasi-sexual relationship, and Meg's attention spent on Stanley causes us to make something of a red herring investment in her development as a character; her attachment to Stanley seems doomed to tragedy as he is clearly neither a suitable son-replacement or sexual interest. This thread is expended soon with the arrival of Goldberg and McCann and is put paid to in the end of Act One in which he awkwardly and angrily responds to the infantilising birthday gift she makes of a toy drum. Instead, when we see Goldberg extract information from her so easily, we recognise that her function in the drama is as unwitting and oblivious instrument in Stanley's downfall. By setting up these quasi-family connections at the outset, though, Pinter establishes an everyday, domestic location for a grim story of torture and abduction.

The play takes on a specific drive and direction from the entrance of Goldberg and McCann, and their assertive confidence in being in the right place alongside their alert interest in Stanley (and his later response to learning of Goldberg's name) indicate to an audience that some significant conflict is about to occur. From this point on, the play moves with steady inertia along lines of tension between Goldberg and McCann's pursuit of Stanley and his attempts to evade their attentions. Dramatically, then, the play's structure is quite simple and its 'story' is quite one-dimensional. It is the ambiguity of that which is at stake, and the truth of who these three men are and what they are to each other, that maintains the keenest of interest as the drama unfolds. Any sense of clarity is first kept at bay by the negotiated, secret plans to hold a birthday party for Stanley, as this in itself partially defers our desire for clarification: when we hear Goldberg and Meg's conspiracy to surprise Stanley with a celebration, we anticipate a potentially comedic but certainly dramatic confrontation, and expect that to provide a first measure of what the two strangers are to Stanley. As such, the build to that scene allows for something of a dramatic climax to develop, and this is constructed throughout Act Two with interactions between Stanley and first McCann, then Goldberg and then all three men together.

Though Stanley at first tries to bypass McCann to get out of the house, he clearly also cannot help but attempt to communicate with the stranger, and undermine any confidence he might have in his mission. In seemingly polite conversation, he embarks on a series of reminiscences of his life in Maidenhead, a respectable market town thirty miles west of London, through which he subtly constructs a genteel background for himself. He narrates his past there as one in which he would make use of the Boots Library and frequent the Fuller's teashop and he recalls living 'well away from the main road' (33), which is to say in a leafy, well-to-do suburb.[7] That his language is deliberately coded in order to suggest he is the wrong target for McCann's attentions is revealed when he later asks, 'You knew what I was talking about before, didn't you?' (36), and again when he blows his own cover by referring to having lived in Basingstoke (much further west from London than Maidenhead, but an equally suitable fictional choice for projecting supposed respectability). In this way, Stanley comes across as wily but faltering, and he later shifts to more determined strategies by professing to be the landlord and claiming that the room in which Goldberg and McCann are to board is already let. As Stanley's manoeuvres shift from subtle subversion to the overt 'Get out' and Goldberg and McCann progress from the cunningly polite to the undisguisedly threatening ('you're beginning to get on my breasts') (39–40), Pinter clearly builds up the tension. This erupts finally in a scene of out and out interrogation, in which the two men throw bizarre and non-seque-torial questions and accusations at Stanley in machine-gun bursts of verbal assault. These start in relatively realistic mode with enquiries about his recent whereabouts, accusations of poor behaviour towards his hosts, and straightforward demands to know where he comes from, why he came to this place and why he stayed. They then become more personal, with accusations of his having betrayed some unnamed organisation and then of murdering his wife, or of jilting her at the altar, before shifting to broad theological or philosophical enquiries and then concluding with the clichéd nonsense questions about a chicken's motivations in crossing the road, and whether it came before or after the egg. While this rapid, seemingly random and bizarre accumulation of charges and questions is deployed to terrify and destabilise Stanley, it also disorients us in the audience, leaving us no time to process what is being said, and in this way an uncomfortable alliance between us and Stanley is established. But if the accumulation of words is garbled or absurd, the tenor of all that is said to Stanley is a coherent series of variations on the same theme: he has evaded his responsibilities and is unable to account for himself. This renders him incomplete, they argue, and Goldberg sums up his condition as 'You can't live, you can't think, you can't love. You're dead' (46). At this point we might realise that their project with Stanley is more one of correction than it is of punishment, and this raises a nagging concern about the authority these men have to conduct any such correction.

Pinter, though, has not furnished us with a straightforward victim in the shape of Stanley, and this is why any empathic alliance we have with him is uncomfortable. His early introduction to us is anything but sympathetic, and his treatment of Meg comes across as opportunistic and contemptuous. When the girl next door, Lulu, seems to show an interest in him, inviting him out to accompany her for some fresh air and lunch, he rejects her advances (which at their simplest are merely friendly in nature) before abruptly inviting her to run away with him, but with no destination other than 'nowhere' to offer. We cannot help but agree with her assessment of him as 'a bit of a washout' (20). By the time we hear Goldberg's criticism of his character, we might find ourselves in agreement with his concerns: 'Why are you driving that old lady off her conk? [...] Why do you treat that young lady like a leper?' (41). When Goldberg and McCann's interrogation is interrupted by the sound of Meg beating the birthday drum, and thereby heralding the start of Stanley's birthday party, we watch as the intense, private confrontation dissipates and flows into a strained social event. The scene is unarguably charged, and this makes for gripping drama, but the charge comes as much from our concern for Stanley's volatility as it does from the as yet unclear consequences of the threat the two strangers pose for him.

Under pressure of this obligated social event, Stanley buckles and lashes out violently. Unable to escape his turn in a game of blind man's buff, the blindfolded Stanley bumps into Meg and begins to throttle her, until he is forcibly pulled away from her. At that moment, there is an unexplained blackout on stage, effectively pulling the blindfold over the audience's eyes just at the moment Stanley manifests this homicidal behaviour. The action continues with the characters stumbling in the dark, and when McCann's torch finally discovers Stanley, he is giggling and bent over Lulu spread-eagled on the table, which might appear as though he has been caught in the act of sexually abusing her. We could clarify Stanley's behaviour here in terms of his hitting out against those who are effectively complicit in empowering Goldberg and McCann against him, but his assault on female targets in this way is a dispro-portionate moral breach that weakens our empathic links with him. His giggling demeanour might be read as a pathetic regression to an infantile state or as helpless, fractured nerves. Either way, it assists in our dismissal of him. In this way, Pinter positions us as audience to Stanley's downfall, on a par with Meg, Petey and Lulu and by undermining an empathic bond with this hapless victim, he more effectively opens up a moral enquiry. Act Three sees that fully exploited.

The seemingly bizarre events of the previous night are first readily explained away. Petey contextualises the blackout by explaining he had to put a shilling in the electricity meter when he came home, and Goldberg contextualises Stanley's behaviour in terms of a nervous breakdown. While the audience might forgive the author's cunning with the former, we are more likely to see through Goldberg's duplicity with the latter. When we eventually see Stanley again, we notice immediately that the process of correction has begun in earnest overnight: the slovenly, unkempt individual we first met in his pyjamas jacket is now clean shaven and wearing a funereal dark suit and white collar. He is greeted by a barrage of short, clipped promises from Goldberg and McCann who, like some forbidding music-hall double act, roll off guarantees that from now on they will 'watch over', 'advise', and 'make a man of' him and that he will be 're-orientated', 'adjusted' and 'integrated' (76–8). Their routine, which covers over two pages of the printed text, serves as something of a dramatic threshold in any performance, sealing Stanley's fate and ending all doubt that he is to be taken away from his adopted home. When we then hear that he can no longer speak, the dreaded realisation that he must have been tortured underscores the disquiet that the play has established. As though with a badly bruised or cut tongue, he repeats twice the muffled syllables of a garbled sentence that seems to refer to Goldberg's waiting car ('Uh-gug ... uh-gug ... eeehhh-gag [...] caaahh') (78), before being led out to be bundled into it. Petey makes ineffectual moves to stop this, indicating that he could get a doctor and that Stanley can be looked after well at home, but when Goldberg insidiously turns on him, offering to take him too, he backs down all too readily. By way of saving face, he suggests glibly to Stanley 'don't let them tell you what to do!' when that horse has so very clearly already bolted (80).

The play ends as it started, with Meg and Petey exchanging glib chatter. For Meg, her world is as yet unchanged, but we have witnessed the devastation of her adoptive son figure, and have despaired at her husband's inability to voice effective resistance. Through Petey, we might hope for some final words that salve the wound, but all he can offer is to maintain Meg's illusion a little longer, and claim that Stanley is still in bed. This ending is deliberate, as to conclude the play with Meg's despair would have closed down any possibility for ethical thought within an all too compelling response of sympathy. Instead, Pinter baffles us with Petey's impossible position between a shaming failure to intervene and a noble but ultimately hopeless care to protect his wife. His impotence to respond has been paralleled in our own experience of the drama. Stanley may break, but Petey's words 'don't let them tell you what to do' resonate within us at the end of the play, as we see that Stanley clearly *is* letting them tell him what to do, that he has no choice and that no-one can or will help him. This stimulates in us an indignation that we must take with us from the theatre, and this is exacerbated somewhat by the blissful ignorance that Meg demonstrates and Petey perpetuates. She precedes the final curtain with her insistent assertion that it had been a 'lovely party' (81), in direct contrast to what we have just witnessed. Without sermonising, without pointing to particular incidents or socio-political contexts, and simply through his the theatrical contract that *The Birthday Party* demands of its audience, Pinter activates the conditions in which ethical judgements have to be made about the treatment of humans by the representatives of organised ideology, and the circumstances in which such treatment takes place free of effective resistance.

When a journalist from *Jewish Quarterly* asked him in 1960 why he had made Goldberg a Jewish character, Pinter replied that he 'only knew that one of the men who called for Stanley was a Jew and the other an Irishman' and that he had 'no desire to write a whole play about Jews or a Jewish situation'.[8] In other words, his plays were not concerned with representing the plight of victims and appealing for corrective measures, but instead were composed to demonstrate the construction of victimhood by authoritative systems, with Judaism and Catholicism as established doctrinal belief structures being as good as any to represent such systems. By making persecutors of Black, Jewish and Irish figures in *The Room* and *The Birthday Party*, groups that were either significantly socially disadvantaged or subject to racial abuse in the UK at the time, Pinter arguably universalised the condition of threat to personal freedom and individual expression. In a letter to the play's director Peter Wood in 1958, Pinter referred to the Goldberg and McCann as '[d]ying, rotten, scabrous, the decaying spiders, the flower of our society. They know their way around. Our mentors. Our ancestry. Them. Fuck 'em'.[9] On one level this is a consciously un-focussed, anti-authoritarian revolt against the ever-present third person plural who steer and judge our lives, and a finger stuck up in their direction. In political terms, this might be construed as a weakness, as a failure to declare the enemy and the precise means by which we ought to address them, but it might also disguise the author's own uncertainty about the provenance of the anger or conviction that drove him to write. If Pinter's concern was to exploit the potential of the theatrical medium to allow an audience to feel the discomfort of the vacant gap where ethical judgement needs to be made, then that gap is more resonant without the socio-political specifics that risk rendering the question redundant. We know beyond moral doubt that the circumstances that permitted the Holocaust to take place are to be condemned, but to ask how such circumstances could come about in civilised society is to ask how it might be that we too could see them being established and, like Petey, fail to resist, or even facilitate their growth. Politically, one might argue that to raise consciousness of that, to activate such ethical enquiry, is of more value than to conform to an unquestionable, ready-made moral conviction.

While Pinter sought to stage the individual's plight against the demands of tradition and orthodoxy, he does not construct villains who are immune from the dysfunction that such systems pervade. McCann's hope that their 'job' of admonishing Stanley and reintegrating him into whatever system he has escaped would be 'accomplished with no excessive aggravation' is clearly unfulfilled (24), and even the resolute Goldberg suffers a breakdown in confidence towards the end of the play, when he finds himself unable to complete the sentence 'I believe that the world…', no longer able to recall the solid social or ethical premises that guide and justify his actions (72). In *The Dumb Waiter*, also written in 1957, a similar uncertainty has become considerably more established in the character of Gus, and that short one-act play can be considered as an exploration of the consequences of the doubt and aggravation that Goldberg and McCann experience in fulfilling their duties.

Like Goldberg and McCann, Ben and Gus are two henchmen of an unnamed organisation. We understand that, rather than the 'special treatment' and 'integration' of their targets, their job is simply to kill and they are equipped with holsters and revolvers for that purpose. We learn that they are sent out around the country to attend to a 'job' once a week, and that this involves waiting at a given location until their victim is delivered to their door. We learn also that they are part of an organisation with 'departments for everything',[10] including clearing up the corpses. The two men have been through a series of tests, and this suggests a well-organised system for the elimination of undesirables. Whether Ben and Gus are hitmen for an underworld gang of organised criminals or are agents of governmental authorities is unclear; their identities are only defined by their activities, which they carry out obediently, furnished each time only with the bare minimum for comfort (a bed, sheets and a teapot) and information on a 'need to know' basis. Again, Pinter offers his audience no more information than the characters possess, and this serves to have us share in their bewilderment as things on this particular 'job' take unexpected turns.

The dumb waiter of the title is the apparatus that indicates the two men are lodged in the basement of what might once have been servants' quarters of a large house, or the kitchen of a café; it is the name of the miniature lift used to carry prepared meals and other items from one floor to another. The title of course also suggests other possibilities, as Ben and Gus are both 'dumb', in that they are ignorant of the circumstances that lead to the selection of victims for any of their assassinations, and 'waiters' in both senses of the word – much of their occupation involves waiting, but they 'wait' in the intransitive sense in as much as they serve. We might acknowledge the influence of Beckett here, whose play *Waiting for Godot* had caused something of a sensation in London a couple of years previously, in 1955, and Pinter is in part paying homage to the author he already admired. As with Beckett's drama, *The Dumb Waiter* opens with some comic business over footwear, and involves two people passing the time until a given event will release them from that burden. Both plays involve a double act that, in classic music-hall mould, has one member who manifests a sense of control and patience and another who is a little dim-witted and needs correcting or encouraging. In both plays, one partner is more obsessed with nutrition and comfort than the other, structuring a kind of mind/body separation and binding between the two. Whereas Beckett's play offered a perspective on humanity's persistent yet occluded investment in determining meaning in human activity, Pinter's purpose is quite distinctly within an ethical frame, as signalled by the occupation given to Ben and Gus. For all its comedy, we cannot look past the fact that the play centres around two men who kill for a living at the behest of an organised system.

The dramatic progression has two lines of interest that hold our attention as the play advances. One is the manner in which Gus is beginning to query the conditions of his employment and, eventually, the nature of what he does for a living. The second is the odd behaviour from outside the room that bemuses and eventually terrifies these two men: toilets that do not flush, or do so inexplicably, at unexpected times; an envelope containing matches that is shoved under the door; a dumb waiter that descends with notes demanding that more and more complicated dishes be sent up. The ambiguous tension between these two lines, as they develop, is where we might look for any meaning but, of course, that ambiguity keeps any ready understanding at bay. What is clear is that what used to be an efficient killing team is now showing signs of weakness, as Ben slowly loses patience with his bumbling and inquisitive partner.[11] 'You've got a job to do. Why don't you just do it and shut up?' (127), he tells Gus as he asks questions about their latest target. But Gus openly criticises their employer for what he perceives as deteriorating conditions of employment (no window, no radio, bed sheets he suspects have already been slept in, an empty gas meter) and begins to show signs of scruples in his recollection of how the death of their last victim, a girl, made a 'mess' the like of which he had not seen before. He tries to clarify this in terms of gender, musing how women 'don't seem to hold together like men'. This distinction serves to activate in the audience a moral alarm at, first, the dispassionate discussion of the murder of a girl and, secondly, the gruesome image of a freshly dispatched corpse with a 'looser texture' that 'didn't half spread'. Scruples, of course, are of no use in a man who is paid to kill without asking questions, and it is noteworthy that Gus is interrupted mid sentence by the first descent of the dumb waiter when he utters the words 'it was that girl made me start to think' (130–1). At this precise point, the two lines of dramatic progression intersect abruptly.

The notes in the dumb waiter contain orders that are impossible to fulfil, starting with a demand for the working-class British fare of tea, steak and chips, sago pudding, soup, liver and onions and jam tarts, followed by European dishes (Macaroni Pastitsio, Ormitha Macarounada) and later oriental food (Bamboo shoots, Water Chestnuts with Chicken, Char Siu and Beansprouts). Pathetically, the men can only offer the snacks that Gus has with him – an Eccles cake, chocolate, biscuits and crisps – and this makes the requests for more complicated cuisine something of a mockery of their impotence, a hostile gesture. It is also, of course, extremely funny and the play becomes something of a macabre parable, where we find ourselves laughing at the desperate reactions of these men to their being manipulated in this way. While Ben seeks to maintain a dignified and deferential demeanour in response to these impossible demands, Gus cannot, and interprets the bewildering experience as an unfathomable and unfair test: 'What's he doing all this for? What's the idea? What's he playing these games for?' he decries passionately, only for the dumb waiter to respond with a demand for Scampi, causing him to lose it altogether and scream that they have nothing left into a speaking tube attached to the device (146).

The play then comes to a swift and surprising end. As Gus leaves the room to get a glass of water, Ben receives some orders down the speaking tube, leaving now no uncertainty that whoever was up above holds organisational command over the two men. To further remove ambiguity, Pinter has Ben speak out loud the orders he is given: that their victim has 'arrived and will be coming in right away' and that the 'normal method [is] to be employed' (148). He calls for Gus, but his partner fails to appear. The other door then opens suddenly and Ben aims his gun at the open space. Gus stumbles through, seemingly shoved, and the two men stare at each other, both in no doubt what this arrangement must mean. Their shared gaze both conjoins and separates the two partners and that tension is emphasised by a 'long silence', forming a strained closing tableau to the play. Gus's constant questioning of the conditions of his employment, and his growing unease at despatching female targets seem to have marked him out as unfit material for the organisation which employs him.

If *The Dumb Waiter* might be considered as an exploration of the aggravation that Goldberg and McCann experience as willing components of a self-sustaining system of authoritarian power that relies upon and establishes obedience in those who are subject to it, then *The Hothouse*, written in the winter of 1958, might be considered a further examination of the processes of correction, obedience and corruption that such power systems exhibit. In this way, the three plays form something of a trilogy that surveys the discourses of systems of power with the grammar of those discourses exhibited in behavioural models as well as language. Stanley's disobedience and his frantic reaction to being finally cornered are written off as a form of mental illness that required 'special treatment', and the institution that is the setting for *The Hothouse* might well be the kind of facility that he is carted off to. The establishment that Pinter constructs is something of a grim Orwellian fantasy, a 'rest home' run by a military man for 'patients' who are 'all people specially recommended by the Ministry' treated 'to help them regain their confidence'.[12] These patients are allocated numbers, used instead of names, reside for months or years behind locked doors in freezing rooms and are subject to the attentions of an elite body of staff (distinct from the 'understaff' in this hierarchical organisation) who might judge that 'for the good of a female patient some degree of copulation is necessary' (219) and provide that remedy personally, recognising nonetheless that 'that sort of thing [doesn't happen] by consent' (268). Members of family need cunningly to breach security in order to attempt to locate their incarcerated kin, who might become prematurely grey and die of 'heart failure', the classic euphemism of many an over-zealous police interrogation. Family are then not informed of a patient's demise, but instead given circuitous excuses and explanations that remove access to the truth. The institution, housed in a flat-roofed building with at least five floors, is equipped with a gymnasium and recreation facilities, but also with soundproofed chambers in which subjects can be connected up to electrodes and monitored from remote control rooms. In all, this is unambiguously a detention centre for the correction of those who, like Stanley and Gus, have lost their way in an authoritarian system that demands obedience.

The play's dramatis personae are all monosyllabically named members of the staff of the institution, bar one member of the understaff, and a man from the Ministry in the final scene. We do not meet the prisoners. Pinter's focus is very much on the self-justifying and self-perpetuating power structure within which each individual component can readily be replaced by the next man. The genealogy of power is traced back to the founding father of the establishment, Mike, whose Stalinesque statue stands outside the building as monument to the moral code that is brutally stamped into its inmates. The current head of the institution, an ex-military man named Roote, is exposed as having killed one prisoner and fathered a child by another, though the evidence for this comes across in hilarious subtextual hints in dialogue between him and his immediate inferiors Gibbs and Lush. Gibbs, too, is a possible culprit for the murder of 6457 and impregnation of 6459, as one might interpret the play as structured around his strategies for undermining and removing Roote's leadership to take control of the institution himself. Inculpating his boss in his own crimes would be effective manoeuvres towards this ambition, and his declaration of Roote's double guilt in the final scene, by obviating the subtextual teases that have led us to that same conclusion, might in fact at the last minute cause us to put two and two together quite differently.

When the compliant Lamb is interrogated as part of a process predetermined to scapegoat him as the illegitimate baby's father, one of the only questions that he is able to answer uninterrupted in full is to define the 'law of the Wolf Cub Pack', which he gives as though learned by rote as 'The cub gives in to the Old Wolf, the cub does not give in to himself' (250).[12] Subservience is printed at the heart of this community, but the old wolves are at each others' throats. Both Gibbs and Lush, who are clear rivals with markedly different approaches, undermine Roote subtly but effectively, and the three men eventually come together in a standoff, all wielding knives, as the thirst to power comes to a head. The attempts to get rid of Roote are hilariously undisguised, from a potentially poisoned Christmas cake to an exploding cigar, but in the end we hear that it is a prisoner revolt that results in his being killed in his sleep. His predecessor, we learn earlier, had 'retired' (196), though that word is uttered after some hesitation as though a suitable euphemism was being selected to avoid a less dignified reality. Lamb also took over from someone who seems to have left inexplicably and without trace. In this way, Pinter constructs a precarious, self-consuming system where the discourse of power is the only consistent, safe element in an ongoing chain of leadership of a world in which 'common assumptions are shared and common principles observed' (252). The root basis of these common assumptions and principles, though, is never articulated, and when Lush challenges Roote to clarify what validates his power, Roote effectively manages to complete the sentence that Goldberg found so difficult to conclude, but does so with brute force rather than words.

Lush On whose authority? With what power are you entrusted? By whom were you appointed? Of *what* are you a delegate?

Roote *hits him in the stomach.*

Roote I'm a delegate! (*He hits him in the stomach.*)
I was entrusted! (*He hits him in the stomach.*)
I'm a delegate! (*He hits him in the stomach.*)
I was appointed! (*He hits him in the stomach.*)

Lush *backs, crouched, slowly across the stage,* **Roote** *following him.*

Delegated! (*He hits him in the stomach.*)
Appointed! (*He hits him in the stomach.*)
Entrusted!

He hits him in the stomach. Lush sinks to the floor. **Roote** *stands over him and shouts.*

I AM AUTHORISED! (306–7)

Where language fails to describe the contours of authority, because no authentic justification can be found for a system that serves only to keep itself intact, then only brute force can be articulate.

On three occasions in the play, Pinter punctuates the farcical realism of its chambers and offices with an audio effect of a very different register. First a long sigh is heard, then a keen, then laughter. These human sounds are given as 'amplified', with the laughter 'dying away', and this suggests that these sounds are being monitored and projected into the world of these senior staff. On the first two occasions this sequence is played, Lush, Gibbs and Miss Cutts seem only vaguely to perceive them (the stage directions indicate that they look up as the sounds are heard). On the third and final occasion, Lush asks 'What was that?' and Roote and Gibbs both affirm that they heard something, but could not identify it, concluding only that '[t]here's something going on' (310–11). These human sounds of true emotion, of passion, lament and humour, puncture the world of power where no such things are expressed. They represent an alien threat, and are a precursor to the prisoner revolt that we might suspect has been cunningly or unwittingly engineered by Gibbs.

It is interesting to note that Pinter decided to shelve *The Hothouse*, unconvinced by it, and it was left unpublished and unperformed until 1980. His career in 1958 was far from established with any security, and his development as an artist must have been keenly important to him. In rejecting *The Hothouse*, Pinter might have been concerned not to pursue a line of creative enquiry that risked becoming a dead end, and though the play is far funnier than *The Birthday Party* or *The Dumb Waiter*, it fails convincingly to open for an audience the ethical gap that both those works achieve at their conclusions. While we can enjoy the contempt with which these authorities are portrayed, we are not rendered complicit or made to recognise our own participation in the power discourses in the potent ways that the earlier two plays are able to achieve in performance. Recognising that he has written 'out of hatred for these people and for the authorities which they represented, and for the procedures that were authorised',[14] Pinter might have felt caution over his motivations, and promoted for himself a more detached approach to theme and character, as is evident in the contemporaneous *The Slight Ache* and *The Caretaker*. In doing so, he moved away from the polemic of critiquing authority to return to an abiding concern for issues of how dominance is achieved and articulated.

The Stranger on the Threshold
A Slight Ache, The Caretaker

Speaking in 1966 of his screenplay of *The Servant*, Pinter recalled what attracted him to adapting Robin Maugham's novella, and thought back to his artistic development in the late 1950s:

> The violence [in *The Dumb Waiter*] is really only an expression of the question of dominance and subservience, which is possibly a repeated theme in my plays. I wrote a short story a long time ago called 'The Examination', and my ideas of violence carried on from there. That short story dealt very explicitly with two people in one room having a battle of an unspecified nature, in which the question was one of who was dominant at what point and how they were going to be dominant and what tools they would use to achieve dominance and how they would try to undermine the other person's dominance. A threat is constantly there: it's got to do with this question of being in the uppermost position, or attempting to be.[15]

Returning to unpack some of the underlying principles behind that short prose piece 'The Examination', Pinter approached his first radio play *A Slight Ache*, by, in effect, returning to first principles. The project, a commission he had received from Donald McWhinnie at the BBC, was an opportunity for being heard on a significant platform that reached a national audience, but also very clearly represented a fresh start for the young author: *The Birthday Party* had been a commercial flop, *The Dumb Waiter* was yet to be produced, *The Room* had yet to be produced professionally. What is more, writing *A Slight Ache* must also have been something of a professional thrill and creative challenge for Pinter, as he knew that McWhinnie had been the one who produced Beckett's first work for radio, *All That Fall*, in 1957. The creative stakes were high. The £60 he received to write what would become *A Slight Ache* would have covered his household rent for six months or more,[16] and this would give him time not only to write that play but an opportunity to experiment and consider his next moves as a writer, which would include the composition of *The Caretaker*. If these two plays were conceived as the first steps of a fresh start, they were to become the hinge that opened the first phase of his success and public acclaim.

A Slight Ache is conspicuous among Pinter's early plays as perhaps the least grounded in any kind of social reality. Even the foreboding *The Room*, set in an indistinct, ill-defined lodging house, clarifies some of its obscurities as it progresses and signals social reality in the nonetheless meaning-resistant figure of Riley. In *A Slight Ache* the threatening, invading presence might still offer some sense of social identity (as both vagrant or ineffective matchseller) but his presence represents an irritation that cannot be treated. The affluent Edward and Flora find their idyllic lifestyle in their comfortable country house marred by the presence of this silent, immobile matchseller at their garden gate. Once this problem is established over an alfresco breakfast, Edward resolves to confront the man, and the play progresses as both he and Flora seek to elicit some response from him that might enable them to clarify his intentions, his motivations or his very being.

Perhaps with a conscious or even perverse aspiration to avoid the kinds of soundscapes that were commonly associated with radio drama, Pinter structured *A Slight Ache* around silence. In its original recording, broadcast on 29 July 1959 on the BBC Third Programme, the matchseller does not at first indicate his presence with any sound, and we do not here any breathing or shuffling of feet when either Flora or Edward engage with him, for example. In fact, the production seems deliberately to promote an economy of silence. There are no domestic sounds of knives on plates, tea being poured or teacups meeting saucers in the opening conversation over breakfast and even when an irritant wasp arrives it too makes no sound. These are notable omissions, and suggest that an artistic decision was made about the auditory behaviour of both interlopers, wasp and matchseller.[17] It is only when Flora steps outside to address the tramp figure, and we hear distant birdsong and the sound of the garden gate creaking as she opens it, that the production finally establishes the kind of sonic atmosphere that would have been expected in broadcasts of this sort. This shift creates a kind of opening out, as though Flora has stepped out of some sterile world into a real, recognisable panorama of countryside sounds. There is an implication here that the matchseller inhabits the real world, and that Edward and Flora are distant from it, and it is the nature of that interstice between modes of being and perceiving that the play explores by activating a challenge to Edward's superiority, achieved through the matchseller's obdurate silence. A class-based, and therefore political, reading is possible here, though the density of the fantasy that follows seems alert to disallow that. It is most likely that Pinter took the opportunity of this commission to profit from the sonic possibilities of radio to explore a dramatic adaptation of the conceptual basis of his early Kullus writings. In 'The Examination', Kullus is invited into a room and interrogated by the story's unnamed narrator, who confesses that Kullus 'journeyed from silence to silence, and I had no course but to follow'. Ultimately, failing to extract any response to his questions, he recognises that 'we were now in Kullus's room'.[18] This domination and reversal of territorial position through the imposition of silence play well on radio, as the matchseller's indefatigable presence causes as much of an irritation to the listening audience, who expect as much clarification as Edward to the mystery that he presents.

There was one notable exception to the silence of the matchseller in the original radio broadcast, and that is made as he ascends the staircase to Edward's study after being invited into the house by Flora. Eight footsteps can be heard, first fading away from Flora and then up toward Edward as the sonic space shifts from downstairs to his desk. To emphasise this, we hear Edward count the approaching footsteps from four to eight (though this was not transferred to the published script). This purposefully indicates that the matchseller is a real presence, and not a grotesque figment of the troubled mind (the splitting of the audio effect into two, segued between the two perspectives of upstairs and downstairs, further distances the possibility that he is some manifestation of one or another character's imagination). This technique offered a means of expressing a palpably physical presence who remained silent, and who would later morph in appearance to resemble different people, transforming from stocky to slim, from an old man to a youth.

The strategy of silence nonetheless promotes Edward and Flora's projection of their own fears and fantasies onto the matchseller. Edward seeks to prompt some response from the tramp-like figure, first via the hospitality of offering a drink, a place to sit, and a concern for his comfort, and then by implying the esteem in which he himself is held amongst the village folk, and more widely for his writing of 'theological and philosophical essays'.[19] When these tactics gain no response, he tries empathy, revealing that he too had been 'in commerce' and worked at the mercy of the elements. Throughout, his self-importance and insincerity are betrayed by various indices of a comfortable existence or pompous indulgence, including references to exotic foreign trips off the beaten tourist path and a hilarious itinerary of proffered drinks. When Flora takes over from her husband, who is exhausted from the fruitless confrontation, she manifests a sexual curiosity for the matchseller. She first indicates that he reminds her of a man who raped her, then offers to mop his brow with her chiffon, before asking his thoughts on women and sex and then undressing him in preparation for a bath. She concludes her seduction with an understanding that he is ill and dying, and offers to tend to him. Edward orders her to leave in demeaning terms, and seems to carry on where he left off, with more assertions of his own strengths of character. Pinter adds a note of nostalgia to Edward's recollections of possessing poise and command (including his killing of the irritating wasp that very morning). He sneezes, falls to the floor, and complains about the germ in his eyes, an intensification of the 'slight ache' he had complained of to his wife at the play's outset. Flora returns, indicates to the matchseller that all is prepared, and takes him by the hand to go and enjoy lunch by the pool. In a final gesture of reversal, she hands the tray of matches to Edward and exits with her surrogate husband. If this silent, hooded figure of decay represents mortality to Edward, or at most a brutal puncturing of his middle-class apparatus to reveal the vacuity of being, he offers Flora the bodily renewal of love and sex.

The gendered differentiation here perhaps weakens the clarity of the play's closure, and this may well have been intended. In the next chapter, a more focussed and driven approach to gender is detected throughout Pinter's output over the next five years. There is a hint of artistic indulgence in *A Slight Ache*, and its oneiric qualities no doubt originate in Pinter's taking advantage of the nature of a new medium. References to monks and monasteries, three-sailed schooners, and memories of floods of biblical proportions contribute to an unfixed sense of time and location in the play that perhaps permit a universalising approach to attributing meaning to any of its elements. The play's broadcast represented by far the largest audience he had enjoyed to date, and was a first step in the process of establishing his name. That would be consolidated by the broadcast in March 1960 of his next radio drama, *A Night Out*, but more firmly established on the London stage with the May 1960 production of *The Caretaker*, which was to represent his commercial breakthrough. The original production ran for over a year, transferred to Broadway in New York, and later was made into a film.

In further exploring strategies of dominance in *The Caretaker*, Pinter contextualised these now in terms of personal need, and the expression of care between people. In this respect, the title is quite precise, as the play focusses on what it means to take care and offer care, and the implications for interpersonal behaviour when the balance of those things is impossible to achieve. The play is set wholly within the only habitable room on the top floor of a West London house. This is cluttered with the detritus of a building in the process of being renovated, assorted junk, and various ornaments and household appliances and fittings. A bucket is suspended from the ceiling. Amid all this clutter, an idiosyncratic Buddha statuette stands on top of a disconnected gas stove. The very first scene of the play is a silent one, in which the twenty-something character of Mick sits on one of two beds – the other being covered in a mound of assorted stuff – and looks around at all the objects in the room, one by one. In this way, the first moments of the play invite us and afford us the time to look in detail at the jumbled, dirty set, before a word is uttered. We might assume the leather-jacketed character onstage lives in this room, but as soon as voices are heard offstage, he stands up and silently leaves, quietly closing the door behind him. Then the characters of Aston (in his early thirties) and Davies (an old man) enter, and the apparition of Mick lingers in our memories as an inexplicable presence elsewhere in the house or beyond as the two men converse.

We quickly learn that the mild-mannered Aston has just saved Davies from some altercation at his place of work, a café, which resulted in the old man losing his meagre job of clearing tables and mopping the floor. Davies's protestations over the incident reveal that he was far from innocent in bringing about any conflict, but Aston offers no judgement either way, and is calm and generous in seeking to make the old man comfortable. He offers him a seat and some tobacco for his pipe, then proposes to return himself to the café to collect the old man's belongings. Later, he offers him a bed for the night and five shillings (representing small change to get by, between £5 and £10, or $8 and $16) to see him through the next few days, and by the end of the first act he has shown the man how to use the electric fire and given him keys to the room and the house. This generosity eventually peaks in the offer of a job and permanent residency, in the form of caretaker to the house once it has been fully renovated and let out. Aston's unquestioning munificence activates a couple of key responses in the audience; first, we might experience a concern that he is making himself vulnerable to ready exploitation and, secondly, we might wonder what he stands to gain from the seemingly selfless capacity to offer charitable assistance to his fellow man.

The first of these concerns is promoted forthrightly by Pinter, in the manner in which he writes the character of Davies as evasive, selfish and opportunistic. His linguistic mannerisms involve deflecting both charity and criticism, so he will respond to an offer with turns of phrases such as 'if you like', 'Good luck', 'best of luck' or to suggestions that he makes noise in his sleep by blaming the Asian family next door.[20] Such casual, ugly racism falls from his mouth from some of his first words, finding quarrel with the Blacks, Greeks, Poles and 'all them aliens' (6) that frequent the café where he worked, not to mention the Scottish co-worker with whom he got into a fight. He is suspicious of Aston's 'black' neighbours, to the absurd point of being concerned about whether they enter the house to use the bathroom. He later suggests that he might stand a chance of getting a job in a café he knows in Wembley because, he reasons, customers 'want an Englishman to pour their tea' (25), a statement that resonates with some ambiguous irony as his name is Welsh, though he avoids confirming that national status when asked directly. This overt fear of all that is 'foreign' has a visual counter-point onstage in the form of Aston's statue of the Buddha, which appears as out of place amid all this clutter as Davies so clearly is, and acts as an emblematic visual analogue of the younger man's calm and selfless character.

Aston's motivations in being so charitable to a homeless old man come across as nothing but innate, unconditional altruism, which chimes with popular conceptions of Buddhist philosophy. The only demands he makes upon his guest are in the form of conversation, and this suggests that he lacks regular human contact. He shares two odd reminiscences which come across as tentative forms of revealing something about himself. In the first, he recalls a time he was poured a pint of Guinness in a thick mug, but that he could not drink it because he only likes to drink from a thin glass. In the second, he talks of a time in a café when a woman made a sexual advance, which he considered 'a bit odd' (23). These two recollections – both positioned as having happened 'the other day' and having occurred in social spaces – suggest a delicate disposition, a man uncomfortable in everyday situations that do not conform with routine expectations. When, at the end of Act Two, we hear Aston's long monologue about the time he was sectioned as a minor and treated with electroshock therapy, we get a complete sense of him as a gentle, damaged individual. We cannot help but be drawn in by his testimony, and its length conspires to maintain our focus. This caps our investment in him, and the details of the recollection evoke our sympathy unremittingly. In particular, the reference to his mother signing the permission forms is particularly painful in suggesting the betrayal of the most fundamental of human bonds, that between a mother and child. This, in turn, finally colours our appreciation of Mick's objectives in entrusting Aston to repair, refit and decorate the house. We recognise this as something of a kind but hopeless project that might rather serve some long-term therapeutic purpose. In the short-term, it is clear that Aston's plans to build a shed (once the garden is clear) so that he can begin to address the many and various snagging issues in the house, from floorboards to leaking roof, is so ambitious as to be untenable, and as if to emphasise this the plug he is fiddling with at the beginning of the play is still in hand at the end.

In response to being asked if he thought his play was a comedy, Pinter explained in 1960: '*The Caretaker* is funny, up to a point. Beyond that point it ceases to be funny, and it was because of that point that I wrote it.'[21] If the point in question is Aston's speech, then there is no doubt that Pinter is demonstrating himself to be a deeply humanist writer. We can only rely on ourselves to take care of one another, and Mick's spontaneous smashing of the Buddha figure might at the most obvious level represent his frustration at the responsibility of being his brother's keeper, but might also be read as Pinter's rejection of all systems of thought that pretend to instruct and contour what should be our primary instinctive motivations. As Aston's speech closes the second act of the play, we return from the interval drinks prepared to see how its revelations might have adjusted characters' behaviours. Even the slightest gesture of empathic generosity from Davies would shift the play significantly in his favour, and his failure to do so establishes the trajectory for the rest of the play.

What Pinter establishes with the odd coupling of Aston and Davies, then, is the meeting of two lonely men who are, circumstantially at least, able to profit from one another's company.

Davies's loneliness is articulated in part by a series of geographical references that not only locate his homeless migration around the west of London (Acton, Shepherd's Bush, Watford, Wembley) and also imagine him on inhospitable routes on the periphery of the city (The Great West Road, The North Circular Road) but also further beyond at distances that would be trying, if possible, on foot (Sidcup, Luton). His identity is fragmented by this lack of fixed location, and this is further exacerbated by his admission of living under the assumed identity Bernard Jenkins, and the instability of his purported real surname (as either the Welsh Davies, or more broadly Celtic Mac Davies) which sets his ancestry still further outside of London. He repeatedly asserts that, should he be able to get down to Sidcup (which projects a leafy, respectable middle-class environment), he would be able to get his authentic papers that will permit him a fresh start.[22] The fact that these papers have been looked after by an acquaintance for fifteen years or so might generate just a whiff of suspicion about the circumstances in which a man who claims a past in the military services sought an alternative identity towards the end of the Second World War (given the date of the play), and we might further note that Sidcup was the location for the Army Pay Office. His hard life on the road might account for the shifty, evasive nature the old man exhibits but it is ultimately his failure to recognise and reciprocate authentic human care that sows the seeds of his downfall. Instead of taking Aston's kindnesses with appropriate humility, he allows his distrust of all that is different to him, and his natural opportunism, to snuff out the opportunities that are so evidently laid out before him.

When Mick first returns at the end of Act One, the audience still do not know his status in this house. His furtive, burglar-like departure at the beginning of the play remains unclarified. When he assaults Davies, who has been left alone rummaging through the junk, and utters the words 'What's the game?' (27), we are as likely to apply that question to him as to Davies, about whom we have already formed a pretty good impression. He soon bamboozles Davies with a set of speeches in which he claims the tramp reminds him of various people, whom he locates either mostly on the other side of London (Aldgate, Camden Town, Dalston Junction, Finsbury Park, Highbury Corner, Shoreditch), south of the river (Putney), or in straightforward vagrant terms out on the road into London ('the other side of the Guildford by-pass') (32). Geographically, then, Mick suggests that Davies is in the wrong territory, and by clarifying that he is both Aston's brother and the owner of the property, he trashes any legitimate claim Davies might protest he has to be in that room alone. From our point of view in the audience, we know that Aston has given the old man clear permission to stay, and our attachment to Mick is double-edged. We might feel some sense of relief that he has come to correct the level of exposure to exploitation that the trusting Aston has created for himself, but we recognise that Mick's verbal and physical assaults are disproportionate to the level of threat presented. A dramatic hiatus occurs when Aston returns, the pace being further slowed down by a couple of drips of rainwater into the suspended bucket, which adds comic punctuation to the scene as all three look up on each one.

Unwilling to assert any authority over his brother, or undermine him in front of this unwelcome guest, Mick resorts to playing a longer game for the rest of the play, applying different tactics of domination. These move from the terrifying use of the vacuum cleaner in the dark (Davies manifests an illogical fear of household appliances such as the electric fire or the disconnected gas stove), to allowing him the space to openly criticise Aston, to linguistic traps through which Davies is obliged to deny a set of skills as interior decorator that Mick has deliberately misunderstood he possesses. In these ways, Mick gets Davies to dig his own grave and causes him to have the confidence to deride and threaten Aston. Wielding the vocabulary of his xenophobia, the old man suggests to Mick that his brother 'should go back where he come from' (69), revealing a confused response to the revelation of Aston's mental illness that finally disassembles the bond of generosity that gave him access to the house. The final scene has Davies pleading to remain to a silently resolute Aston. His final questions, 'What am I going to do?', 'What shall I do?', 'Where am I going to go?' (75–6), might usually demand a sympathetic response, but any chance of this has been consumed by his contemptuous behaviour. If the play has been a game of domination for a right to remain in this space after the offer of care from Aston to Davies, Mick's care for Aston has necessitated a strategic scheme of manipulation of Davies's myopic selfishness. Care has been taken to correct an imbalance, when a care tendered unconditionally was not taken with appropriate reciprocity.

Pinter would expand significantly on the theme of our caretaking of one another in much of his later writing. Encouraged by the success of *The Caretaker* in 1960, his first impulse in the first years of the new decade was to explore the rich dramatic prospects of conflict between the sexes, and develop and sophisticate the simple female archetypes that had populated his first plays. The tensions and parallels between maternal and sexual impulses embodied in Rose, Meg and Flora had barely broken beyond the membrane of symbolic value, and in plays that follow, a bridge from metaphor to interpersonal experience is constructed in the representation of female characters.

CHAPTER 2
THE COMPANY OF MEN AND THE PLACE OF WOMEN

The Male Church
The Dwarfs

Between 1952 and 1956, as either a jobbing or 'resting' actor, a young Harold Pinter began the task of writing a novel, *The Dwarfs*. Autobiographical in part, it charts the ebb, flow and decay of relationships between three young men – Mark, Len and Pete – and a young woman, Virginia. The novel focusses in part on the nature of friendship between men, how they negotiate what they mean to one another and what value their interactions have to their individual development. Pete explains the nature of that male friendship to his girlfriend Virginia:

> They were hardly one in dogma or direction, but there was a common ground and there was a framework. At their best they formed a unit, and a unit which [...] was entitled to be called a church; an alliance of the three of them for the common good, and a faith in that alliance.[1]

That 'faith' – an unmeasured trust between the men – is to be tested through the novel, most notably in relation to Virginia. The three friends are very different in temperament, and it is only their banter over art, literature and art criticism that sees them at their best together. Len, a railway porter who has a precarious relationship with the mysterious dwarfs of the title, exhibits behaviour that indicates a possible mental illness which the other two either do not notice or choose to dismiss. After an aborted trip to Paris, he is hospitalised with a bowel condition. Mark is portrayed as a womaniser and vain hedonist. He is referred to in his absence by Len and Pete as 'a sexual mechanic' and he himself seems content to play to this stereotype (54). Pete is an office worker who comes across as a superior-minded thinker, detached from his own emotions, able to witness them and comment upon them. Virginia is Pete's girlfriend, though she eventually tires of his treatment of her and separates from him. The novel is a series of scenes between permutations of all four of these characters, with occasional brief interventions by Len about his dwarfs.

Late in the novel, Virginia contacts Mark after she splits from Pete, and the two seduce one another in a brief scene which ends with her informing him that Pete thinks him a fool. This betrayal of friendship – a friendship, Mark now takes it, based upon an invention of mutual respect – is later pitted against the perceived betrayal of sleeping with his friend's ex, and the two men spend over ten pages of the novel's penultimate chapter unpicking what they feel about one another. The discussion has been prepared by an earlier statement by Len to Mark:

> Occasionally, as I say, I believe I perceive a little of what you are, but that's pure accident. Pure accident on both our parts. The perceived and the perceiver. It must be accident. We depend on such accidents to continue [...] You're the sum of so many reflections. How many reflections? Whose reflections? Is that what you consist of? What scum does the tide leave? [...] What have I seen, the scum or the essence? (151–2)

Len's pragmatic, existential doubt over what we can truly know of one another communicated solely through our actions is tested fully in Pete and Mark's final stand-off, in which scum is weighed against essence, perceptions are listed and applied not only as character traits, but as reasons for friendship to end: failing to share one's perceptions of one another, and thereby permit false assumptions to continue between friends, being led 'up the garden' (175). The decay of the men's friendship is mirrored throughout the novel in the metaphor of putrefying food and drink, to which Len is most susceptible, most notably in his aversion to a camembert he claims made him ill in Paris, prefiguring his hospital treatment.

The presence of Virginia in this otherwise all-male friendship is not portrayed as disruptive by Pinter, but Pete clearly demarcates areas of conversation in which she might have no right to participate. When she first appears in the novel, she is not presented in the company of her boyfriend Pete, and thereby as defined through him in such ways, but instead we meet her on her own, reflecting on how he would respond to her aesthetic notions of how she disrupts the sunlight in the room by moving through it. A page of his imagined, pedantic, phenomenological dismissal of her introspection then follows, inserting his domineering presence into their relationship before he is materially present. Her gentle derision of his attitudes establishes her as emotionally intelligent and tolerant. Pinter seems to side with her in the manner in which he too, as author, frequently ascribes agency to a room throughout the novel as a form of transferred epithet for what is happening in it: 'The room settled' (23); 'The room is moving' (29); 'The room grunted, slapped' (129); 'The room stopped' (170). In sharing the aesthetic predisposition of the narrative voice in this way, Virginia is presented as a sympathetic and even reliable character.

Virginia's neutrally expressed satisfaction with her own body, wearing a loose dressing gown after a bath, is dismissed by Pete as vulgar and exhibitionist: 'you're behaving like any other little tart who must show herself off or cease to exist' (85). This reveals much about the particular masculine perspective that Pete manifests and Pinter is critiquing. Earlier, Pete explains his attraction to Virginia in terms of how she avoids easy representations of femininity: 'For example, you don't need to clutter yourself up with ornaments of provocation, that kind of stuff [...] you do not have to go in for titillation, like the rest of them' (40–1). He may have a point that gender is a culturally constructed performance, but he removes individual choice and expression from his disdainful equation. In a later drunken party scene, a woman removes her clothes and overtly toys with her own objectification as an expression of her own pursuit of pleasure. As an inebriated consumer of this spectacle, Pete makes no judgement, and surrenders to the atmosphere by finding a bedroom with a girl named Brenda. His attraction to Virginia, then, is based upon a hypocritical basis that she excludes herself from a code of sexual attraction that he otherwise enjoys as its beneficiary. He drunkenly tells Brenda 'women are women. It doesn't do to forget it' (127), indicating a distinction of some sort that is important to him, a behavioural distinction between the genders that is innate, beyond performance.

Virginia asks Pete for a break in their relationship, a break which becomes permanent. With perhaps typical macho dismissal of her reasons, Pete tells Mark that she has 'changed her spots [...] mixing with some crowd in Soho, that's all. She's gone gay' (155–6). Mark later puts it to Virginia that he has heard she has been 'gadding about', which she dismissively confirms (159). Virginia's degeneration, as Pete wills to see it, is then presented as an individual choice, and her and Mark's mutual seduction concludes it as straightforward sexual independence. Towards the novel's end, as part of the concluding argument between Mark and Pete, Mark berates Pete's attitude to women: 'Your behaviour to Virginia [...] has been criminal for years' (170). He offers an egalitarian view that erases Pete's hierarchical view of people's relative worth: 'You exist, but just remember that so does she, in her own right' (178).

The importance of this novel to an appreciation of the corpus of Pinter's dramatic writing lies in the key strands of male friendship, and the betrayals that undermine it, and of the various representations of women that spring from within that setting. Pinter returned to the unpublished manuscript of *The Dwarfs* in 1960 to rework the material as drama, first for the radio and then for the stage. It was broadcast on the BBC Third Programme on 2 December that year, and first staged in September 1963 at the New Arts Theatre, London. The play has only Len, Pete and Mark as characters, and there is no mention of Virginia. Len is more clearly positioned as a hinge between the two others, and the play focusses on the interaction between the three men as friends. The dwarfs are mentioned in dialogue, with Len indicating more overtly than in the novel that they are in place to observe, manage and assist in the brewing trouble between the friends.

The repeated presence of and reference to food and drink becomes more readily symbolic on stage than on the page, as we witness characters prepare tea, bring on glasses for wine or whisky, offer beigel, and handle biscuit tins and apples. This physical carrying and manipulation of food and drink might present or underline notions of sharing, hospitality and mutual sustenance that are aspects of friendship scrutinised by the play. These are then tempered by all the references to rotting and decay, from the first scene where a solid-ified, fortnight-old pint of milk is fruitlessly shaken over a teacup, to Len's business gargling with wine before spitting it back in to his glass and shelving the bottle he had thought to share, to mention of the cheese that is the cause of Len's diarrhoea. Even Mark's Portuguese toasting fork – as an ornament, disconnected from its original utility – adds to this metaphorical field more obviously than it might in the novel. On the page it serves more straightforwardly to locate its owner as a Sephardic Jew than as the index of hospitality it adopts when wielded on stage.

With his dramatic adaptations of *The Dwarfs*, Pinter tried to concentrate on the failures within the friendships of men, who become victims of the perceptions they project of themselves, failing to profit from the nurturing potential of their alliance. The fractures that threaten the solid bonds made between men were to become closely examined across a number of his works. We have already seen how in *The Caretaker*, Pinter examined the failure to profit from generosity in an environment of potential mutual care-taking. Prior to the success of that play, he had relied to a certain degree on the footholds offered to him by a number of commissions to write for radio and television. He continued to write for the screen throughout his life, but the period between the two key plays *The Caretaker* (1960) and *The Homecoming* (1965) saw a proliferation of writing for TV and film. In fact, nearly two-thirds of his output in those years was for media other than the stage. For the cinema, he adapted *The Servant* (1963), *The Pumpkin Eater* (1964), *The Quiller Memorandum* (1966) and drafted a screenplay for *Accident* (1967). For television he wrote *A Night Out* (1960), *Night School* (1960), *The Collection* (1961), *The Lover* (1963) and

53

Tea Party (1965). As discussed above, he adapted his unpublished novel *The Dwarfs* for Radio (broadcast in December 1960) and then for the stage (1963). The television works were each soon adapted to stage plays (*The Collection* and *The Lover* first, in 1962 and 1963 respectively) and it is in this form that most of them are published for us today in Faber's *Plays 2* and *Plays 3* collections. These television plays, then, soon entered the canon of Pinter's writing for the stage, and today are encountered by actors, directors and audiences in that form. The psychology of male groupings is explored in *A Night Out*, *The Collection* and *The Homecoming* (and in the screenplays to *The Servant* and, much later, *Sleuth* (2007)). We also see various representations of women and femininity in those plays, and also in *Night School*, *The Lover* and *Tea Party*, culminating in the remarkable *The Homecoming*. In considering the plays of the early 1960s, up to and including that last play, we can examine how Pinter was at that time seemingly fascinated by these discourses of gender interaction, and the manner in which men and women construct 'narratives' of one another as part of the process of negotiating their relationships, and how these 'narratives' could be corrupted or corrupting.

Untenable Archetypes
A Night Out, Night School, The Collection, Tea Party

In his book *Sex on Stage*, Andrew Wylie claims that Pinter achieved 'an idiosyncratic view of gender politics' which he characterises as the 'terrible pain of reconciling masculine alienation with feminine reassurance'.[2] While it would not be accurate to say this characterises all of Pinter's inter-gender behaviour, it captures well some of the early explorations of this territory. *A Night Out* (1960) first puts masculine alienation in operation against feminine reassurance in stark terms, and delineates gender roles in stereotypical form. In it, we have an overbearing mother, flirtatious and manipulative young girls and a prostitute who seeks to project herself as more respectable than her profession might allow.

In the opening scene we meet a young man, Albert Stokes, combing his hair and polishing his shoes in preparation for a night out. His mother, with whom he lives, feigns to have forgotten he has told her he was attending a works retirement party and applies what we assume to be routine emotional blackmail to get him to stay at home. In trying to get him to go into the cellar to get a light bulb to replace the faulty one in a spare room that was once his late grandmother's bedroom, she invokes a doubling and reinforcement of her maternal role (she refers to 'Grandma's room' five times) to make him comply. When this fails she further invokes parental authority and shame, insisting that he does not 'go messing about with girls' through a coercive implication that it would upset his dead father.[3] Our introduction to Albert, then, is as someone very heavily tied to his mother's apron strings by a combination of his own lack of independence and her passive-aggressive manipulation. The mother seems motivated by an emotional need to keep her son in an immature form, and therefore incorruptible by the opposite sex, who might take him from her.

In the next scene, we hear more of Albert from his work colleagues, who are waiting for him at a coffee stall. We learn that he has performed badly at a recent works football game, after being moved to 'left back' position from his usual 'left half'. As a result of the shift to a defensive position that he was not accustomed to, Albert exposed the team, and was blamed for their failure. The football analogy situates Albert into a team environment that parallels the work environment, and now he is on the way to a social environment with the same group of people. Here too he is put in a defensive position when Gidney, a self-assured co-worker (who notably plays the key 'centre half' in the football team) puts two girls up to pretending to be attracted to Albert. When one of these girls is furtively goosed by the elderly Mr Ryan, in whose honour the party is being held, Albert gets the blame. Gidney then goes after him and seems happy to add this supposed infraction to his recent football failings as a reason to tear a strip off him. Knowingly pushing his buttons, Gidney tells Albert he is a 'mother's boy' which triggers a quite significant release of anger. Albert punches Gidney, and a scuffle ensues.

An audience at this stage would probably have a good deal of sympathy for Albert. He is an abused innocent, trapped in an emotional bind by his mother and dismissed in his only community of peers, who represent both his social and professional life. Like Stanley before him, he is mollycoddled at home and resented and punished for retreating from everyday social interaction. An audience's sense of pity for him is rewarded by the fact that he does show some mettle in standing up for himself, verbally and eventually physically. He talks sensibly back to his mother, offering logical reasons for why he cannot fix the light bulb for her immediately, and undermining her invocations of his father and grandmother by pointing out that they are no longer among the living. At the party, he responds politely but incredulously to the girls' fake attention, and when Gidney seeks to reprimand him he stands his ground verbally. As such, he is not represented as without spirit or self-respect, and when he snaps and punches Gidney, we as audience are encouraged to feel the bully got what he was asking for: we accept a moral compromise for a minor victory scored by our oddball hero.

From our seat on the stalls, we might at this point expect Albert to somehow redeem himself from this altogether forgivable moment of weakness. His fight with Gidney bears the hallmarks of a typical dramatic moment of crisis, after which we expect the rest of the play to fall easily into place: his masculinity asserted and his reputation defended, Albert may come out of the experience purged and ready to get the rest of his life equally under control. The investment we make in Albert, however, is quickly turned against us. He returns home at midnight (having clearly spent the interim in a brooding funk of resentment) to find his mother asleep amid her scattered game of solitaire on the kitchen table. She wakes and gives him both barrels of her emotional torment, taking his disarray as evidence of 'mucking about with girls' (360). She places his dried up dinner on the table as an emblem of his shame, and berates him at length for treating the house like a hotel and not appreciating her efforts.

Albert says nothing, then bangs the table, grabs the clock that she has deliberately placed there to mark his absence and raises it above his head. The scene ends with a blackout and a scream from his mother. Instead of taking the usual root of a dramatic hero who might fight against the odds to demonstrate his worth, he instantaneously descends in our estimation to a maniac capable of matricide.

Back out in the urban landscape, he meets a prostitute who solicits his custom and invites him back to her flat. His docile acceptance of this suggests a change of spirit, perhaps a new-found machismo, ready to be tested. The Girl (Pinter does not grace her character with a name) is not rendered as a prostitute in stereotypical mode – in fact she displays none of the erotic signatures that other Pinter women of this period exhibit – but instead she is presented (and presents herself) as another maternal figure. The lure of sex here demurs to the fear of the maternal. Once in her flat, the Girl begins to manifest a discomfort with her profession by using two distraction tactics. First, she professes to respectability by pointing out a photograph of a girl she claims to be her daughter, stating that she is in a boarding school near Hereford, implying she is both a mother and a person of means. Secondly, she gives Albert a series of house-proud instructions as to his behaviour: he must not walk heavily on the floor, he must not swear, he must not sit on her stool, he must use a handkerchief if he coughs. The scene comes to replicate the previous one, with his mother berating him, and Albert snaps and offers a similar response. He grabs her clock from the mantelpiece and threatens her with it, equating her to not only his mother, but the girls whose behaviour had earlier caused his undeserving oppression: 'You're all the same, you see, you're all the same, you're just a dead weight around my neck' (371). He grimly declares that he 'finished the conversation' with his mother, that he 'finished her' and appeals that he 'loved her, really' (371–2), all very determinedly in the past tense, leading us to assume that he not only killed his mother but that, consequently, he represents a present danger to the girl. Albert then uses a set of commands as a mode of threat, one that menaces the Girl and causes us to fear the worst of his motivation:

Albert Get up.
Girl No...
Albert Get up! Up! *She stands.* Walk over there to the wall. Go on! Go over there. Do as you're told. Do as I'm telling you. I'm giving the orders here. *She walks to the wall.* Stop!
Girl [*wimpering*]. What... Do you want me to do?
Albert Just keep your big mouth shut for a start. *He frowns uncertainly.* Cover your face! *She does so. He looks around blinking.* Yes. That's right. (372–3)

For Albert, controlling a woman through a sequence of commands is less about erotic fulfilment and more out of a desire once and for all to give a woman orders rather than receive them. His instruction for the Girl to cover her face is frighteningly typical of real scenes of manipulation of this sort, where a male aggressor senses a need to depersonalise his victim by rendering her as body without face, as well as seeking to limit her ability later to recognise or describe him. That Albert has no specific orders to give once he has the Girl's compliance indicates that control itself was his goal, not control for any specific purpose. His decision then to ask her to collect his shoes and put them on his feet, and lace them, is simply pathetic. Watching from our seats, these last instructions mean we witness the Girl bend down before Albert and, in demeaning her thus, he demeans himself in our eyes. He humiliates her further by flipping her half a crown in mock deference to her profession.

The final scene contains the play's dramatic punch line. With a smile and a confident demeanour, Albert returns home in the cold, early hours of the morning. He saunters across the hall and throws his jacket and tie across the kitchen. There, he sits and stares at the ceiling with a satisfied look on his face. And then we hear his mother's voice. She is very much alive and waiting to confront him for what turns out only to have been an empty threat of violence, an unresolved expression of frustration and impotence. She offers to forget it and take him away on a holiday and, as though talking to a young child, tells him 'you're not a bad boy, Albert, I know you're not' (375). Accordingly, Albert's physicality reverts to type: 'His body freezes. His gaze comes down. His legs slowly come together. He looks in front of him' (374).

Albert might have gained our respect but he lacks a dignifying strategy for coping with his emotional straightjacket, and his abuse of the Girl renders any humour from the regaining of control by the matriarch in the final scene somewhat suspect. It is as though an important question about male behaviour remains unanswered in favour of the comedic satisfaction of the ultimate emasculation of an insecure man, both admonished and absorbed by an infantilising maternal system he cannot escape. The theatrical and comedic imperatives, then, dominate over ideological concerns in this play. In order to be initiated, our laughter has to be grounded in a recognition of the stereotype of the overbearing matriarch, and the angst of the male experience in its shadow. This involves, as Drew Milne outlines, 'the assumption of male perspectives whose structural blind spots form the basis of unrecognised political exclusions'.[4] As such, then, the laughter is culturally defined by certain presumptions that may be different in different cultures, including our own present-day culture decades after the play was written. Those gender presumptions might merit scrutiny, but *A Night Out* does little to critique them; the comic 'punch line' relies on them.

In his next work, *Night School*, the author complicates issues by taking further the level of dissimulation that the Girl had employed in *A Night Out*. She had pretended that a photograph of herself as a young girl was her own daughter, an innocent and vulnerable lie that Albert exposes. In *Night School* we again see a photograph used to call into question what a woman declares of herself. Sally has taken lodgings with Walter's two elderly aunts, Milly and Annie, who have given her their nephew's bedroom while he is in jail for forgery. Returning home to discover he must now sleep on a 'put-u-up' in the dining room, Walter begrudges Sally her lodgings but is equally beguiled by her. When trying to find his hidden cache of forged post-office books in his old wardrobe, he comes across a photograph of Sally in her guise as a nightclub hostess, entertaining two gentlemen. Sally has explained to her landladies that her income comes from being a school teacher, which may also be true, but Walter seeks to find out more about her by engaging the help of a local criminal, Solto. He then tracks her down to a nightclub, but, equally taken with her, denies her existence to Walter. Realising Walter has discovered her photograph from her conversation with Solto, Sally packs her bags and leaves a farewell note in her room, alongside a self-vindicating photograph of herself as a school teacher.

Pinter was discontent with *Night School*, believing it to be evidence of his 'slipping into formula',[5] and even considered not having it published in his collected works. The printed text now available in *Plays 2* is a revised radio version of the original television script, and this now functions as the available stage script. The 1966 revisions augment the ambiguities embedded in the 1960 original and render the character of Walter as seemingly more conniving and calculating. Handing the photograph of Sally as hostess to Solto comes across to us as a deliberate ploy to undermine Sally's respectable alibi and regain his bedroom without recourse to confrontation. Dissimulation and creative self-representation are used as narrative devices here, and the play is something of a sketched experiment in that regard, embellished by some mild comedy in the characterisation of the food-obsessed elderly aunts. Both Walter and Sally offer constructed representations of themselves to steer the other's impressions: Sally by projecting herself as a school teacher, and Walter by telling her he acts as a 'gentle gunman' for an armed robbery gang.[6] Sally, then, seeks to disguise an occupation that involves her making use of her sexual allure, while Walter seeks to make himself more attractive by claiming an edgy and dangerous occupation (but carried out with a 'gentle' disposition). Albert (who claimed to the Girl to be an assistant director) and the Girl in *A Night Out* employed the same tactics of course, and Pinter is repeating himself here, slipping into formula, to match women who seek to protect themselves from judgement against men who feel an insecure need to pretend to be something they are not when confronted with sexually expressive women. In both cases, the men read the women's dissimulation as suspect, as a reason to distrust and fear manipulation, due to the consequent magnification of their own inadequacies.

These issues of distrust and dissimulation formed the basis of a much more successful and engaging play, *The Collection*, first broadcast on television in May 1961, and transferring to the stage the year after. Pinter here begins to develop the issues he had explored in *A Night Out* and *Night School*, although now the ingredient of sexual jealousy is poured into the mix. The play's dramatis personae is comprised of a married couple and a gay partnership, and in this way Pinter begins to dissolve some of the gender presumptions that had informed the comedy of the earlier plays. Harry and Bill live together in the former's house in Belgravia, an affluent part of London not far from Buckingham Palace. The play opens with Harry returning home in the early hours to find his house phone ringing. He answers it to receive some curt demands to wake Bill, which he refuses to do. This incident incites suspicious behaviour and questions over breakfast, but Bill insists he does not know who might have been calling him at that hour. We soon learn that it is James who wants so insistently to speak to Bill, to confront him about having slept with his wife, Stella, in a Leeds hotel during a trade exhibition the week before. The play then unfolds from a series of differing versions of what happened between Bill and Stella, and the characters' responses to these.

Whatever happened at the Leeds hotel is an event that drives the whole drama, and the various nuanced narratives that we hear of what happened cross-reference one another confusingly. An audience are unlikely to come to a conclusion over which elements might be true and which made-up. The kaleidoscope of variants simply cannot be held and processed by a mind attentive to an ongoing performance. This is an important theatrical fact, in considering plays such as this; confusion and ambiguity are key to the audience experience, and clarity is deliberately inaccessible. As a result, our natural desire to want to know the facts of the matter is necessarily displaced, and instead we might begin to consider the motives of the characters. Our expectation as audience, when we first hear James's accusation of Bill, is to take this as a factual statement that drives that character's motivations towards the second man, and that the drama will progress in the pursuit of a resolution of that conflict: a satisfaction of James's dishonoured position. The detail James gives of the Leeds tryst indicates either a very thorough confession by his wife, or the results of a particularly intense interrogation of wife by husband. Bill denies having seduced Stella at first, offering a second narrative in which she kissed him as they came out of the lift together, but they then went their separate ways to their own rooms. This alternative scenario might be quickly dismissed as a self-protecting lie, soon exposed when he seemingly confirms details of the accusation against him, placing himself in Stella's room. James recounts his conversation will Bill to Stella, implying that Bill had confirmed her story but suggested that she had 'hypnotised' him.[7] When Harry then goes to talk to Stella, in an attempt to clear up the mess that is disrupting his household, she declares to him that she hardly saw Bill in Leeds and that it is James who has 'dreamed up' the 'fantastic story' (136), portraying him as an excessively jealous husband. We are here obliged to reconsider what we have made of James, and indeed of Bill's decision to acquiesce to the story, if it was made up. We are further confused when Harry, returning home to find Bill and James close to fighting, opts to offer a different account to the one we have heard him told. He states that Stella confessed to being the one who made the whole story up. We detect perhaps a subtle tactic: if James knows that Harry has spoken to Stella – whether Stella spoke the truth to Harry or not – then James cannot continue to maintain a position of authority over the certainty of what happened in Leeds. This fifth version of events is then countered by a sixth, in which Bill declares that Stella and he together made up a story of their seduction, spending two hours together in the hotel lounge constructing a fantasy of what they would do together if they were to go to her room.

Bill's final confession throws us further. It sounds credible, which erases as unlikely what we have heard so far. But it is in fact only a recounting of a story-telling exercise: how Stella and James played a game of describing what they might do with, to and for one another. In this way, we note that the infidelity described was a constructed narrative all along, but one that was pursued in a form of a sort of erotic parlour game. The nothing that happened was anyway an infidelity of sorts (in the form of a shared titillating narrative) but not one that James can manfully pursue at the level of the stakes he has raised. The final version of events is all that James has left to take back to Stella, and the final scene has him telling her what she and Bill had done, which she receives 'neither confirming nor denying' (145).

The gay couple Bill and Harry are not represented with the sorts of stereotyping that, for example, the mother in *A Night Out* is, and Pinter seems to include gay characters here as a means simply to engender ambiguity of motivation in a story of narrated desires, while offering such partnerships the dignity of equal emotional disquiet. Sexuality is wielded subtly by Pinter as part of the battle of wits between James and Bill and an ambiguous bond is established between them, which takes on some of the traits of attraction and flirtation. At the first meeting between them, when James barges into the house, he keeps Bill wrong-footed by employing convivial conversational tactics, dismissing his denials as the words of 'a wag' and then offering Bill a drink in his own living room (121). He later belittles his wife by indicating he prefers Bill's company to hers and employs the words 'man', 'bloke' or 'masculine' nine times in short succession, as if verbally to activate her exclusion through gender. By pointing out to her how he shared a laugh with Bill, he displaces her as the subject of an affair by instead making her an object of male derision. When he later successfully reduces her to tears – effectively by erasing the significance of her story through not only its confirmation but with an implied friendship with her fantasised object of desire – he goes further and employs the inference of attraction behind the euphemistic description of Bill as 'a man's man'. 'I do understand, but only after meeting him' he continues, 'I can see it both ways, three ways, all ways' (131–2), suggesting a strategic migration of sexual attraction that further excludes her.

Stella is very much a peripheral character in the play, which concerns itself mostly with male attitudes to infidelity and with the dilemma that what we know of one another is dependent upon a necessary belief in what we are told. When she speaks, it is mostly in response to others, and she gets no real opportunity to define herself.

As such, she is something of a narrative device, employed by her author to get the drama between men in motion. When her husband makes her suffer, it informs us about him, rather than gives us any insight into her character's emotional reality, and she exists more in the play in the manner in which the other men talk about her, than as a physical presence. In his second encounter with James, Bill offers a definition of female behaviour that clarifies Stella's supposed deportment in Leeds in a way which subtly abases her husband:

> Every woman is bound to have an outburst of ... wild sensu-
> ality at one time or another. [...] Even though it may be the
> kind of sensuality of which you yourself have never been the
> fortunate recipient [...] That's a husband's fate, I suppose. (139)

His words here emphasise a not uncommon cultural positioning of women that would exclude their personal sexual expression from the union of marriage. By way of commiseration, Bill suggests that 'the system's at fault, not you', implying an understanding of a 'system' of gender interaction that both explains women's unruly behaviour and exonerates men's repressive responses to it, while also perhaps implying an invitation to leave the system for an all-male alternative. Harry later seems to speak the language such a system advocates when he suggests to James that he might simply 'go home and knock [Stella] over the head with a saucepan' (142) as a ready solution to the situation that would avoid the need for masculine confrontation. In appealing to an assumed innate set of gender values, Bill and Harry are attempting to pull James away from the lack of clarity that has arisen from a series of conflicting narrations of infidelity. What Pinter is doing, though, is drawing our attention to such assumed values, within a drama of uncertainty. When James finally confronts Stella with a version of what happened in Leeds which she neither confirms nor denies, he might be regarded as attempting to clarify an uncertain past episode by asking her to acknowledge (whether true or not) a version that he can cope with, and thereby a narrative of her as his wife that can cause their relationship no further damage. 'That's the truth, isn't it?' he insists, but Stella's 'friendly, sympathetic' face gives nothing away (145). The 'truth', Pinter seems to suggest, is not a set of established facts but a negotiated story, especially where verification is not available.

Pinter wrote his first screenplay adaptation shortly after completing *The Collection*, turning Robin Maugham's novella *The Servant* into a script for a film. It was directed by Joseph Losey and was released in November 1963. Michael Billington considers the film to be an 'extension of [*The Collection*]'s pre-occupation with the politics of domestic power and the equivocal nature of sexuality'.[8] The possibility of a latent homosexuality had been exploited in the portrayal of James and Bill's association, and Pinter wove a similar tension between the characters of Barrett and Tony in his screenplay. In part, this attraction between men is established in both play and film by the implication that the two men have 'shared' the same woman, a sexual meeting of men by heterosexual proxy. *The Servant* portrays a moral collapse that is brought about through a combination of fraud, ambition and aimless gluttony on one part and vacant character, misguided trust and flaccid ambition on the other. Between the two are revealed the vacuous prerogatives of social codes that lead to opportunism and assumed rights. The moneyed Tony is doing up a house and seeks a gentleman's gentleman to keep the place in order. He employs the seemingly servile Barrett, but slowly we note how Barrett takes control of the layout and decor of the house, acts in a subordinate manner, invites in his girlfriend Vera (saying she is his sister) and develops a Mephisthophelean grip over Tony. Pinter's very early short prose piece *Kullus*, written in 1949, shares thematic shape with *The Servant* in the manner in which Barrett slowly takes control of Tony's house and soul. Pinter read his 1955 prose piece 'The Examination' (in which the Kullus character was revisited) on BBC radio on 7 September 1962, and perhaps his returned attention to it had been prompted by his work on that screenplay. He then resurrected the character and scenario one final time in 1963, when approached to provide an original screenplay for a project that aimed to film original screenplays by him, Samuel Beckett and Eugène Ionesco. The result was *The Compartment*, which was never to be filmed due to a failure to assure financial backing. Only Beckett's script, entitled *Film*, came of the project. The unused script was later retrieved and converted by its author to a television piece with a new title of *The Basement*, broadcast by the BBC on 20 February 1967. The central Kullus motif of a room being taken over by an invading agent is expanded here in the screenplay and eventual TV production, and the medium permits the slow visual transformation of the room and allows for ambiguity of perspective to distort and extend visual possibilities.

Tim Law is alone in his basement flat reading an erotic book when an old friend, Charles Stott, knocks on the door and asks to be invited in, out of the pouring rain. He eventually indicates he has a girl, Jane, with him, and asks is she might join them. He then takes her to Law's bed and makes love to her. In subsequent scenes, Stott slowly takes over Law's flat and Jane becomes Law's lover. The scenes swap between internal and external, night and day, the basement flat's decor and furnishings change radically, and seasons come and go rapidly. The inclusion of a woman as a love and lust interest who is willingly 'shared' as a manipulative manoeuvre to facilitate control over someone, as with Vera in *The Servant*, is a diversion at this stage from the manner in which Pinter was writing and developing female characters. Sally in *Night School* and Stella in *The Collection* might not be fully drawn characters, but they offer intelligent challenges to the male figures and masculine narratives of gender. If the shawled girl in *Kullus* was an early prototype, she offered little other than mystery and sexual allure, and in returning to that scenario for expansion as *The Compartment/The Basement*, Pinter was perhaps taking time to inhabit fully an old creative impulse about manipulation and domination before returning to develop his female characters as something more than narrative devices.

The Basement exploited as fully as any of Pinter's screenplays the freedoms the medium offered him as author, and one key manner in which the work was to articulate itself on screen was in an ambiguous shift between a realist expression of objective reality and subjective perspectives. Pinter can be seen to be thinking through further possibilities of the blurring of the subjective and the objective in a short prose piece he wrote the same year as *The Compartment*. The result,

Tea Party, was soon adapted as a drama for television and presented on BBC TV in March 1965. The prose version was published in *Playboy* in 1965 and the script was not to make its debut as a stage play until 1970. With *Tea Party*, Pinter returned to considering the implications of a 'system' of gender understandings and the impact that has upon men (and again we can note that any impact upon women is still not central). The distinction that Bill in *The Collection* draws between female sexual behaviour outside and inside of marriage – the desexualisation of the wife and the provocative availability of the single woman with her own sexual agenda – is something that haunts the character of Disson in *Tea Party*, the chief executive of a firm of sanitary ware producers. In the introductory scene he is interviewing an attractive young secretary, Wendy, who complains that her previous employer would touch her inappropriately. Pinter has her cross and uncross her legs four times during the scene, a signal employed in his other works to denote sexuality. We also learn that the following day Disson is to get married, and in this way the mutually repelling narrative strands of married life and libidinous desire are introduced with an early promise of comedic entanglement. This is humorously echoed in Disson's respectable middle-class business of constructing apparatus for the sanitation of bodily functions.

Disson's gender insecurities manifest themselves as a curious form of visual impairment, which deteriorates to full blindness. His friend and optometrist, Disley, hints that his experiences of faltering eyesight are psychosomatic in some way ('I only deal with eyes old chap [...] Why don't you go to someone else?').[9] Our attention, then, is drawn to consider some psychological failing or problem. This visual impairment first occurs during a game of Ping-Pong with his brother-in-law, Willy, watched by his stepsons Tom and John, and then in his workroom, when he nearly saws through Tom's fingers. Later, full blindness inflicts him while dictating a letter to Wendy. In the first two instances, then, his problem arises in domestic, recreational contexts and in both he is challenged in some way by his sons. In the first, John encourages Willy to beat his father by attacking his forehand, and in the second John annoys his father by preferring his homework to the instruction in woodwork Disson wishes to give him. We might recognise that in these scenes Disson is being mildly undermined, and we have noted earlier that he is sensitive to any challenge to his authority or masculinity. Immediately after marrying Diana, for example, he asks her if he makes her happier than 'with any other man' (102).

Disson's brother-in-law Willy represents something of a challenge to Disson over the course of the play, on both a social and sexual scale. We learn in the second scene, when Willy takes on the job of best man at Disson and Diane's wedding, that Disson is marrying into a family of social high status (and from his own parents' dialogue later that he comes from humbler origins). Disson invites Willy to take on the role of his right-hand man at the firm, and, to his surprise, Willy suggests that his sister, Disson's new bride, might act as his secretary. In this way, Pinter intersects Disson's domestic life with his professional life and adds an erotic interest (in the form of Wendy) that then intersects with both (she passes through the door between Disson and Willy's offices, and Disson's paranoia at what happens in that room has him at one point peering through the keyhole). This blurring of his environments, and the placement of his wife outside of the domestic sphere, and in close relation to the sexually intriguing Wendy, are the cause for his loss of focus. 'I don't like self-doubt. I don't like fuzziness. I like clarity' he states (105), and we see quite clearly that he cannot hope for clarity in the scenario established around him. This sets up in us both an expectation of comedy, as a respectful man seeks to maintain his dignity, and also of pity, as we see him set against a paranoid disposition that slowly leads him to mental crisis.

That pity we experience as audience is double-edged, as we recognise that Disson is instrumental in setting up the environment within which his psychosis might grow. When his son refers to him as 'Sir', affecting the kind of inter-generational respect he has learned that his uncle Willy adopted as a child, Disson tells him he must not do so. This seemingly trivial dialogue serves a deliberate and precise function: it simultaneously enacts the social difference between Disson and his wife's family and Disson's reluctant consciousness of that, and it has him correct his sons by recommending, ironically, a dilution of the respect he is due. Inviting his brother-in-law, and subsequently his wife, to occupy the adjacent office to his, while sharing his own with a sexually attractive and available secretary, seems equally bound to create a conflict. Disson has seeded his own downfall.

Wendy's complaint that her previous boss had touched her inappropriately becomes, in retrospect, something of a self-fulfilling prophecy. Her portrayal is key: she must be neither too overt in her sexual availability nor too unaware of her power to attract. When Disson complains of her wriggling as he dictates a letter, and presumes her chair to be too uncomfortable, he proposes that she sit on his desk. The scene acts as an initiation of mutual seduction between them, both in his suggestion of adopting a non-conventional seating position that would put her on display and in her delibera-tions in doing so, emphasising her high heels. Her final words 'There should be no difficulty in meeting your requirements' (109) resound with all the deliberate ambiguity of a clichéd secretary/boss flirtation, turning the vocabulary of their everyday professional interaction into a series of codes that titillate via double meaning. These codes soon take more deliberate form, as game-playing. Disson has Wendy tie her chiffon around his eyes and, only when he is thus sightless, she permits him to touch her. By fetishising blindness this way, Disson gets access to his desires while maintaining a distance from the disre-spectful behaviour through visual deniability. Game playing, then, is the permissive conduit to a release of sexual tension and later Disson initiates a mock-football game using a table cigarette lighter as a ball, explicitly to enable him to grab Wendy's arm. When later he loses his vision altogether in her presence, and asks her in his genuine concern if it is her he is touching, she naturally accuses him of playing a game and 'being naughty again' (124).

Disson's own blurring of his professional and libidinous behav-iours combined with the blurring of his professional and domestic boundaries continue to manifest themselves problematically for him in instances of hysterical blindness (such as Pinter used in *The Room* and *A Slight Ache*) and in an associated paranoia about the exploits of his wife, Willy and Wendy, even to the depths of painfully entertaining the thought of incestuous interaction between Diane and her brother. During the final tea party, which Disson hosts in his office to celebrate his first wedding anniversary, he sits with a tight bandage around his eyes and imagines what is going on around him, including an image of his sister and Wendy lying head to toe on his desk and being caressed by Willy. In having a character reach such a state of crisis over seemingly irreconcilable aspects of femininity, it is as though Pinter collapses any sincere interrogation into ready comedy again. By expanding on the motif of game-playing as a means to access otherwise repressed erotic instincts, he was to find more fertile routes forward with his enquiry around gender.

Negotiations and Contracts
The Lover, The Homecoming

A common trope throughout these gender plays of 1960–5 is the fetishistic control of a woman through a series of orders, and we have already considered a (cowardly) example of that in *A Night Out*. The first root of this can be found in the novel of *The Dwarfs*, in a game that Mark initiates with Virginia:

> – I've never seen your legs above your knees.
> – No.
> – Lift your skirt up.
> – Like this?
> – Yes. Go on.
> – Like this?
> – Leave it?
> – Like this?
> – Uncross your legs.
> – Like this? (161)

The implied desire in Mark's requests is met with an acquiescing enjoyment at being sexually appreciated by Virginia, whose repeated 'like this' demonstrates an acknowledgement of the rules of the game and a willingness to comply and receive the inferred reward of physical contact that might follow. That same fetishistic behaviour re-appears in *Night School*, when Walter offers Sally a few glasses of brandies and eventually commands her to sit down, stand up again, turn around, sit down again, cross and uncross her legs. Wendy and Disson's interaction in his office in *Tea Party* is of this genre: a mutually enjoyed testing of boundaries that facilitates erotic interaction.

With *The Lover*, Pinter took the act of game-playing between partners to an extreme. Written for Associated Rediffusion, *The Lover* was first broadcast in March 1963 and opened in a double bill with the stage version of *The Dwarfs* in September of the same year at the Arts Theatre, London. The drama is generated by the adjustments made to the role-playing arrangement of a married couple, Richard and Sarah. Not all is revealed to the audience at once, and so our discovery of what is going on between the two is part of the comedic pleasure of the piece. The scene opens on a quite conventional, middle-class environment that would not at all be out of place in a Noel Coward play of the 1940s: a detached house 'near Windsor' with 'tasteful, comfortable' furnishings.[10] Sarah in a 'crisp, demure dress' is dusting and tidying as Richard, with his briefcase and bowler hat, crosses the stage to kiss her goodbye for the day. His first line immediately sets awry any pre-conceptions this setting might establish for us: 'Is your lover coming today?', the husband asks, to which his wife responds with a causal, affirmative 'Mmmm'. He enquires whether she and her lover will be going out or staying in, and what time he ought to come home, as though politely concerned not to disturb his wife's antics with another man. Richard leaves, and the lights fade on Sarah continuing her dusting. The lights then rise immediately on scene two, later that day, with Richard returning home and receiving a whisky poured for him by Sarah. Following some seemingly trivial exchanges about the weather and traffic, Richard enquires dispassionately about her afternoon with her lover. As the play establishes itself, then, it seems set on offering us a polite comedy with a bizarrely casual attitude to extra-marital sex.

Despite our laugher, we might detect subtle tensions between the pair onstage, buried in the subtext. These start with a series of seemingly inconsequential contradictions: after refuting his wife's suggestion that perhaps the traffic on his way home was bad, Richard states there was a 'bit of a jam' after she suggests he was 'just a little' late (150); when Richard reminds Sarah that she had once said her lover was interested in gardening she agrees but then dismisses the notion; when Richard asserts that the room gets warm with the blinds down, Sarah dismisses it with a simple 'Would you say so?' (152). At first, we might just sense that Richard is disguising his jealousy behind questions about the lover and this seems confirmed when he asks if Sarah ever envisions him hard at work during her unfaithful trysts. She seems to seek to exacerbate his discomfort by suggesting that the thought just adds to her pleasure, only then to deflect his question by stating she knows such an image of him at work would anyway be fictitious, as he spends those afternoons with his mistress. Things seem to tense up a gear when Richard retorts that, in fact, he does not in fact see any mistress but a 'whore', 'a common or garden slut' (155). This can only add to the hilarity activated by moral shock.

The distinction that Richard seeks to draw between a mistress and a 'whore', and by extension between these and his wife, then becomes the focus of the discussion. Justifying his outspoken language by strategically invoking a frankness between them that she cannot deny him, he dismisses the wifely qualities of grace, elegance and wit as unimportant in a 'whore' who is simply 'a functionary who either pleases or displeases' (156). When Sarah declares that she finds his 'attitude to women rather alarming', he seizes the moment to draw a distinction between his different relationships with women; in seeking a relationship outside marriage, he states, he was not looking for a duplicate of his relationship with his wife, but for 'someone who could express and engender lust with all lust's cunning' (157). 'The dignity' he declares 'is in my marriage', and we note a distinction between marital and extra-marital sexuality that dictates these characters' attitudes and behaviours. The discussion continues in the bedroom, when in the next scene we see the two in their night attire, preparing for bed.[11] Sarah seems unsettled by the conversation, and points out he has never made such enquiries before about her lover. They conclude before sleep that there is no jealousy at play, and Sarah states that she finds their arrangement 'beautifully balanced' (161).

The play has thus far presented itself in straightforward and quite traditional terms. It comes across as a piece of light, drawing-room entertainment, which communicates primarily through revelatory dialogue, though with much more forthright language than the kind of genre it is emulating. Entertained by the extra-ordinary open marriage, and the manner in which the husband and wife clarify and justify their positions within it, an audience are carried along within a frame of humour that seems grounded primarily in the unsettling of normative cultural expectations around marriage. Where Pinter builds his drama up by subverting our expectations of character type, he then progresses by subverting our expectations of the established theatrical discourse. As the lights dim on Richard and Sarah in bed, we might feel we have the measure of this play, as that frame of comedic subversion is straightforwardly understandable and enjoyable. We expect to derive more pleasure from perhaps some further complication between characters, planted by the suggestion Sarah has made that all four might meet for lunch in the village. As the play progresses, though, we soon realise we have been had.

The next scene repeats the sequence of the first, with Richard preparing to leave for work and Sarah attending to domestic duties, this time making the bed. She informs him that her lover will be coming again and, following a quick fade up and down of the lights, we find her preparing for him by putting on a tight, low-cut black dress and high-heeled shoes. The doorbell rings. We expect her lover to be in the frame when she opens the door, but instead there is the milkman. This is clearly a gag, making reference to that well-trodden twentieth-century British urban mythology of housewives misbehaving with milkmen, and deliberately deferring the audience's first sighting of her lover, increasing the anticipation for that inevitable next development in the drama. It is also a joke at the audience's expense, in that in referencing the milkman as indulger of married women's unspent sexual appetites, Pinter is teasing the audience. So our surprise is all the more keenly felt when the lover finally enters. Sarah addresses him as Max, but we see it is Richard, without a tie and in a suede jacket. What Pinter effects here is a sudden and confusing shift in theatrical discourse: we thought we were appreciating the performance in one way, and then we realise that we need to read it differently, but lack the information yet to know quite how. In forcing us as audience to start from scratch in this way, we realise that everything we have heard before between these two was simply not as it seemed. What we read as a jealous and enquiring subtext in Richard's words, for example, needs to be re-evaluated. What does it mean that they might discuss their extra-marital affairs if, in fact, they were referring to their behaviour as themselves in a different guise? How do we consider Richard's explanation that he does not have a mistress, but makes use of a prostitute in the afternoons? The subtle tensions we noted between the two now need to be reconsidered, and what follows begins to chart the shifting territory of this married couple's erotic and emotional lives.

After some flirtatious crossing and uncrossing of legs from Sarah, Richard/Max collects a bongo drum from a cupboard and begins to tap it. Sarah joins him and they engage in an odd game of tapping the drum and scratching and intertwining fingers. Then, lighting cigarettes, they role play first an act of sexual harassment, with Richard taking on the role of violator with wandering hands, and then an act of the rescue of a damsel in distress, with Richard offering to defend Sarah from his first adopted role. What Pinter spells out quite clearly with this sequence is that this married couple enjoy a very active and varied sex life, which they achieve through game and role-playing. He also presents a clear demarcation between this overtly expressed sexuality and their other roles as husband and wife. During their role-play, both make reference – in their alter-egos – to being married, and to being married as a means to deny and undermine sexual interaction. Sarah fends off Richard/Max as an assailant with 'I'm waiting for my husband' and Richard/Max later turns down the attentions of a gratefully rescued Sarah with '[m]y wife's waiting for me' (165–6). Marriage, then, is used as an index of sexual erasure, which foregrounds all the more this channelling of sexual energy through role-play and games.

Pinter is enacting and mobilising that set of cultural assumptions that might, quite falsely, separate libido and desire from the dignity and honour of the state of marriage. When, in *The Collection*, Bill taunts James with this, by pointing out that, as her husband, he is by definition exempt from any possibility of enjoying Stella's unbridled eroticism, Pinter is wielding the cultural positioning of marriage as a lever to lend credibility to narratives of infidelity. In *Tea Party*, Pinter employed the same set of cultural assumptions to cause a character distress through an inability to reconcile or breach the 'barrier between the erotic and the platonic', to employ D. Keith Peacock's distinction.[12] In *The Lover*, Pinter goes further in examining how cultural expectation dictates human behaviour and interaction, by allowing his married couple to bypass cultural codes that might separate them and directly access their desire for one another through games.

Once the seduction of the afternoon is complete, and their desire is consummated beneath the living room table, Sarah and Richard converse as their alter-egos Mary and Max. Just as they had previously played the game of closeting their erotic existence by references to her lover and his mistress, now they speak from the other side of that convenient barrier and speak of their husband and wife. Richard had sought to speak of Max, and now Max wants to speak about Richard, and he asks Sarah why she thinks 'her husband' puts up with his afternoon tumbles with her. We begin to see that the discomfort that we suspected Richard was experiencing with his wife having a 'lover' earlier was perhaps a manifestation of an overall dissatisfaction with the game-playing they are engaged in. Just as Pinter has tricked his audience with a shift in theatrical discourse at the centre of the play, so Richard unpins the structured game-playing in his marriage from within it, by using its own distinct and separated discourses, those of husband/wife and of lover/mistress. As Max, he talks of how he can no longer go on deceiving his wife, and refers to his earlier revelation (as Richard) that he (as Sarah's husband) sees a prostitute and not a mistress: 'She thinks I know a whore, that's all. Some spare-time whore, that's all' (169). As with the multiple narratives that keep the characters guessing in *The Collection*, Richard recognises the two dominant narratives of his marriage, and seeks to complicate, multiply and overlap them verbally for strategic effect. When he goes as far as to suggest having a word with Sarah's husband, she begins to almost come out of role:

> **Sarah** Stop it! What's the matter with you? What's happened to you? (*Quietly*) Please, please, stop it. What are you doing, playing a game?
> **Max** A game? I don't play games.
> **Sarah** Don't you? You do. Oh, you do. You do. Usually I like them.
> **Max** I've played my last game. (171)

The last line is an important punctuation mark in the conversation, and holds more than one meaning. Max is making clear he wants to renegotiate his relationship with this married woman and, in doing so, Richard, through his role as Max, seems to be making clear he is tired of the role-playing that defines their sexuality. To underpin it further, he then takes advantage of the rules of the role-playing to invent some children, much to the hilarity of the audience. Calling off an affair for the benefit of children is a not uncommon argument, an appeal to decency. When Sarah counters with seductive lines, to bring him back to the game as she would have it, he then invents a distaste for her figure, arguing that she is 'too bony' and that he has a taste for 'enormous women. Like bullocks with udders' (172). The deliberate mis-gendering here is emphasised when Sarah tries to correct him. Richard is limited, it seems, to the terms of the role he is trying to shake off or re-negotiate, and in his confinement he comes across as grasping at straws to dismiss the relationship as it stands. Similarly, when he returns later that evening as himself, he continues within the assumed limitations of the role of husband. Actors and directors need to decide if this limitation is psychological – is the character somehow restricted to only articulate himself in one or the other guise – or is it strategic; does he want to re-negotiate the erotic/platonic interface of the relationship by manipulating the game-playing terms of engagement in order to adjust those same terms?

Perhaps with a hint of cruelty, Richard then returns home after a 'dreary conference' (a sideways swipe at their afternoon conversation) and asks Sarah if she has had a good day and if her lover came. In response to her sulky dismissal of his pseudo-polite questions, he suggests that '[p]erhaps things will improve' and pays her some warm compliments that centre around his pride at having a beautiful wife that others might covet (175). He soon comes to the point and insists that she breaks off her relationship with her lover. To Sarah's shock, he gets the small drum out from its cupboard and asks her what it is for, if it has anything to do with her illicit afternoons, before tapping it as he had done so previously that day as Max. He ignores her appeals to stop and then adopts a role-playing posture, asks for a light for his cigarette and tells her that her 'husband won't mind' (182). Transforming from Richard to Max before her eyes for once, the line is an invitation to follow what he is up to, and to join in. Earlier in the play, before we realised that he was, in fact, her 'lover', Richard makes an observation about the closeted separation between their erotic daytime lives and their polite, suburban evening lives. 'Your poor lover has never seen the night from this window', he points out, and asks if Max doesn't 'get bored with these damn afternoons? This eternal teatime?' (159–60)

What perhaps dawns on us in the audience at the end of the play, when we see Richard make his sexual advances towards his wife, and deconstruct and re-arrange the narrative apparatus of their erotic interplay, is that he does not want to bring an end to their sex games, but that he perhaps wants to integrate them more fully into their evening lives, as a married couple. His business-like dismissal of her lover was not quite an act of erasing that part of their lives, then, but a translation of it from afternoons to evenings and a consolidation of his roles of husband and lover. The play ends, nonetheless, without clarity on this point. Following Richard's reference to 'her husband', Sarah continues according to the previous game, and improvises the line 'my husband's at a late-night conference' (183).

Despite the re-arrangement, it seems that, verbally at least, the two still cannot admit the expression of their sexual desires into their marriage without role play. 'Would you like me to change?' Sarah asks, meaning that she might change her clothes from the house-wifely to the tight dress and high heels, but indicating also her willing flexibility if a new schema of sexual play is being initiated. The following final words of the play are both mildly shocking and suitably oblique. Kneeling on the floor, facing one another with Sarah leaning over Richard, he answers: 'Yes. *Pause.* Change. *Pause.* Change. *Pause.* Change your clothes. *Pause.* You lovely whore' (184). The pauses here are pregnant with erotic tension, but also allow the emphasis on the demand for 'change', its possible various meanings (other than changing clothes) and defer the articulation of that final defining word. Is it a man simply 'talking dirty' to his wife as part of a temporary shared subscription to debasement for mutually stimulating excitement, or is it a defining stamp of the base utility of a woman for a man? After all, the word has been used previously in the play in a dismissive and functionary manner. The plays ends, then, charged with both eroticism and a certain uncom-fortable ambiguity. The command for 'change' comes from within an established, unchanging role-play game, the rules of which seem very much intact, to the seeming content and amorous advantage of both characters.

Some might argue that the early TV plays in the 'Armchair Theatre' format simply represented televised adaptations of dramas conceived theatrically, but the evidence really obviates such a perspective where Pinter's screenplays were concerned. His partici-pation in television drama, for him, was far from a simple adjunct to his work for the stage, and he later recalled the early 1960s as 'the days when television was really active and imaginative and lively and unafraid'.[13] Upon examining his television scripts, it becomes clear that he sought to make full use of the potential of the medium. Take for example the representation of the character of Sally in *Night School.* The television audience's first visual impression of her is of her naked legs, casually flipping off her shoes. After sitting, she picks up a pile of exercise books and starts making corrections.

Pinter's original screenplay explicitly states that we do not see her face during this establishing sequence.[14] Her objectification as a potential focus of erotic interest, then, is her first introduction, and the camera's gaze ensures that such a presentation of her is more efficiently achieved than might be realised in a staged version. This cutaway to Sally in her room, of course, did not feature in the final script for Radio and theatre: the strategy is only appropriate to the screen medium. There is a comparable moment in *The Lover*, where Richard's wife Sarah prepares herself for his return in the role of her lover Max, and on screen she transforms from his wife to his mistress. The scene in the television broadcast lasts just over three minutes. It starts with the camera tightly following the trajectory of stockings being pulled up Sarah's legs, focussing on the female form. It ends, following a brief camera pan to concentrate on Sarah's legs again, with her opening the door to her lover Max. At one point the actress, Vivien Merchant, has clearly been instructed to hold her hand unnaturally high after zipping up the back of her dress, rather than let it fall naturally. This facilitates a clear and uninterrupted view of her rear as the camera pans down her body. What we are invited to watch in the original television version, then, is the transformation of Sarah from wife to mistress, and a deliberate and lingering focus on the female body.[15] It is an invitation to enjoy the female form, and a preparation for a scene of sexual tension that is to follow. This is, straightforwardly, addressed to conventional male heterosexual triggers of desire. It invites conventional perceptions of Sarah as sexually aware, and self-preparing as an object of sexual delight for a man to enjoy. The printed stage play, however, omits this transformation scene altogether, and cuts straight to Richard's return home. If the scene as performed on screen were played out on most conventional stage spaces, it could not command the same lingering voyeuristic focus that a camera can direct. It could, in fact, be quite boring for an audience. In another play, Pinter nonetheless managed to achieve a similar effect, with greater challenge to the construction and possession of feminine definition, in lines he gave to the character of Ruth in *The Homecoming*:

> Look at me. I ... move my leg. That's all it is. But I wear ...
> underwear ... which moves with me ... it ... captures your
> attention. Perhaps you misinterpret. The action is simple. It's
> a leg ... Moving. My lips move. Why don't you restrict ... Your
> observations to that?[16]

There is a great leap forward here between 1962 and 1965 in
the manner in which women are represented, though they both
adopt the same arguably male-dominated vocabularies of gender
construction. Both create a deliberate focus on aspects of female
form that are presented in a sexually provocative manner. Whereas
the camera in *The Lover* invites a slow appreciation of Sarah's body,
conspiratorially protected by the distance between audience and
action that the medium allows, in *The Homecoming* Ruth controls
that invitation to the onstage characters – and to the audience by
extension – in a manner that allows a critique of the male gaze
by foregrounding it. Male heterosexual members of any audience
might feel a discomfort at the invitation occurring live before them
which parallels and is exacerbated by the awkwardness the moment
creates onstage. In finding a verbal, dramatic stage equivalent to the
camera's voyeurism, Pinter begins to deconstruct the discourses of
desire and negotiation of desire.

In the works discussed in this chapter so far, Pinter clearly has
employed a perceived duality of women as fertile soil for his dramas
and *A Night Out*, *Night School* and *Tea Party*, certainly, rely upon
such cultural coding for their comedy to be effective. With *The
Collection*, and certainly with *The Lover*, though, he appears to
have been adopting a direction of foregrounding and ironising the
cultural assumptions that underpin and steer his characters' behaviours. Both those plays end with something of a question mark, as
though to leave us to wonder if the characters have learnt anything.
In doing so, he leaves a space where we ourselves might consider
what our own responses are. Without directing such responses, he
opens an opportunity for us to govern ourselves through our own
reflection upon the subject matter presented, and this is a variation
of the ethical gap we see being opened in his earlier plays. *The*

Homecoming represents the apogee of this particular development in Pinter's writing, both in terms of its handling of gender and homosocial behaviour and in terms of its manner of constructing a theatrical discourse to leave that space for audience reflection at its close. Elizabeth Sakellaridou charted Pinter's development in his treatment of female characters, from manipulating archetypes to objective consideration of feminine reality to an androgynous stage of 'fullness and perfection' in which his female characters are both 'independent' and 'autonomous'.[17] She locates one hinge in his work with *The Collection* and *The Lover* as plays with 'women as the central object of his examination' before considering how an amalgamation of Stella and Sarah of those plays forms something of a basis for Ruth in *The Homecoming* as 'a turning point in the dramatist's feminine characterisations' in part because 'her female psyche becomes the focal point of the male writer's scrutiny'.[18]

Pinter's screenplays for *The Servant*, *The Pumpkin Eater*, and later for *Accident* were important opportunities for him to explore further the landscape of male/female and male/male interaction, and there must have been some profitable creative to-and-fro between his adaptations for the screen and his own writings for stage and television. Pinter's construction of the last two of these screenplays framed the writing of *The Homecoming*. *The Pumpkin Eater*, based on the recently published semi-autobiographical novel by Penelope Mortimer, must certainly have been a creative experience that stimulated in him a series of reflections about marriage and sexuality that he had already been processing in his recent works. The film charts the isolating and demeaning pressures on a woman who is mother to numerous children and wife to a philandering husband. As in *The Collection*, the reality of infidelity is constructed by measuring its psychological impact. Jo's daily reality centres around her numerous children and her love for her husband, and she finds herself defined frequently by her role as mother and wife, including by her psychiatrist (whom other men, not she, decide she should talk to), rather than by any sense of ambition or personal identity. Jake, who defines himself by his work as a screenplay writer ('I have to work! It's my life') fails to recognise that Jo cannot be satisfied by her definition by the roles she fulfils ('Where's mine? Where's my life?').[19] The multiple children, and the numerous previous marriages, serve to reinforce a sense of enclosure or entrapment within gender type, and Pinter captures this through Jo's seeming lack of certainty or memory concerning her previous marriages, which is of a piece with his frequent application of uncertainty and the unreliability of individual perspective or testimony.

Accident, adapted from Nicholas Mosley's novel of the same name, was written in the summer of 1965. Here, Pinter takes the lack of freedom to do the right thing that Mosley embedded in his work and demonstrates instead a human failing to be true to oneself. He exposes his own fascination – through the observation he constructs – with how we interact with the codes and rules of 'normal' social and moral behaviour, and how these are constructed and manipulated by us. The betrayals he documents in this film are ultimately not people's betrayals of one another (to have extra-marital affairs is presented as a norm, much as it is later in his own play *Betrayal*) but betrayals of themselves, of their own integrity and dignity. Notably, whereas in *The Servant* or the television dramas, the female characters suffer as foils to the men, or act as narrative devices, pushing the men into their difficult corners, with *Accident* (as with *The Pumpkin Eater*) a concern for women as individuals is much more evident, and one of the most piercingly refreshing pieces of dialogue in the screenplay is given to Stephen's wife, Rosalind, when in quite straightforward terms she dismisses Charley's infidelities with the young teenager Anna as 'pathetic', 'puerile' and 'banal',[20] releasing her contempt for her husband Stephen – who so evidently desires the same girl – as much as for Charley.

The similarities between *Accident* and *The Homecoming*, written very close to one another, become evident if compared side by side. In both there is an elusive central, powerful female, desired by a social group of men around her who find themselves bound together by her. Their coming together as a masculine group is in some way defined by her, and revolves around her. Both works even feature a professor of philosophy. It is also difficult to like any of the characters in either the play or the film. Both works generate their dramas by examining the interaction of a set of established attitudes to women with a woman who challenges those attitudes by taking control of the factors (male physical and emotional needs) which inform them. If the necessary inclusion of a female catalyst or foil within processes of male interaction is a determinable theme in much of Pinter's writing in the 1960s, it was in many ways resolved and re-defined in *The Homecoming* and *Accident*. The characters of Emma in *Betrayal* (1978) or Anna/Sarah in *The French Lieutenant's Woman* (1981) are clearly highly evolved versions of this new female character, in total possession of their own sexual identities, and not simply extensions of male desire.

The Homecoming has its origins in a sketched dramatic draft of three scenes between a man, his partner and another man who shares their lodgings.[21] Much of this brief, rejected draft finds its way into the second, third and fourth scenes of the play: Teddy and Ruth's appearance at the family home, Teddy's brief conversation with his brother Lenny and Ruth's confrontational dialogue with Lenny that follows it. That original sketch, now held in the manuscript archives of the British Library, concludes with the three unnamed characters seemingly prepared for a three-way sexual tryst. In returning to that draft in 1965 and reconfiguring it as dialogue between a man, his wife and her brother-in-law, Pinter fleshed out the greater context into which this negotiation of sexual sharing of a partner might have resonance. He imagined an all-male family inhabiting a house together, and the alignments of power between them cast by family connection, strength or income generation. The first scene very clearly presents these alignments and the tensions that threaten or keep them in place.

The play opens with a man in his thirties reading a newspaper in a living room. He is interrupted by a man of seventy in a cardigan, cap and walking with a stick, who enters from the kitchen, rummages in a drawer, and asks after the whereabouts of the scissors. The younger man insults him and tells him to shut up, and this provokes a threat of physical assault with the walking stick from the old man, and verbal assertion of his physical prowess. We learn from the ensuing dialogue that the two are father and son, with the younger indolently dismissive of the older's cares or claims. The father's vicious warnings to his son are undermined as so much hot air by the confidence of Lenny's responses, unmoved from his seated comfort. Max invokes his past prowess and feared reputation in a dogged attempt to extract some respect from his son, and in doing so reveals a history of gangland connections and brutality that may have resonated in the mid 1960s with the infamy of organised criminals such as the Kray twins (arrested in 1965, the year of the play's composition, for running a protection racket in London). Max recalls how he and a man named MacGregor were 'two of the worst hated men in the West End of London' (16) and how people would stand in silence when they entered a room. When Lenny repeats his request for Max to shut up, he retorts viciously 'I'll chop your spine off' (17) but it is clear by now that there is no weight behind such threats. The play, then, starts off with violence carried about impotently within language, but wielded with a delusional and misplaced confidence.

The exchange between Max and Lenny is not light on exposition, with first the detail about MacGregor and then, more significantly, the revelation that Max has been married to a woman who is clearly no longer around. His reference to her is a bizarre mixture of affection and hostility: 'she wasn't such a bad woman. Even though it made me sick to look at her rotten stinking face, she wasn't such a bad bitch' (17). This skewed reminiscence is a first, shocking revelation of the deep-seated misogyny that characters in this play are to articulate as effortlessly as breathing. But its internal contradictions are also presented as characteristic of Max's expression; just seconds later he refers to himself as Lenny's 'lousy stinking father' (17) and later employs insults for his sons that might ordinarily be thrown at female subjects: 'bitch' (24) and 'slag' (88). This cross-gendering, though, seems quite deliberate on Pinter's part, and Max's role in the family is clearly presented as both paternal and maternal, in traditional terms. In this first exchange, Lenny berates his father for being unable to cook, and we learn from this that while Max might attempt to air the spent currency of his youthful thuggishness, his role now in the family is firmly in the kitchen. This is later consolidated by his own admission that it was he, not his wife, that would bathe his children and put them to bed, behaviour that would not have been altogether normative in households of this type in 1965. When he later rejects his brother and youngest son's request for food with 'Go and find yourself a mother' (24), he inadvertently emphasises not only the lack of a maternal figure in the household, but also his own adoption of that role. Later, he even goes as far as removing his wife from the role of childbirth, stating 'I gave birth to three grown men! All on my own bat' (48).

Pinter delivers further exposition about the missing wife, whom we learn was called Jessie. Max's brother, Sam, is introduced as employed as a chauffeur through an exchange about his day's work and reputation, before reminiscing about how he would take his brother's wife Jessie out for drives of an evening. This recollection is part of an exchange that seems heavily laden with subtext. It starts with Sam skilfully deflecting his brother's inferences about his homosexuality by rejecting Max's queries about whether or not he had ever had sex in the back of his cab as simply an instance of his professionalism, before consolidating that with the qualifier 'I don't mess up my car [...] Like other people.' We know immediately from Max's response that this is a loaded comment, that marks the victory for Sam: 'Other people? What other people? *Pause.* What other people? *Pause*' (23). Max attempts to equalise by again undermining Sam's masculinity through talking of his potential to marry, but Sam quickly uses this as an opportunity to speak of Jessie. Coming on the back of the exchange about libidinous activities in the backs of cabs performed by 'other people', reference to chauffeuring Max's wife around in the back of his cab sets the cap on his minor victory, acknowledged neatly in Max's submissive, softly spoken 'Christ' (24). The richness of this material, to be rendered by directors and actors through lengthy work in their rehearsal rooms, is found in both the clear subtextual impact that is being activated, and also in the ambiguity of what is being suggested: what was Jessie's status as wife, given what Max has implied of his underworld connections? Why was she being escorted around town? Who, if anyone, misbehaved with her in the back of the cab? Not Sam, we would be led to believe, if his implied homosexuality is presented in relation to this past. A few pages later, he returns to the issue, and brings Max's old partner MacGregor into the picture, implying that Max wouldn't have trusted Mac with Jessie. If he's twisting a knife in old wounds, we do not get a complete picture, just hints and inferences that will only be explicitly tied up in a final-scene exclamation from Sam, mid-heart-attack, that 'MacGregor had Jessie in the back of my cab' (86).

The first scene of *The Homecoming* plays a traditional expository role, then, whilst depositing a series of uncertainties embedded in the bits of family history and relationships it maps out. In this way, Pinter established a context into which he could insert material from his old draft scenes between two men and a woman, and re-write it for the nascent characters of Teddy, Ruth and Lenny. Teddy is a British academic in the United States. He returns to his home for the first time in six years in the middle of the night, and we see him open the door with a key and enter the house with Ruth. We learn unambiguously that this is another of Max's sons (he refers to 'my father's chair' and 'My room') and that Ruth is most likely his wife (she speaks of their having children) (28–9). So far we have seen conflict between characters as a default position, not a driver of plot, but now we are presented with the mystery of a son returning home with his wife in the middle of the night to a house he seems to have left some while ago (he refers to his bedroom being empty). Given the harsh misogyny and cross-gendering of roles we have witnessed, as audience we might wonder what is in store for Ruth. With small details offered in quick succession, though, Pinter introduces her as neither defined by her relationship with Teddy nor dependent on him. She refuses her husband's offer of a drink, declines his suggestion that she might go to bed and queries his obvious intent to stay a while with his family with the passive-aggressive, faux-innocence of the question 'Do you want to stay?' (29). She then asks for the key to go out for a walk, in the middle of the night, after just arriving, and as Teddy states he is going to bed. Her seemingly idiosyncratic behaviour indicates that there is to be a dramatic tension between this independent woman and the harsh, masculine environment that has been prepared for her entry by her author.

There is a further emphasis in this scene on the lost mother, as Teddy explains that the open-plan living room and hall were created by knocking down a wall after her death. With that one simple, seemingly incidental explanation, Pinter fuses the exposed domestic interior of the stage space in front of us with Jessie, the absent character rendered ever-present in an internal adjustment of a domestic space that ensured, Teddy declares, that the 'structure wasn't affected' (29). We might not have time in the theatre to reflect on the metaphoric possibilities that are pregnant in this statement, but Pinter has Ruth sit down immediately after it, as some visual punctuation point that places her firmly within that frame established in relation to the missing matriarch. Perhaps, here, we might first be being invited to wonder whose homecoming we are witnessing. Pinter presents a vital new female presence, framed by an ambivalent female absence. All that is required now for the drama to get truly underway is a meeting of this independently minded woman with those that wield a narrative of gender that belittles the female, and Pinter quickly delivers with what must be one of the most potent scenes in his whole body of work.

Returning from her nocturnal stroll, Ruth enters the house to be met by Lenny, seated, in his dressing gown. Immediately, he is put on the back foot when she corrects his 'Good evening' with 'Morning, I think' (35), denies that she is cold upon his enquiry, and refuses his offer of a drink (though he gives her a glass of water anyway). These small details are gifts for actors: Lenny plays calm and unsurprised when an unknown women enters his house with a key, and tenders three common gestures of welcome from a hospitable host; Ruth rejects all three. By these very subtle means, Pinter establishes both the game (to hold onto some position of collected measure and control within an unexpected situation) and the tactics of the players (the tendering and rejection of hospitality) before any stakes are raised. After some banter about a clock's ticking disturbing his sleep, which establishes his need to control his environment, Lenny finally asks Ruth questions to find out who she is, but offers no acknowledgement of her status as his brother's wife. On learning that she and Teddy have stayed in Venice on their visit together to

Europe, he makes an odd claim that he would have served in the Italian Campaign in the Second World War if he had been old enough. The bizarre statement asserts some ownership of the frames of the conversation before he asks to hold her hand, followed up by a physical move toward Ruth (as Pinter notes in the stage directions) to consolidate those manoeuvres for control. When she asks why he wants to hold her hand he launches into a long speech, by way of answer, about his encounter with a syphilitic prostitute and the violence he meted out on her.

Lenny's speech contains information that gives the audience a greater sense of who this man is, all of which adds to the picture we have had of him from his belittling of his father. His talk here of how the woman had a chauffeur who was 'an old friend of the family', who could have been relied upon to stay quiet if he chose to murder her, confirms any suspicion we might have formed that this family operate within a context of organised crime. Disturbingly, by pointing out that he was able to act with impunity with a woman, and doing so in direct response to being asked why he wants to hold her hand, Lenny seems to making a statement of his right to act as he chooses with and toward Ruth. When she calmly responds by questioning a detail in his story ('How did you know she was diseased?'), his reply ('I decided she was') makes overt the masculine discourse in operation; he defines and controls any female presence he encounters (39). As if to fortify any effect his words might have had, he embarks on another, longer speech, in which he again recounts his encounter with a woman to whom, again, he did violence. This time the victim is an old woman for whom he had volunteered to help move an old mangle, universalising the anti-female stance.

These speeches might be taken as strategic warning shots, as clarification of status and declaration of behavioural expectations. If the first few scenes of the play have painted the context for the drama, then here Pinter sets in motion the central conflict of the play: the male presumption of a right to define, construct and own women, and female strategies of resistance that include taking control of the vocabulary of that male discourse. Upon ending his second speech,

Lenny returns to the far more subtle tactics that the scene had opened with, by playing the considerate host and taking an ashtray out of Ruth's way, and then offering to take her glass. This sets in motion a series of responses from Ruth in which she takes utter control of the situation.

> **Lenny** And now perhaps I'll relieve you of your glass.
> **Ruth** I haven't quite finished.
> **Lenny** You've consumed quite enough, in my opinion.
> **Ruth** No, I haven't.
> **Lenny** Quite sufficient, in my own opinion.
> **Ruth** Not in mine, Leonard
> *Pause.*
> **Lenny** Don't call me that, please.
> **Ruth** Why not?
> **Lenny** That's the name my mother gave me. *Pause.* Just give me the glass.
> **Ruth** No.
> *Pause.*
> **Lenny** I'll take it then.
> **Ruth** If you take the glass ... I'll take you.
> *Pause.*
> **Lenny** How about me taking the glass without you taking me?
> **Ruth** Why don't I just take you?
> *Pause.* (41–2)

The short exchange contains six pauses, all of which precede Lenny's lines, indicating a space for thought in which he contemplates his response. Ruth makes no such hesitations. She is clear, unambiguous and assertive. Not only does she render impotent the warnings in Lenny's stories that might indicate a woman who demands too much of him is at risk of violent correction, she employs the same tactic of implicit threat in return. Here, the words 'I'll take you' are deliberately ambiguous in ways that must cause translators of Pinter's works minor headaches, as they simultaneously contain the threats of being overcome by violence or of being forcefully seduced. And Ruth wields these after having first adopted the maternal voice, by using Lenny's full name as any parent might when chastising a misbehaving child. She follows through by offering him a sip of the water he had sought to remove, thereby folding his own petty mechanism of manipulation back upon him. Moving towards him with the glass, she proposes that he lie down and she pour some down his throat, again suggesting both violation and seduction. Finishing the glass of water off herself, she laughs and goes up to bed. The scene is a *tour de force* of the kind of engaging verbal combat that established Pinter's reputation.

People interested in the process of playwriting would do well to visit the British Library and read the archived three-scene draft that became those early scenes of *The Homecoming*. That rejected manuscript represented the foundation to this most remarkable play, and by returning to it and adapting it Pinter recognised that a dramatic crisis could be constructed from the suggested sharing of a sexual partner, and how this might speak to cultural discourses of gender. He set about re-writing those scenes by establishing a domestic context for the conflict to ferment in, and then examined the consequences in scene after scene. It is a clear example of his frequently declared *modus operandi* that he would start with some characters and let them tell him what happens to them. Clearly, what had to happen next was that Ruth and Teddy would make an appearance before the whole family in the morning, and this had to be to mixed responses. Max is surprised to see his son after breakfast, and, with reference to Ruth, asks with no concern for tact 'Who asked you to bring tarts in here?' and protests that 'We've had a smelly scrubber in my house all night. We've had a stinking pox-ridden slut in my house all night' (49). The 'pox-ridden' description recalls Lenny's statement that his decision that a woman is diseased is enough to qualify her as such, and confirms the mind-set of the household: to have a woman overnight must mean she has been paid for her services, which must therefore mean she is syphilitic. What is more, Max's statement here that 'I've never had a whore under this roof before. Ever since your mother died' (50) both adds to this misogyny and represents either another disrespectful dig at his wife, or a statement of literal fact which might explain why Sam used to chauffeur Jessie around (that is, between clients). The scene ends with Max's acceptance of Teddy's explanation that Ruth is his wife (which triggers another assumption about women when he asks how many children she has produced) and the reciprocated offer of 'a cuddle and a kiss' between the two men. Act One closes, offended members of the audience might leave at the interval, and the rest of the drama can unfold in the second of two acts.

The play starts again with a civilised conversation over coffee (notably furnished by Ruth) as Max recounts an idyllic represen-tation of their family life when the boys were young and Jessie was the backbone of the family. This rosy image soon deteriorates to his complaints of a 'crippled family, three bastard sons, a slutbitch of a wife' (55). As with the earlier statement describing Jessie as a 'whore', this reference to his sons' illegitimacy could be either a base insult or a statement of the literal. That Pinter gives Ruth and Teddy three sons too, and has Max ask after their legitimacy, sets in motion the suggestion of a cyclic, irrevocable process.

The rest of the play is a series of negotiations between Ruth and the men of this household, starting with her own husband who seems to have changed his mind about staying a while, and makes excuses for why they ought to pack and leave that day. Lenny interrupts this by requesting a dance with Ruth before she leaves, and kisses her as they do so. Joey returns and witnesses this embrace, and concludes 'She's a tart' (66) before taking gentle hold of Ruth and leading her to the sofa, where he first kisses her before lying on top of her. Pinter gives Ruth no lines or stage directions during this. She acquiesces to the kisses and caresses until she suddenly pushes Joey off her and demands food and whisky, and insists it be poured into an appro-priate glass. In one brief scene she shifts allegiance from Teddy to his brothers, and makes demands in return for the physical attention she grants them. Shortly after, when Joey returns from having spent some time in the bedroom with Ruth, he explains that he 'didn't get all the way' (74), indicating that if Ruth is employing her sexuality for anything other than self-gratification, she is successfully manipulating these men. Ignoring Teddy's protests, Max suggests that they invite her to stay, and pay her a stipend to which they will all contribute. Lenny goes one further, and suggests that she earn part of her keep by working as a prostitute, with limited hours to ensure she has time to fulfil any domestic obligations, which they later list as cooking, cleaning and bed-making, but imply bedroom duties too. To put the cap on their convenient re-definition of her, they even suggest she is given a different name. The conversation is clipped, business-like and focussed. Teddy can do little more than protest that she would get old quickly, which is readily dismissed, though he maintains a dignified silence when it is suggested he might procure American clients passing through London.

Ruth comes downstairs and the final negotiations begin, with Teddy revealing his family's plan for her. She takes control of the conversation and bargains ruthlessly, demanding a flat with three rooms and a bathroom, a personal maid and a wardrobe of new clothes. She refuses to return the cost of these, indicating that the men would have to consider their financial input as 'a capital investment', thereby demonstrating that she is far more skilled in business negotiations than they seem to be. In this mode, she concludes by stating that '[a]ll aspects of the agreement and conditions of employment would have to be clarified to our mutual satisfaction before we finalized the contract' (85). They fare Teddy well and crowd round Ruth to form a final stage tableau that places Ruth centrally, with Joey and Max kneeling at her feet, Sam prostrate on the floor having suffered what seems to be a heart attack, and Lenny and Teddy standing.

The play's ending is shocking on a number of counts, not least the indifference with which the characters respond to Sam's sudden demise, which seems therefore to function as some macabre comic bass note to the composition. Teddy's seeming acceptance that his wife might abandon him and their children is as outrageous as the casual nature of both the suggestion to Ruth and the acceptance by her that she might stay and function as a sex worker. It is the altogether abnormal nature of these interactions that impacts upon an audience, and demands a reaction from us as the lights dim on that final tableau. A response of moral outrage might be one, but Pinter seems to be trying to do something more than shock for the sake of it, and one concern might be to again foreground the discourses of interaction between the genders. As with *The Lover* and *Tea Party*, the tensions between the platonic and erotic in marriage are set in motion, but rather than being reconciled they become the terrain of negotiation for improvement for Ruth. As with *The Collection*, the manner in which a woman's domestic duties and status vis-à-vis men are culturally inscribed are foregrounded, but here they are tested, and vulnerabilities exploited by Ruth. While it might seem that the play concludes with Ruth's debasement, all that is certain as the curtain closes is that she has gained control of this family as some new quasi-matriarch, and there is no evidence that she will ultimately yield to their will. She has shown no signs of such a possible outcome, but only temerity, resistance and strategic superiority. Nonetheless, as Milne argues, it 'is difficult to perform Ruth as a positive image of female self-determination, since her power depends on her recognition and confirmation of the misogynist fantasy within which she is forced to perform'.[22] If she succeeds at the end by having manipulated the grammar of an ideological structure that would have her as its victim, and overcomes that outcome, that grammar nonetheless remains unaltered. The degree to which Pinter succeeds in proposing that it should be altered very much depends on how well a production highlights misogyny as a redundant mode of social interaction.

Within all the negotiations that take place in *The Homecoming*, none of the characters gains our respect. An audience are left with no-one to admire in the drama, which seems only to chart the modes by which advantage is negotiated between people. In one of his later speeches, Teddy explains that his scholarly writing concerns itself with perceiving modes of human interaction, and proposes that '[i]t's a question of how far you operate on things and not in things. I mean it's a question of your capacity to ally the two, to relate the two, to balance the two. To see, to be able to *see*' (69–70). He goes on to explain to Lenny that he, Teddy, operates 'on' things, that is to say has an objective ability to watch the manner in which people behave with cool, critical distance whereas Lenny and the family operate 'in' things, the victims of whims and circumstance. Pinter first employed this distinction in his novel *The Dwarfs*, when Pete accuses Mark of 'operating on life and not in it', which Mark immediately interprets as being accused of being a 'ponce' of some sort (that is to say, a man who lives off another's earnings) (79). There is a biographical relevance here, in that one of Pinter's friends cast the exact same accusation at him. In *The Homecoming*, Teddy proudly adopts the role of ponce, in Mark's terms, by claiming that to operate 'on' things is to have real insight, the ability to see, and is in some way superior to those merely operating 'in things'. But Pinter is not here justifying a mode of behaviour of which he himself once stood accused; Teddy is clarifying his ruthless stance, and his author is preparing us for the moment he will stand by and watch his wife bartered rather than display any emotion that might betray his vulnerability. Ruth's final words to him 'Don't become a stranger' (88) seem quite knowingly to deflate this objective stance, and suggest that he may as well be a stranger for all their years of marriage.

With the character of Ruth, Pinter concluded a journey through perceptions of female plurality, and male responses to it, that had begun with Victoria in *The Dwarfs*, had been interrogated through The Girl and Sally in *A Night Out* and *Night School*, complicated with Stella and Sarah in *The Collection* and *The Lover*, and explored further through the processes of adapting prose for the screen with *The Servant*, *The Pumpkin Eater* and *Accident*. While there was more to his artistic portfolio than issues of gender, *The Homecoming* seems to have represented a significant achievement in his creative life, as what followed was a period of relative creative stagnation, and a search for new forms of expression and a different approach to the realities of interpersonal relationships.

CHAPTER 3
PRESENT CONTINUOUS, PAST PERFECT

Contours and Shadows
Landscape, Silence, Old Times

With the international success of *The Homecoming*, Pinter's reputation as a significant playwright was confirmed. His creative output, however, subsequently diminished quite rapidly. Between 1965 and the turn of the next decade he wrote just two short plays, *Landscape* and *Silence*, and a sketch, *Night*. *The Basement*, although broadcast in February 1967, was, as we have seen, essentially a re-working of a 1963 text. His screenplay output during this period was also slim, with just two, *The Quiller Memorandum* (1966) and *Accident* (1967), and he returned to a 1964 draft screenplay of *The Go-Between* in 1969, which was eventually filmed and released in 1971. His creative flow had clearly not dried up altogether after *The Homecoming*, but in 1968 Pinter talked of how his creative life had become 'constipated',[1] and complained about how '[w]riting becomes more difficult the older you get, at least it does for me'.[2] In 1970 during his acceptance speech for the German Shakespeare Prize, he publicly admitted that 'at the moment I am writing nothing and can write nothing. I don't know why. It's a very bad feeling, I know that, but I must say I want more than anything else to fill up a blank page again'.[3]

A part of his artistic activity that became all the more important to him at this stage in his career was collaboration. This took the form of both actual relationships and virtual ones (with authors such as James Joyce and Marcel Proust). Notably, he began his creative relationship with Simon Gray in 1972, directing *Butley*, the first of nine Gray plays he would direct in his lifetime. He had directed the first play from someone else's pen in 1967, Robert Shaw's *The Man in the Glass Booth,* and formed Shield Productions in 1970 with a group of friends. James Joyce's *Exiles* at the Royal Shakespeare Company's (RSC) Aldwych Theatre was to be one of their first productions in 1970, directed by Pinter. His relationship with the RSC had been established when *The Collection* was staged by them at the Aldwych in June 1962. That production had been co-directed by Peter Hall and Pinter himself and that rehearsal process marked the beginning of a fruitful collaboration between writer and director that was to last over a decade. After their 1965 production of *The Homecoming*, Hall and the RSC presented the debuts of *Landscape* and *Silence* in 1969 and of *Old Times* in 1971.

Correspondence between Beckett and Pinter in 1969 indicates that he was closely familiar with Joyce's play at the time of writing *Landscape* the year before. Ronald Knowles points out[4] that Beth's line 'if they touched the back of my neck, or my hand, it was done so lightly. Without exception. With one exception'[5] mirror Robert's words in *Exiles*; 'All then – without exception? Or with one exception?'[6] We might speculate about the inspiration Pinter found in *Exiles* during a period of creative difficulty, before the purgation of any 'writer's block' with *Old Times* in 1971. Indeed, this latter play was written immediately after the rehearsal period for *Exiles* and during the run of the first performances of the play in the Winter of 1970/71. As late as December 1971, when Pinter told Mel Gussow that he believed 'the past is not past, that it never was past. It's present',[7] he was deliberately or unconsciously echoing the character of Robert's words from *Exiles*: 'the past is not past. It is present here now' (108). Even the play's title can be found, perhaps quite coincidentally, within that play's dialogue when Robert invites Richard to his home: 'You must come some night. It will be old times again' (47).[8]

Another creative spur was adaptation, and Pinter's continued experience in writing for the cinema was to offer him renewed creative avenues of exploration that would benefit his writing for the stage. In writing the *The Pumpkin Eater* screenplay, Pinter had made use of his first shifts in time in any of his works. The opening scenes are set in the 'present day' before taking cinema audiences back to 'ten years earlier' to track the gradual decay of Jo and Jake's marriage. On one occasion, the present time intrudes in the story as it progresses, to establish the sterility of Jo's present life as consequent of what happened in the past.[9] With his later screenplay for *The Go-Between*, Pinter frames a series of events over three weeks in 1900 with a series of seventeen brief interventions in the present (set as approximately 1950–70), where the chief character of Leo as an old man revisits the Norfolk village which was the location for the disastrous events that he witnessed and participated in as a boy. This interjection of the past, the location of difficult memories, into a developing painful narrative that is the basis of those recollections adds to the pathos of the film, a marker of all the scars that we carry from past disappointment and tragedy. At one point in his screenplay, Pinter allows a synapse between past and present ('Village Street. No cars. Day. Time neutral')[10] as though to indicate to Losey that time might collapse into one shared moment in the centre of the film. The expression is poetic, and the cinematic response can only be to allow a moment of ambiguity that might cause an uncertainty in its audience, one that allows them to feel the emotional impact of remembered past on present experience. Later in the decade, in adapting *The French Lieutenant's Woman* for the screen, Pinter was concerned to capture the structural principle of the novel as a faux-Victorian book that nonetheless declares itself as written in the present time. Eschewing voice-over as essentially counter-cinematic, he replaced the novel's narrative voice by applying a structure of a 'film within a film', using the dual presence of the actors and the characters they embody to dovetail the emotional relationship of the latter into the affairs of the former in a manner that artfully borrowed the structure of the past declaring itself in the present. Using the motif of life copying art, he captures the manner in which a past moment is rendered perfect, untouchable, unrepeatable in experience, and this is captured precisely in his filmic solution to the double-ending of the novel in which he stages a repeat of the 'happy ending' from the film that is being shot within the film. Steven H. Gale points out that this parallels the ending of *The Lover*, in the manner in which this 'dream-like event mirrors Mike's sensitivity at the film's conclusion, for even though he has lost Anna/Sarah, it is likely that he will live in a continuing fantasy instead of coping with reality'.[11]

Typical cinematic discourses usually do not involve needing to warn of or clarify for an audience any leap backward or forward in time (or across a life/art divide), as this can quickly be adduced by a series of visual indicators, not least the visual age of the characters, their clothing and their environments. A different set of conventions dictate how we read staged material, however, and leaps between times need to be clearly marked verbally as well as visually (or textually, in an interruptive Brechtian mode). When struggling with his drafts of two voices that would eventually come together as *Landscape*, Pinter brought the past and present together on stage in three ways chiefly; first in the recollections that his two characters, Beth and Duff, utter; secondly in the manner in which these two sets of recollections interact and interfere with one another, bringing the certainty or significance of past events into relief; and thirdly in the static stage image of the characters' present condition, which slowly insinuates itself as a sterile, unending moment that in some way is a consequence of what is being recounted. Memory, then, is the hinge between past and present on stage and an alternative to enacting the past, as in film, is to engage with it at length through dialogue. *Landscape*, by consequence, is a quite static play, and we are invited to listen to its two characters' interweaving monologues, our gaze drawn from one to the other as the performance progresses.

When the lights rise at the start of a performance, we see Beth and Duff seated in the kitchen of a country house; a man in his early fifties 'at the right corner' of a long table and a woman in her late forties 'in an armchair, which stands away from the table, to its left'. In the dim background, Pinter notes, are 'a sink, stove, etc., and a window'. At no point in the play does Pinter indicate that either Beth or Duff move from these positions, but in a rare (and therefore significant) note to actors in his script, he explains that '[b]oth characters are relaxed, in no sense rigid' (166). Given the domestic setting, we might immediately assume that this is a husband and wife couple, and our first interest would be to expect to get a confirmation of that in some form and discover something of their relationship, what they are waiting for, how they might speak to one another. An arrangement between Beth and Duff though is soon apparent: they do not seem to hear one another's words.

Beth speaks first, and these first sentences are delivered in a mixture of past, present and future tenses, causing a certain immediate disorientation about whether her words are a memory, a future ambition or a present daydream. Settling into speaking mostly in the past tense, she talks of being on a beach with a man, whom she recalls lying down beside and speaking to of having children together. She indicates that she is probably recalling these incidents by correcting herself about whether she spoke words to some passing women or just thought them. 'I am beautiful' she states, and describes the remembered man's position, reclining in the sand (167–8). As such, the play opens with an evocation of a self-aware, contented woman and a man she once loved. It is a gentle introduction, with pleasant imagery. When Duff then speaks he offers a story of being caught in the rain with only strangers, 'youngsters', for company, offering a contrast to her recollections of sun and intimate company.

Duff very clearly addresses Beth directly, and continues to do so throughout the play, although she never overtly acknowledges his words. He makes frequent suggestions about things she might do, which collectively suggest she is in need of encouragement to go out. He proposes that she might join him for a walk one day, that if she did so she might recognise people they might meet, and that they might one day go sit in the garden together. Later he proposes they go up to the drawing room and share a drink one evening. Beth responds to none of these suggestions, and the manner in which they are offered suggests the encouragement of a carer, trying to bring a reticent person out of her shell. But they might also come across as the appeals of a husband for his wife's company, indicating that such normal interaction is a thing of the past. 'Do you like me to talk to you?', Duff asks at one point and, for want of an answer, he replies for himself, 'I think you do' (179). Later, irritated at getting no response, Duff resorts to a sulky passive-aggressive tactic: 'at least now, I can walk down to the pub in peace and up to the pond in peace, with no-one to nag the shit out of me' (182). What Pinter establishes with Duff's questions and that petulant rejoinder is that, for Duff, Beth is a silent, unresponsive, diminished presence. This is a reasonable cause of his aggrieved sadness.

This effective separation of the characters from one another is the theatrical discourse that we glean from our seats. We begin to accept that this husband and wife couple are in different worlds, that he cannot hear her (and that perhaps what she is uttering is her private thoughts) and she will not or cannot, for whatever reason, hear him. We need make no more sense of it than that in the theatre, and can just concentrate on the words within that frame. The play, then, does not offer a story or dramatic conflict in the way all of Pinter's previous material had, but instead offers a series of images, moods, seeming memories, that interplay and interact with one another as we hear and process them, and do so in juxtaposition with an image of a husband and wife talking in a kitchen. Conflict of a sort does begin to appear, in the form of Duff's frustration with his unresponsive wife, and is also implied in references to some past infidelity (or infidelities) that predate the present stagnant state of this marriage. There is no resolution sought or offered for this conflict, only a verbally brutal release of vexation from Duff in which he imagines, or recalls, a passionate (or non-consensual) sexual encounter with Beth, which he locates after an episode where she was banging a gong for supper when there was nobody but him to hear it and no food on the table. This burst of sexual fantasy represents something of a release of pent-up energy in the play at the end, but it is a morally ambivalent episode – his description of Beth's conduct with the gong is clearly a recollection of her manifesting troubled behaviour – and it effectively belittles Duff while also confirming his sorry emotional isolation. The last lines of the play go to Beth, and return to the beach and the sun, the tender touch of a remembered lover and her declaration 'Oh my true love, I said' (188). This love rendered in the past tense goes to emphasise that separation and isolation of this couple in and from each other, as the last dramatic silence falls and the lights dim.

Although the two characters seem to speak in separate monologues, there is a dialogue of sorts between them, and deliberate symmetries and asymmetries. Where Beth speaks of summer, Duff speaks of rain; where Beth has a lover for company, Duff has his dog (missing, when first mentioned); when Beth talks of going to a bar for drinks, Duff talks of an encounter in a local pub; when Beth recalls contemplating having children, Duff bemoans boisterous youngsters who shared his shelter from the rain, 'making a racket' (169). In addition to these contrasts, there are a few moments of connection. Beth, for example, recalls how her lover referred to her concentration when arranging flowers as a 'grave' look, and Duff later recalls how he would describe her as 'grave' when she was young (176). Detailed close reading, then, might encourage us to think that Beth is recalling special moments with a younger Duff, but there is no time for close reading during a performance, and such details may or may not be captured and acknowledged by individuals in an audience. Mention of another man, Sykes, might equally cause us to wonder. Sykes was their employer, and they tended to his house before inheriting it together. Beth recalls wearing the blue dress he bought her and sitting on her own in it and looking down at children playing in the valley, and Duff recalls her coming to bed late one night after serving Sykes and his guests. These references simply fall in our ears, and we might put together connections as we hear more, or we might remain in a pleasurable uncertainty, finding the structure of the piece, the rhythm and imagery of the words, simply appealing.

A series of fifteen pauses throughout the play offer some structuring to what we hear, and each allows us to digest what precedes it before the play resumes a new section. Shortly after Beth's recollection of sitting in her blue dress watching children playing, there is a 'long silence' (185), making something of a subtle climactic moment to that memory. We might think the play has ended there, as the silence lingers across the auditorium. This momentaneous self-consciousness we might experience as audience invites and activates our increased attention as the final section begins and Duff's rhythm of delivery speeds up. The result is a dwelling within us of the isolation and sadness that Beth remembers and Duff embodies, a sense of what could have been (the children she observes), before this being wound up in Duff's torment and semi-violent narrative of sexual domination, a story in which he re-takes his wife's lost attention and affection, resisted and refracted away by Beth's oblivious continuation of her blissful memories. And we take them to be memories, of course, when we hear them in the theatre; they have a structural integrity, with no contradictions, that facilitate this assumption, although in reading them we might wonder how narrativised these necessary stories have been by her, and for her.

Landscape made its stage debut in double bill alongside *Silence* at the Aldwych Theatre in July 1969. This similarly short play is a natural partner for *Landscape*, in that it pursues some of the same creative strategies, and goes further in experimenting with stage discourses. Again we have characters talking, separated from one another, and again we have a division between past and present through evoked memory. *Silence*, though, multiplies the layers that *Landscape* set in play. The marred love story here involves three stage characters, not two (although the old landowner Sykes might have been inferred into a love triangle in *Landscape*, the character was not present to offer his testimony). Time is banded across various strata in *Silence*, with at least two past times and an ambiguous present occupied by the three onstage. Here, the isolation of the characters is emphasised further than in the previous play, with all visual references to any real world removed, and three actors standing in 'three areas' with 'a chair in each area' which might simply indicate stage space for each character being delineated by a separate pool of light.[12]

Both Rumsey (forty) and Bates (in his mid-thirties) have had a relationship with Ellen (in her twenties), whom they both knew as a child. Ellen appears to have been more emotionally attached to Rumsey, who rejected her, and more sexually attracted to Bates, whom she rejected. All three offer recollections of the relationships, and describe their present states of solitude. As they speak, they offer testimony not only of their pasts, but give details that would suggest they are older than the age given in Pinter's script. So, for example, Bates complains of being called 'granddad' by his youthful neighbours and Ellen speaks of her elderly drinking companion who asks about her 'early life' and her 'youth' (194). A twenty-something actress speaking these lines before us might cause us to wonder if we are to understand these lines, and consequently Bates's reference to being disdained for his age, as older manifestations of these same characters, speaking through an actor's body aged in accord with the time being remembered, rather than the moment from which memory is recalled. This notion is reinforced by two movements during the otherwise static play, when a character moves and joins one of the others in their area. First Bates moves to Ellen and speaks with her, and later Ellen moves to Rumsey. The conversations that take place during these might be considered to be the theatrical equivalent of cinematic flashbacks, as the actors here inhabit characters their own age, playing scenes that took place in the past, before returning to their area and performing that character as much older, recollecting past intimacies.

A recurring image in the three recollections is of some presence in a tree, first mentioned by the 'little girl' Bates remembers taking for a walk. 'I see something in a tree, a shape, a shadow. It is leaning down. It is looking at us', he recalls her saying, and remembers telling her it was probably a bird (198). He repeats this explanation in his first line after the flashback scene between Ellen and Rumsey, thereby foregrounding it as important, and twice later he draws attention to shapes in the trees. This creates a sort of visual leitmotif in the mind's eye of the audience member, but one that is unclear, an indistinct blur in a tree, which we might mentally overlay with an image of a bird looking down, regarding. It is faintly disturbing, and remains within us as a token of something not quite defined, not quite complete. This contributes to other examples of uncertainty, such as when Ellen refers to some kind of personal ontological crisis when she states 'I sometimes wonder if I can think' (194) or when Rumsey wonders if, when a horse approaches him, the horse experiences any need of him. All of these uncertainties speak to two key aspects of this play which resound in its poetry: we cannot truly know one other and we cannot know or control what others want of us. As with *Landscape*, there is a tacit warning that in failing to negotiate our mutual needs for company and comfort, we must accept or suffer isolation instead.

The indistinct object in the trees that troubles Ellen as a child also acts as a kind of creative chimera, a by-product of Pinter's writing process which finds itself captured in black ink on white paper: in trying to capture an expression, sometimes that expression is left incomplete, and articulating experience cannot always be resolved in neat, clear and directly communicative symbols. Beth in *Landscape* captures this creative phenomenon well when she reflects on 'the basic principles of shadow and light' in drawing, and goes on to recall how the 'shape of the shadow is determined by that of the object', before then curiously insisting that '[s]ometimes the cause of the shadow cannot be found' (185–6). She trails off with that thought over a set of three pauses, allowing us time to puzzle a little at what she might mean by a shadow with no object to cast it. Perhaps she refers to false memories, created by a troubled mind to make sense of past trauma or present unhappiness. Perhaps she means memories of people who are no longer present to merit that memory, or occupy it, re-enact its significance, either because they have been taken by death (Sykes) or distanced from that possibility by some interpersonal failure (Duff). The imagery of a shadow with no object to cause it is not dissimilar to that blot in the trees remembered in *Silence*: a presence that draws attention, that troubles, but which does not fully declare or resolve itself. How better might art capture the nature of memory as a phenomenon of the present time, a stain in the present from past spillage? By contrast, the comfort of happy memories is something that is elusive, impossible to contain and hold still, like the sand in which Beth attempts to draw a man and a woman, but which renders the figures unrecognisable, 'slipping, mixing the contours' (178).

The spectre of the past in *Landscape* and *Silence*, captured in unreliable, uncertain or possibly fictional memories, is something that haunts the plays' characters in their present existence. Pinter also soon realised that the past represented a space that could be vied for, fought over, defined and re-defined at will, as a means to take some control of a present moment, and we see that being employed in his next two full-length plays, *Old Times* and *No Man's Land*. A sketch he wrote in the late 1960s, *Night*, was a first outlet for this theme. It was first performed at the Comedy Theatre, London in April 1969 within an anthology of short pieces by various authors entitled *Mixed Doubles: An Entertainment on Marriage*. Pinter's sketch is a charming and doleful piece, in which a husband and wife dispute details of their early courtship. Man (neither character is named) recalls their first walk together, and recollects details of putting his hand under Woman's coat on a bridge and touching her breasts. Woman recalls standing by some railings, not on a bridge, and recollects their interlocked fingers, and how she found him a gentle, caring man, and wondered what move he might make. Man remembers standing behind Woman, and Woman remembers staring Man in the eyes, and rejects his version as the memory he has of an evening with another girl, on some other night. We never learn what the real version of their remembered first date should be, and they seem happy to accept the discrepancies as they both fold together into a contented present, where they are married and have children. Their pasts become multiple narratives of remembered 'women on bridges and towpaths and rubbish dumps' and 'men holding your hand and men looking into your eyes' which suggests an indifference to, and acceptance of, the inconsistencies in the narratives that have led them to their present moment, but which might represent threats to the integrity of their current lives.[13]

This focus on established married life continued with *Old Times*, which features another husband and wife pairing, Deeley and Kate, and her old flat-mate Anna, who has come to visit. The kernel of this play might be traced back to the early 1960s, and the plays in which control of a narrative was a key feature, such as *The Lover* and *The Collection*. The abandoned draft from that time of a series of scenes between a woman and two men, most of which was recycled in the construction of *The Homecoming* as dialogue between Teddy, Lenny and Ruth, contained a final scene that did not make that transition. In it, A returns to join in the dialogue between B and C and all three discuss night attire and the possibility of a sexual tryst between them all. In a hand-written note that accompanies the typescript, Pinter made these notes:

Jealousy
A of B & C
C of B & A
B of A & C

Now, if we replaced A, B and C by James, Bill and Stella, the first two lines of that note make some sense, if we recall *The Collection*, and it may be that the drafting of the A, B, C play was abandoned to follow that inspiration first, by adding Harry into the sequences of potential jealousies. *Old Times*, though, gets closer to imagining a narrative centred around such a circulation of jealousy within a triangular arrangement and some lines are imported from this abandoned draft, suggesting that Pinter returned to it for inspiration. Negotiating jealousy within marriage was a theme of the James Joyce play *Exiles*, although it is not openly declared and debated, but becomes a subtle tool of manipulation. If Joyce's play acted as something of a creative spur for Pinter at this point, even more direct parallels with the play can be found later in his *Monologue* and *Betrayal*, in which, as in *Exiles*, the relationship between two men is defined by their shared love of one woman, and her reciprocated love for them both. In *Old Times*, Pinter partially inverts that triangle by having two female characters and one male and the issue of sharing a partner is not a feature, or at least not explicitly.[14] Instead, Pinter maps out a territory of implied threat that destabilises characters through undermining their narrative construction of themselves. This structure perhaps also owes something to Pinter's experience rehearsing and performing the role of Garcin in Jean-Paul Sartre's *In Camera*, broadcast as one of the first productions in the BBC's 'The Wednesday Play' series in 1964. Sartre's play, like *Old Times*, is populated by one man and two women who vie with one another in shifting strategies of domination and alliance to hold on to their narrativised constructions of their projected identities and sense of personal worth. Set in an imaginary limbo after each of them has died, the impenetrable and resistant truth of their pasts inserts itself uncomfortably into their present predicament. The experience might well be one of a series of sources of inspiration that later coalesced in the writing process of Pinter's 1971 play.

Old Times is set within realistic decor: a converted farmhouse near the sea with 'spare modern furniture',[15] including two sofas and an armchair in the first act. The two sofas (as opposed to just one) indicate a wealthy environment, and serve also to maintain a visual symmetry in the second act which takes place in the bedroom, and which has two divans and an armchair. Pinter states clearly in the setting notes that the 'divans and armchair are disposed in precisely the same relation to each other as the furniture in the first act, but in reversed position' and this implies symbolic relevance to the placement of such real items (285). Despite this qualified realism, Pinter does something peculiar and notable with space and time as the play begins, in the manner of his experiments in *Silence*. Kate and Deeley sit and chat about her old friend Anna as though they were awaiting her arrival. Deeley is asking for details of her, as though trying to get a full picture of this guest that is about to arrive, and Kate supplies him with answers. The first line of the play is Kate's answer to a question we do not hear: the play starts mid-conversation. All the while a woman is standing upstage, in the dim light and by the window. We do not yet know for certain who this figure is, but her silent, indistinct presence insinuates itself on the conversation and we might infer that it is the person to whom the speaking characters allude. Is she actually there, in the room with them (Pinter does write 'at the window') or does she occupy some liminal, theatrical space, on stage but not quite in the scene? Whereas in his other works, Pinter has deferred any adjustment to the theatrical discourse that dictates how we read what happens in front of us (the delay in the 'reveal' of Richard as his wife's lover in *The Lover* is a prime example, overturning the expectations of farce), here he starts at the onset with a dislocated set of frames. We cannot immediately work out the grammar by which what we are watching can be interpreted: if Kate and Deeley are talking about Anna, and she is there in the room with them, is this some sort of game? Or is she is simply waiting to enter the scene, invoked as a presence but not present within the scene as played? The play that follows makes most sense if we decide upon the latter, but for those first few moments in performance the ambiguity resonates, and so is deliberate.

The opening conversation establishes Anna's hair colour, body type and whether she is married or not, but does not really concern itself with such trivial details. Deeley seems to be trying to get a generic sense of who Anna is and used to be, and makes the curious assertion that he will be able to tell if she, Anna, has changed by watching Kate. This is a notable comment as it introduces a theme of how identity is the property of those who define us. As the two continue to discuss Anna, the conversation in places comes across as something of a mutually agreed negotiation of her identity, as though they are together inventing the character. For example, Deeley wonders if she is a vegetarian at one point, and later Kate points out that he indicated that she is (he clearly did not, and could not know if she is a stranger to him). Later, the fact that Deeley is surprised to learn that Anna and Kate lived together might indicate that this 'fact' has just been made up. Having a female character upstage in the dark, but clearly within the delineated space of the room the two speaking characters inhabit, might lead some audience members to understand that the character is being constructed in front of us, summoned up from some uncertain past that Kate claims not to fully remember, and details of which take even her husband by surprise.

Pinter then uses a kind of jump-cut, offering another nod to his experience of writing for the cinema, and transferring some of its grammar to the deliberately dislocated stage discourse he has set up with Anna's silent presence. She suddenly walks downstage into the lit acting area and joins Kate and Deeley mid-sentence, continuing in a monologue addressed clearly at Kate about what the two of them used to get up to together in their shared youth in London. The pace of the monologue (written as one long sentence; Pinter writes with an opening lower case after each question mark to indicate a continuous stream) shifts the gear of the performance, and it goes on long enough to establish firmly a new section of the play, and a new logic whereby we recognise we have jumped forward in time to later that evening. Audiences adapt quickly to shifts like this, but when they happen they can be disconcerting. The pace of the monologue here leaves no time to settle the residue in us of any uncertainty from what the earlier discursive frame (Anna being both present and not present) was doing. Instead, that sense of someone being defined, and the definition mattering in some way to the married couple, lingers and eventually works its way into what the rest of the play does. Anna's sudden animation also serves to puncture the present with a blur of past memories and, just as in *Landscape*, *Silence* and *Night*, the play develops through interaction with the past recalled in the present moment. This time, Pinter has found a way to do this without recourse to static stages that give room to lingering verbal reminiscences.

Much of what follows in Act One is a conversation dominated by Deeley and Anna. Kate's lines barely make it into double figures until the last five minutes of this act. In this way, Pinter establishes a kind of adversarial position between Deeley and his wife's old friend. The conversation contains some very subtle undermining of one person's position by the other. For example, after Anna's long introductory monologue about London in the past, Deeley artfully dismisses the subject with 'We rarely go to London' (256). When Deeley responds to her enthusiastic words about their home, and tells her that he often leaves the place for his line of work, Anna disguises a retort in a complement to their environment in 'No one who lived here would want to go far' (257). When Deeley declares he knows the island where Anna lives (we later learn it to be Sardinia), her response, after a pause, to his 'I've been there', is the non sequitur 'I'm so delighted to be here', clearly deflecting the possibility that she herself might become the subject of their conversation (260–1). In polite conversation, such understated challenges have a plausible deniability that means they cannot be easily challenged as rude, but when we note them occurring we recognise an awkward tension between people.

In this testing conversation, Kate's husband and friend spend much of the time talking about her, so much so that she foregrounds their definitions of her by redundantly, and therefore pointedly, asking 'Are you talking about me?' (261). This narrative around Kate is first signalled by a Freudian slip Anna makes saying to Deeley 'You have a wonderful casserole [...] I mean wife' (258) through which Pinter refers back to the opening dialogue (when the casserole was first mentioned) and, in this way, Anna turns the tables on that opening scene. In equating Kate with the housewifely duties of food preparation, Anna establishes a set of definitions of Kate as staid, domestic and fixed, to which Deeley has already inadvertently contributed by noting how she stays at home when he travels. Anna then recollects how Kate used to cook up a good stew when they lived together. The choice of vocabulary here might be significant. To all intents and purposes, there is no difference between a stew and a casserole – both involve the slow cooking of meat in liquid – except perhaps a register in the choice of the words where the Anglo-Saxon derived vocabulary denotes a lower class than the Latinate word.[16] We might therefore take Anna's reminiscence of getting the same food, with different names, in both past and present as an indicator that Kate has stayed put in all but class, wealth and environment.

Deeley and Anna then engage on an agreed line of definition by considering evidence of Kate as a dreamer, as always divorced from the present moment, and this resolves itself in a series of excerpts from songs they sing at and with one another. Pinter's choice of songs is from a bygone era (even in 1971) and they are referred to by Anna as 'lovely old things' (264). With one exception, all of the songs are from musical theatre and film between 1928 and 1937, but also became standards that had commercially popular iterations in the 1950s, when these characters (and Pinter) would have been in their twenties. The songs, then, represent and signify the past in a material way through deliberate, shared nostalgia, and a nostalgia that is doubled by the memory of a 1950s popular cultural reiteration of 1930s show tunes, here in the early 1970s.[17]

As well as setting a tone of shared nostalgia, a currency of the past that is spent in the present, the songs also continue the definition of Kate by Anna and Deeley, and begin to establish a challenge between them for ownership of that definition, with Deeley's 'they can't take that away from me', 'I've got a woman' and 'all the things you are, are mine' taking on a tone of deliberate possessiveness in this context (265). This is embellished by the theatrical experience; the fact that the actors begin to sing creates a delightful and entertainingly odd moment that puts the two singers in overt competition, while emphasising the possessive content of the lyrics. Singing these complimentary lines towards Kate also comes across on stage as a manifest attempt to gain her favour, to woo her. The sequence is punctuated by a silence, allowing the moment to settle awkwardly onstage before it starts abruptly again with a monologue from Deeley which opens as though mid-flow in a way that suggests we have leapt forward in time again. He tells a story of how he once went on his own to the cinema to see Carol Reed's 1947 film *Odd Man Out* (another example of nostalgia for cultural artefacts from his youth) and locates the cinema near a bicycle shop where his father had bought him his first tricycle (another example of nostalgia being doubled, folding one era back on another). After some dismissive commentary about two usherettes sharing a joke about self-pleasuring, he describes how he met Kate in that cinema and light-heartedly suggests it was the film's star Robert Newman that brought them together. In dismissing the brief suggestion of lesbianism with the reference to the usherettes, and in making a point about Kate being the only other person in the cinema, Deeley is creating a narrative of their relationship that excludes all other female intervention. Anna makes a few comments to permit herself into the narrative, firstly by declaring information that indicates she knows the film and then making something of a game-changing announcement, one that explicitly declares her awareness of the rules of the current game and forewarns of her tactical mastery of them:

> There are some things one remembers even though they may never have happened. There are things I remember which may never have happened but as I recall them so they take place. (269–70)

The second sentence here is the testimony of an author, and is the stated premise that is the very engine of this play. We have seen the taking control of a narrative within a relationship being equated to seemingly taking control of that relationship, in *The Lover* and *The Collection*, but what Anna's statement here implies is that the construction of narratives of the past have real implications to present configurations between people, and Pinter takes this and applies what he has learned from *Landscape* and *Silence* about how the past invades and colours the present. Unlike those plays, though, the past becomes a space of territorial negotiation and confrontation in *Old Times*. Giving Deeley no time but to release an exasperated '*What?*' to her statement about memory, Anna launches into her own narrative of times past that inverts the exclusion of the intruding female in Deeley's story, and has a man crying in her and Kate's shared room, a man who is rejected by them both. After some chat about Kate and Deeley getting and being married, Anna then makes her boldest move and remembers a time when she and Kate went to the cinema together to see *Odd Man Out*. Her statement that they were 'almost alone' in the cinema allows for Deeley's presence, but she deliberately unsettles his account of the day he met his wife by re-writing its elements. The title of the film, here, gains evident ironic force.

To consolidate Deeley's exclusion, Anna shortly after instigates something of a flashback sequence (as we see in *Silence*) where she and Kate talk about what they should do with the evening, and if they should invite a male friend around. At this point Kate finally gets to speak again, and the dialogue continues between the two women until the end of the act, marginalising Deeley, who manages just one interjection. This is the third apparent shift in discourse in the course of the first act, with an audience now unclear whether we have a genuine flashback in front of them – a moment from the past being replayed – or a playful re-enactment of the past in the present by Kate and Anna, which Deeley's inability to interject soon suggests. Act One ends after Anna turns to face Deeley as Kate leaves to run her bath, and the gesture is a clear visual statement of contest. If this is the end of round one, then Anna is clearly in the lead and Deeley falling behind. His earlier statement about how he sat to one side in the cinema on the day he met Kate has become something of a marker of his position in the play: 'I was off centre and have remained so' (268).

The play began with a shared narrative construction of a character, continued with a joint construction of the narrative of another character in a competitive mode, proceeds to the telling and the strategic re-telling of a significant past event in a cinema, and the first act ends with an acceleration of that re-telling of the past through a re-enactment of a past quality of friendship. The process of constructing stories is foregrounded on a number of occasions, notably the manner in which characters question the choice of words they or others use: Kate first queries the appropriateness of the word 'friend' to define Anna, Deeley notes Anna's use of the words 'lest' and 'gaze' as being in uncommon usage, and later clarifies his own choice of the word 'globe' instead of 'world' in such a pompous manner as to draw attention to his choice of vocabulary. Deeley's profession, given as film director, also contributes to the theme of authorship, markedly when he bizarrely declares himself to be Orson Welles, the foremost British film auteur (and star of Carol Reed's most successful film, *The Third Man* (1949), which must linger in the background of the chain of references Pinter is activating here). Combined with a theatrical structure of which the reading frame is deliberately shifted between four sections (the latter three separated from one another by silences), these features create a dramatic development that is in flux, is being constructed in front of us by its characters who are each susceptible to deliberate narrative collapse, moving through a collision of testimonies towards an inevitable disintegration.

The second act takes place in the bedroom, and so moves closer to the private heartland of Deeley and Kate's marriage. Anna waits on a divan while Kate takes a bath, offering continuity with the end of act one 'flashback' sequence and their talk of her going to bathe. Deeley enters with coffee, and then launches his first new offensive by declaring that he once met Anna in a tavern in central London and that they then went to a party on the other side of Hyde Park where he sat and looked up her skirt, with her silent consent. He then writes Kate into the reminiscence, having Anna joined by a friend at the party. Anna neatly subverts this by declaring she was wearing Kate's underwear, and so merges herself with Kate as the subject of Deeley's past libidinous gaze. This deflects his attempt at appropriation of her in the past as she folds an inferred sexual availability into a game that she and Kate would play to titillate themselves, thereby turning the gazing men into the women's subjects of either desire and derision (or both). Deeley makes one last grab at owning the past narrative and tells Kate how he had met Anna and looked up her skirt, but ends by also fusing his wife and her friend, stating '[s]he thought she was you, said little, so little. Maybe she was you. Maybe it was you' (307). The stakes are against him. Kate and Anna return to their 'flashback' mode of conversation, and any attempt to get a confirmation of a sexual relationship between the two women in the past, by discussing Kate's body and how it might be dried after a bath, leads only to Deeley's exasperated sense that things have gone too far.

It is Kate who ties up the loose ends, by effectively dismissing both of those who have verbally staked a claim to her, employing the same narrative strategies as them. She recalls for Deeley how Anna had fallen in love with him because of his vulnerability, thereby reducing the sexual link to one of romance that writes him as relatively weak in her narrative. Then she turns to Anna and declares remembering her dead, but the manner in which she describes Anna as dead foregrounds its own fictionalisation, by describing a form of ritual burial, with Anna in 'immaculate' sheets, her face smeared with dirt and covered in faded inscriptions (perhaps a suggestion that she is being smothered by her own fictions). From Anna's passive death in the past, which Kate remembers sitting and watching, she moves to describing an active killing of Deeley, when she plastered his face with dirt from the window box, which is to say she made his appearance match that of the 'dead' Anna in the same story.

What Kate does at the close of the play is effectively erase the constructions of the past that Anna and Deeley had written in order to channel and possess her. In doing so she removes Anna from her past – when she recalls Deeley asking who had occupied the other bed before him, she answers 'no one at all' – and then undermines the premises of her marriage (claiming that neither a wedding nor a change of environment 'mattered') (311). If we consider the play as a set of three characters slowly writing themselves and each other, in a sort of inter-dependent Pirandellian daydream, then Kate's last intervention is a deliberate close of chapter. If we follow the play on a more realistic register, then the ending is emotionally devastating. Now bereft of his scaffold of narratives, Deeley performs a routine that has been foretold in one of Anna's reminiscences. He sobs, approaches the divan where Anna has lain down, hesitates, heads for the door, hesitates, then sits beside Kate on her divan and rests his head on her lap. After a 'long silence', he gets up and goes to slump in the armchair, and Pinter requests 'Lights up full sharply. Very bright' (313). This visual punctuation concludes the drama. A final tableau scene is to become typical of Pinter's writing and only with *The Homecoming* have we before had a play end with a deliberate lingering on a visual arrangement. This new strategy here creates a final image that will linger with the audience, and which acts as emblematic of what the play has achieved. In *The Homecoming* it is the triumph of Ruth over the men she now commands, and here the arrangement of characters on two divans and a chair emphasises their isolation from one another, their failure to define themselves in functioning relationships.

Landscape, *Silence* and *Old Times* form a trilogy of dramas that represent a set of experiments with both memory and theatricality that resulted in compelling plays, and which also very clearly informed Pinter's subsequent writing. The merging of vocabularies of representation from his screenplay work proved fruitful in addressing issues of the remembered past, and we can see an evolution from a sort of irrepressible voice-over from Beth in *Landscape*, to the flashbacks in *Silence* emphasising the emptiness of the characters' present existences, to a playful disruption caused by jump-cuts and flashbacks in *Old Times* that do not declare a straightforward frame for reading them, thereby keeping the tension of uncertainty alive in an audience's appreciation. The subject matter of *Landscape* and *Old Times* is situated firmly in the emotional territory of established married couples, and as such they belong to a continued strand that runs from *A Slight Ache*, through *The Lover* and *The Collection*. Although those earlier plays had been written arguably from a masculine perspective, with a male character negotiating an emotional framework within which a functioning relationship might be constructed, the new work began to adopt a more nuanced approach to gender in which the sensibilities of both male and female experience were more fully explored and articulated. Adding now the dimension of past events invading or defining present situations, Pinter found a new spring of inspiration that would provide for a decade of creative output.

A Foreign Country
No Man's Land

Another exercise in addressing how times past fold into and inform times present, and with a growing focus again on the female experience, can be found in Pinter's 1971 screenplay for *Langrishe Go Down*, adapted from Aiden Higgins's 1966 novel. Pinter had hoped to direct the piece for the screen himself, but the necessary funding could not be found. It was directed by David Jones for the BBC seven years later and broadcast on 20 September 1978. Set in a country house in Ireland in the 1930s, it is the story of three middle-aged women and their relationship with a young German philosophy student, and the action veers between a sterile present of 1937–8 and an eventful past in the summer of 1932. Steven H. Gale commends Pinter's adaptation, stating that 'it is the inter-cutting of images of the actions of the two women in the past and the present that is especially effective in presenting the contrast between their life of passion and a life of dry withdrawal'.[18] Echoing the opening lines of Pinter's 1969 screenplay for *The Go-Between*, which correlates past time in territorial terms ('the past is a foreign country, they do things differently there'),[19] the character of Ellen here says 'my youth was somewhere else'.[20] This territorial mapping of the emotional past, and the interruptive heave it can inflict on the present, was to be fully explored by Pinter in his next, and his most ambitious, screenplay adaptation, of Marcel Proust's *À la recherche du temps perdu*.

Pinter recalled the months of work in 1972 on the manuscript that would later be published as *The Proust Screenplay* as some of the most satisfying of his working life, and Joseph Losey considered the final manuscript to be Pinter's finest work. Pinter stated that he did not seek 'to rival the work' or to just 'make a film centred round one or two volumes' but to 'try to distil the whole work, to incorporate the major themes of the book into an integrated whole'.[21] His ambition, and final achievement, was to secure cinematic solutions to capturing Proust's expression of the present time as a platform for interruptions from or temporary retreat into the past, mediated through and captured in art. By using point-of-view shots, Pinter forged Marcel's subjective experience at the centre of the proposed film's panorama, rendering an internal, personal experience of memory through layered filmic languages of sound and image. The seemingly bold removal of Proust's madeleine/tea episode, in this context, is an obvious choice: the sensory experience of taste is alien to cinematic discourse. In its place, Pinter offers the evocations of past sounds and sites. Pinter locates the bells that transport Marcel back to his childhood, for example, in the screenplay's opening and closing moments, and the reassuring three knocks that Marcel's grandmother would give on the partition wall between hers and the young boy's bedroom are invoked by Pinter at her funeral. Visual devices operate too: the repeated motif of a 'yellow screen' is revealed in the screenplay's final moments to be a close-up of a wall in Johannes Vermeer's painting 'View of Delft', representing a final opening out from an absorbed, obscuring, proximity to detail to a distanced, objective overview of a whole view. He described how 'the architecture of the film should be based on two main and contrasting principles; one, a movement, chiefly narrative, toward disillusion, and the other, more intermittent, toward revelation, rising to where time that was lost is found, and fixed forever in art'.[22]

Pinter's next full-length play to be written after the Proust adaptation, and inflected by the obsession with the past and memory that the screenplay invoked, was *No Man's Land*, commissioned for the opening of the National Theatre building on the South Bank. With this work, Pinter seemed to revert to previous themes and styles, introducing an intruder into a household (Spooner) who would seek to profit from the generosity of his host (Hirst) and establish himself permanently on site as the man's secretary. As such, the play resurrects the Kullus persona, and resembles *The Caretaker* in structure: the intruder insinuates himself into the household, carefully implies a sense of obligation upon his host, presumes to out-manoeuvre him only to discover his host has those who would protect him, and is ousted following a final plea to stay. Spooner, like Davies, may have fallen on hard times but he is no vagrant, and presents a far more wily and educated front. His name alludes to the linguistic wrong-footedness of the spoonerism, and perhaps acts as a badge to his literary aspirations, their failure, and his inability to out-manoeuvre the residents at this Hampstead Heath household. Given this, perhaps Pinter was self-consciously and openly admitting to overtly crafted and self-referential material. The heavy curtains across the window during daylight link back to Kullus's predilection for that arrangement, and Spooner's 'What a remarkably pleasant room. I feel at peace here. Safe from all danger' is tauntingly 'Pinteresque':[23] the author could not have been unaware of such self-referencing and, rather than demonstrating a diminishing of his powers, its intertextuality speaks to the act of writing and a fear of losing creative powers that this play embodies. Spooner's later statement, 'I have known this before. The voice unheard. A listener. The command from an upper floor' confirms this self-referential potential, as this seems deliberately to indicate events in *The Dumb Waiter* (372). When a heavily inebriated Hirst declares at the end of the first scene 'Tonight ... My friend ... You find me in the last lap of a race ... I had long forgotten to run', Spooner sarcastically retorts 'A metaphor. Things are looking up' (338) and this serves both as indicative of the character – part of a series of verbal parries to demean his host – and almost as a declaration of the play's author, simultaneously emphasising a phrase that is key to the play and emphasising the constructed nature of his characters' dialogue. The funereally named Hirst's stagnant creativity might also be read as a lengthy 'note to self': Michael Billington comments that the portrayal of Hirst could represent 'Pinter's nightmare vision of the kind of artist he might, unless he were careful, become'.[24]

No Man's Land is set in Hirst's large, well-maintained house in north London, within walking distance of Hampstead Heath and a pub there named Jack Straw's Castle, where we learn that Spooner and Hirst have just met.[25] The play opens on Hirst pouring drinks for himself and his guest. Spooner is garrulous while his host presents a reticent front, and is near monosyllabic in conversation. We perhaps infer that Hirst has sought solace in both drink and company this evening and, as Spooner clearly does, we might conclude that he lives a solitary life in an over-sized house furnished abundantly with both books and stocks of alcohol. Spooner articulates both a gracious gratitude and a canny nose for gleaning information about his host. He queries a 'we' that Hirst employs and asks about the two mugs he sees on the bookshelves, as if to ascertain whether the man lives alone or not. Spooner's articulate diction indicates (or imitates) an educated background, he declares himself to be both a poet and a mentor to young writers, and the two men speak abstractly of the salvation of the English language and drink a toast, declaring 'through art to virtue' (334). These suggest an indulgent promotion of artistic endeavour over and above lived experience, or at least an easy, middle-class allegiance to the arts as allied to respectability.

When Spooner makes reference to a memory of drinking tea on the lawn of his cottage, and Hirst acknowledges that he did the same, Spooner leaps on the small revelation as a detail that binds the two men and, in so doing, initiates the theme of memory in the play. Memories of real or imagined histories are to be wrapped within the stories of the past that the two men are to begin telling. Here, Spooner links a particular kind of pastoral imagery to a definition of what it is to be English ('A memory of the bucolic life. We're both English') and this seems contrived to further his agenda of generating an accelerated closeness to his host (335). When Hirst makes reference to the ancient English custom of hanging garlands from rafters in churches to commemorate the death of an unmarried person, Spooner picks at the potential implications of such a recollected detail and asks after Hirst's wife, only to construct a possibly all too accurate past of a wife having left the home and Hirst rendered impotent. This strategy of one character manipulating another through rendering a version of personal history that hits a nerve in the present is recognisable from *Old Times* and Hirst's response is to deliver his metaphor about being in a race he has forgotten to run, and to beat an undignified, inebriated retreat, crawling on hands and knees out of the room.

At this point in the performance of the play, we as audience would consider Spooner to have affected some kind of victory, having browbeaten the owner of the room that he now alone occupies. Before he gets to take any advantage of that position, he and we immediately hear a door open and slam shut. A second scene begins as a younger man, Foster, enters the room. This shift is sudden and unexpected; we might have imagined that Spooner would be left to profit from his position, and that we would watch a scene unfold as he takes possession of the room and reveals for us, perhaps, his real agenda. Foster's entry, then, catches us as audience as much unawares as it does Spooner, and with it the play increases in momentum in a way that makes the first scene seem to have been something of a prologue, a preparation for the challenges to follow. Foster acts almost unsurprised to find Spooner in the house, introduces himself as Hirst's son but then immediately speaks of having had a 'night off', indicating that he is an employee of the household. He delivers a long monologue in which he reveals details of a subtly threatening nature. Pinter has delivered this kind of monologue before; Goldberg in *The Birthday Party*, Mick in *The Caretaker* and Lenny in *The Homecoming* all tell stories that function as attempts to unnerve their recipient, to demonstrate knowledge, experience or brutal capacities that might pose a threat if they are not to get their way. Foster ends by asking Spooner to identify himself, and responds to his claim to be Hirst's friend with 'You're not typical' (342), which demeans both host and guest. If we viewed Spooner with suspicion up to this point, as a verbal aggressor of sorts, we now might think him to be at risk himself. Pinter nudges at our allegiances in this way, and the uncertainty this engenders suggests that everything is still for play in this drama.

Foster is soon joined by another manservant, Briggs, who claims to recognise Spooner as someone who collects the beer mugs in a Chalk Farm pub. Spooner confirms this, and there is a remarkably concise exchange between the three men that, while revolving around seemingly trivial details, establishes a verbal jostle to demean and redeem: Briggs's assertion that Spooner collects glasses in a pub places him at the most unskilled end of the labour market and the location of the pub is also more solidly working-class than the suburban Jack Straw's Castle. Spooner retaliates by claiming to be a friend of the landlord, clarifying his activity in the pub as a gracious favour. Foster then claims also to be a friend of the landlord, potentially negating Spooner's claim, and the conversation trails into an acknowledgement of Spooner's acquaintance of Hirst that dilutes the word 'friend' to meaningless proportions. Foster and Briggs leave Spooner no verbal space to stake his claims to respectability, and therefore a right to a presence in the house. The subtext is all swift, challenging parries, while on the surface the subject matter is banal and benign. There is a sober sharpness of wit and wile in Foster and Briggs that sends Spooner onto the back foot. He recovers by responding to their boasts of appealing to Siamese girls with an oblique travel anecdote of his own, and one that portrays him as a man of culture: he talks of the inspiration for a painting from an incident witnessing a fisherman in Amsterdam. Here we see narrativised memory being used again as a means of negotiating status in the present moment, just as it had been wielded in *Old Times*. Foster offers his own, a memory of a conman, that clearly articulates his suspicion of Spooner.

The master of the house, Hirst, then returns into this scenario. He states that he feels refreshed from a brief sleep and craves drink, and quickly consumes even more whisky, eventually straight from the bottle, until he collapses yet again of continued fatigue or accelerated drunkenness. Following Hirst's return, the dramatic balance for the rest of the play is finally established in what remains of the first act. Foster and Brigg's statuses as manservants are confirmed, but we see them behaving in a disrespectful and dismissive manner towards their supposed master, and the tensions between his requests or commands and their inaction or reluctance become evident. Spooner's endeavour to interject himself into this domestic arrangement is also made plain in his attempts to assist Hirst and berate the two servants for their disrespectful attitudes to their elders. Hirst, though, seems to have prepared a defence against Spooner, or genuinely forgotten the guest he previously so generously watered. He demands to know who the stranger is, and rejects the epithet of 'friend' to describe him, stating that his only friends are those whose faces he sees in photographs in his album. This insistent distancing, alongside the hostility from Foster and Briggs, isolates Spooner and he recovers ground by insinuating himself into a dream that Hirst states he has just suffered, suggesting that a drowning companion in that dream represents him. All characters, then, end the act in a precarious state: Spooner's bid to profit from his new acquaintance is a long way from succeeding, Foster and Briggs seem to be far from their master's favour (the manner in which they take the threat posed by Spooner so seriously suggests their tenure is not as assured at is might seem) and Hirst himself is emotionally and physically fragile and in need of support. Spooner's arrival this evening has clearly coincided with or established a threshold moment in Hirst's domestic arrangements. Foster even locks him in the room for the night, switching the lights off as he goes, as though to keep him out of harm's way but secured captive.

No Man's Land quickly establishes an atmosphere of decay and loss, and has a chief character plagued with past events that might constitute regrets. To this Pinter adds Hirst's nightmare of the drowning friend, and places this subconscious activity on a par with memories: Spooner places himself into both, and in doing so foregrounds the territory of negotiation in this play as the oneiric, the uncertain past, the shifting sands of the mind's constructions. If the play had begun with a scenario reminiscent of that of *The Caretaker*, it soon shifts from the material world that obsesses the earlier play's characters to this more metaphoric plane. The claustrophobic atmosphere that prevails supports this, emphasising the interior, self-reflexive world that Hirst and Spooner inhabit. The second act presents the subtle battle to gain advantage in that world, via manipulations of memory and imagined pasts. It opens with something of a prelude between Briggs and Spooner, which re-enacts some of the themes of the first act. Spooner again stakes a claim to respectability (affirming himself as a poet) and Briggs treats him again with diffidence. A key feature of this section is Briggs's story of meeting Foster one day when the latter was looking for driving directions to Bolsover Street. The unnecessary and intricate details of the directions given through London side streets present a complicated maze towards a destination that, Briggs declares, is anyway unworthy of attaining. The directions, and their re-telling, are acts of deliberate obfuscation. The monologue is almost gratuitously metaphorical, although it is unclear what purpose the metaphor of the convoluted directions might serve; it articulates perhaps a suspicion of the need to attain meaning, or acts as a threat to Spooner to give up any ambitions to pursue his objectives. The speech sits in the middle of the play like the Post Office Tower it references: a monolithic, modernist presence that stands out from the apparently more traditional material that surrounds it.

The Bolsover Street monologue also functions to prefigure a speech that is twice as long, issued by Hirst upon his return. Perhaps the obfuscation that confuses and amuses an audience prepares them to be suspicious of the information they are to receive about the supposed past of these characters. Clearly re-invigorated by a night's sleep, Hirst addresses Spooner as Charles Wetherby and goes into a lengthy set of recollections about their shared pre-war past at Oxford. The other names he recalls, including Bunty, Tubby and Burston-Smith, almost suggest a P. G. Wodehouse 1930s lifestyle of the idle rich (and, by extension, a fictive account). He jovially confesses to having seduced Spooner's wife and enjoyed an affair with her. The strategy, it seems, is to belittle Spooner, and thereby to begin a fresh day with the upper-hand. Spooner plays along with the narrative that Hirst seems to be making up and trips up at first by allowing himself to be outranked in their remembrances of the war. He regains ground by introducing another of Hirst's female conquests before indicating his own successful sexual adventures, to Hirst's disgust. This unarmed response allows Spooner to dig further, and accuse Hirst of having manifested a depraved sexual appetite before then driving home a final blow in the form of a criticism of Hirst's command of poetic form. Signalling his defeat, Hirst shouts for a drink of scotch, and retreats back into maudlin alcoholism.

The manner in which the two men engage in reminiscences of names, places and events might easily be, or come across as, an actual shared past. The audience might readily believe that the two men do actually know one another, and the actors' performance might conspire to make this possibility seem assured; they might, after all, need to come to a decision on the matter themselves as they hone their portrayals. That the two characters engaged as strangers in the first act confuses this possibility, and the truth of the matter remains ambiguous (and does not matter to our enjoyment of the play). The seemingly fictional past is contrasted with a real, but equally distant and intangible past, in the form of Hirst's photograph album. Here, there is no doubt, is authentic emotional meaning, and Hirst seems to indicate that he is willing to share something personal with Spooner: 'I am prepared to be patient. I shall be kind to you. I shall show you my library. I might even show you my study' (382).

Hirst's attitude to Spooner certainly manifests patience, and his willingness to engage with him, as friend or stranger, despite the verbal beating he gets in doing so, might come across as a need for change, for a new domestic arrangement, for human contact beyond the inhospitable daily service he receives from Briggs and Foster. Those two mugs that Spooner notices in the first act remain visible throughout the play, after all, as an emblem of human domestic company. Spooner represents for Hirst a viable, if flawed, alternative to his current staff, and articulates some genuine understanding of Hirst's ageing condition and artistic worth. Given Hirst's previous statement that he is on the 'last lap of a race ... I had long forgotten to run' there is almost a desperate late attempt at fresh friendship here (338), but the appeal that is made is genuine and Hirst summons up his most persuasive bid by conjuring up memories of community from the faces that populate his photograph album:

I might even show you my photograph album. You might even see a face in it which might remind you of your own, of what you once were. You might see faces of others, in shadow, or cheeks of others, turning, or jaws, or backs of necks, or eyes, dark under hats, which might remind you of others, whom once you knew, whom you thought long dead, but from whom you will still receive a sidelong glance, if you can face the good ghost. Allow the love of the good ghost. (383)

By placing Spooner's youthful face in the album, and inviting him to contemplate the warmth and camaraderie of long dead friends, Hirst moves close to finally inviting Spooner to stay in his household. He suggests that Spooner should 'tender the dead, as you would yourself be tendered, now, in what you would describe as your life', proposing a form of mutual benefit, a symbiotic existence between past and present, and by extension between the two men now. The speech is a focal point in the play, and encapsulates the prospect of human company against a backdrop of atrophied possibilities, and a progressive interaction between past and present. Here, Pinter almost deliberately inverts the Proustian aesthetic that offers resolution of memory through art: as a work of art, *No Man's Land* suggests here that the past can be accessed, perhaps through fictionalisation, to serve a release in the present moment. Proust's involuntary memory is supplanted with a canny, wilful mobilisation of memory that might bring people together, but in the play this is rendered vulnerable to plundering for selfish ends. In 2008, afflicted by cancer and aware that his last days were approaching, Pinter asked his friend Michael Gambon to recite this passage at his eventual funeral, evidencing the value to him of the sentiment it contains.[26]

Sensing a threat to his tenure, Briggs rudely punctuates the end of Hirst's speech with a negation of the possibility of a connection with past community (and thereby the kindling of present relations) with 'They're blank, mate, blank. The blank dead' (383) and the rest of the play will involve his and Foster's attempts to shoulder Spooner out of any potential allegiance with their master. When Spooner later offers to take up the post of Hirst's secretary and help place names to faces in the album, Foster repeats Briggs's strategy: 'Those faces are nameless' and Hirst makes one last expression of emotional need which also articulates his awareness of his 'last lap' being almost run: 'There are places in my heart ... where no living soul ... has ... or can ever ... Trespass' (388). Spooner eventually makes an extended case for why Hirst might take him in as secretary, cook, companion and 'chevalier', but makes a possible strategic error in offering to host a poetry reading that Hirst might give in the Chalk Farm pub, a backward step for an established man of letters. His suggestions are met with silence.

From here the play moves towards it close. Hirst shrugs off Spooner's lengthy proposals by suggesting that they change the subject, and do so for the last time. Foster and Briggs take advantage of this to ensure that Spooner's proposal is never again contemplated, and, suggesting that winter is now the final subject, suggest that Hirst is trapped, with only their company, for the rest of time. All mention of the past is ended, and replaced by a permanent, unchanging present moment. The metaphorical space becomes all the more claustrophobic, and Hirst seems to lack the energy to resist this final assertion of his decaying self. Spooner, recognising that his bid to join the household has failed, repeats Hirst's words from earlier in the play as an acknowledgement that the game has ended: 'You are in no man's land. Which never moves, which never changes, which never grows older, but which remains forever, icy and silent' (399).

This inhospitable stasis and unoccupied terrain that the term 'no man's land' suggests suitably captures the emotional concern of much of Pinter's writing in the years after *The Homecoming*. Whereas in that play and those that preceded it, Pinter would most often come to some conclusion in which a character or two gains the upper hand over another or others, from *Landscape* onwards (leaving his more political writing aside) he seemed intent on examining the failure to connect, to profit emotionally from the tendered or potential warmth of human company. After *No Man's Land*, he begins to expand the palette of these failed connections, and develops a concern to consider the configuration of the family as a unit that might represent a context for healthy mutual sustenance, and the human weaknesses that threaten or undermine that prospective benefit.

CHAPTER 4
THE IMPOSSIBLE FAMILY

Exiled
Monologue, Betrayal

There were few parent and children family units in Pinter's writing in the first twenty years of his output for the stage, and the majority of the married couples in his work in that period had no children. Rose and Bert, Petey and Meg, Edward and Flora, Stella and James, Sarah and Richard, Beth and Duff and Kate and Deeley are all childless. Albert Stokes in *A Night Out* is a grown man still living with his mother, and her infantilisation of him is part of the play's dramatic grammar, but their arrangement does not represent a functional family situation. Reference to 'the children' in *The Lover* comes in the context of a renegotiation of Sarah and Richard's game-playing, and is clearly an invented detail employed within the characters' constructed narratives to labour a point. Disson has stepchildren in *Tea Party*, but they function to aggravate his insecurities of status, rather than as any index of family unity (other than, perhaps, its tendered potential). We are told, of course, that Ruth and Teddy have three children that they have left at home in the United States, but references to them are peripheral, and Pinter's decision to give that couple children functions in part to offer a parallel of the family structure from which Teddy has removed himself (in itself, hardly a celebration of the benefits of family bonds) and in part to emphasise the extremity of Ruth's decision to stay behind in London.[1]

After *The Homecoming*, there is a notable shift in references to children, and their place within established marriage. In *Landscape*, Beth's recollection of sitting alone, stroking the dog and watching children running through the grass down in the valley activates a sense of longing, or of missed opportunity. In the revue sketch

Night, Woman interrupts the conversation with 'I thought I heard a child crying, waking up' and this neatly serves to indicate the status together of the two characters.[2] It also offers a sense of something comfortable and established being temporarily disturbed before settling again, which might sum up the delightful shuffle of mixed memories that the sketch comprises. These two fleeting references to children in Pinter's late 1960s writing are in stark contrast to any appearance of children before, as both indicate or promise harmony or completion. This trope is extended and developed in later writing, and reference to children and family units becomes a common feature of much of Pinter's subsequent output. His plays *Betrayal* (1978), *A Kind of Alaska* (1982), *Family Voices* (1980) and *Moonlight* (1993) all contain or address family structures, and the yearning to start families, or belong to them, is captured in *Monologue* (1972) and *Victoria Station* (1982). Furthermore, family structures are foregrounded and put under threat in the plays *One for the Road* (1984), *Mountain Language* (1988) and *Party Time* (1991) and are an integral part of the means of expression of at least the first two of those, while fragmented family occurs as an important motif in the third. Later, a narrative of a baby and a mother activated within *Ashes to Ashes* (1996) is central to that play's concerns, and family relations are woven into the chatter in *Celebration* (2000). This chapter offers a survey of Pinter's extended exploration of male interaction in the 1970s and beyond, and how the relationship with women beyond those male relationships develops to embrace the potential of unification within family, and the forces that put such unity in jeopardy.

I considered earlier how Pinter's work as director on a production of James Joyce's *Exiles* in 1970 acted as something of a creative spur in returning to his own writing, and that *Old Times* sprang from the momentum that experience gave him. Joyce's play may also have re-activated a fascination that can be traced back to his novel *The Dwarfs* – the potential for unpacking human relations through examining the shared attraction of two men to the same woman, and the ways in which this defined that male relationship. In his preparatory notes to the play, Joyce queried the degree to which the two men share a physical attraction to one another which they defer and project through Bertha; Robert by attempting to seduce her, Richard by permitting and effectively staging that seduction. According to Joyce, Richard craves 'to feel the thrill of adultery vicariously and to possess a bound woman Bertha through the organ of his friend'.[3] It is this attempt at masculine union via a feminine intermediary and the precarious application of psychosexual impulses in resolving insurmountable desire that may have captured Pinter's imagination.

When, after *Exiles*, Pinter was to return to his earlier interest in homosocial behaviour and male interaction through the intermediary of a woman, it was to chart the dysfunction of that behaviour, and the betrayals to self and to others, that it brought about. Children were to form an important part of that re-examination and Pinter may have drawn inspiration from the position of children in some of the screenplays he had written, most notably *The Go-Between* which he completed in 1969. Whereas in *The Pumpkin Eater* and *Accident*, children featured as part of the broader canvas of the family lives that were being corrupted or dismantled, in *The Go-Between* the central tension of the film is developed in the loving quasi-adoption of a young boy, Leo, by a pair of lovers, Marian and Ted, who employ him as an intermediary in their courtship, recklessly exposing him to the trauma that will result from their ill-fated union. Steven H. Gale notes how Pinter shifted the focus of L. P. Hartley's novel, in adapting it, away from 'how actions based on class distinctions impact upon individuals' to a focus on 'that impact over time on those not directly involved in the application of those distinctions',[4] which is to say the young Leo in his screenplay. This artistic interest in the potential impact of adult machinations on childhood might have been further pricked by the representation of Richard and Bertha's eight-year-old son Archie in *Exiles*, whose attachment to both Richard and Robert activates the potential for a notional joint parentage that I will consider in Pinter's work as a form of 'impossible family'. The shape of such a non-conventional family has been present through much of Pinter's work, in as much as characters have either been adopted or offered to be adopted by established family units in much of his writing, from Stanley in *The Birthday*

Party to Ruth in *The Homecoming*. Elsewhere, characters such as Davies in *The Caretaker* or Spooner in *No Man's Land* have sought to insinuate themselves into established units to take advantage of the mutually sustaining potential of such an environment. By shifting the apparatus of this will to merge onto children in *Monologue* and *Betrayal* in the 1970s, Pinter begins to effectively manoeuvre configurations of family as potent indicators of human potential.

Monologue (1972) recalls the situation of the end of Pinter's novel *The Dwarfs*, and the dissolution of the friendship of two men following their sexual liaisons with the same woman. What the lonely Man in *Monologue* describes is highly reminiscent of Bertha's cerebral attraction to Richard and sensual attraction to Robert in *Exiles*:

> Now you're going to say you loved her soul and I loved her body. You're going to trot that one out. I know you were much more beautiful than me, much more *aquiline*, I know *that*, that I'll give you, more *ethereal*, more thoughtful, slyer, while I had both feet firmly planted on the deck. But I'll tell you one thing you don't know. She loved my soul. It was my soul she loved. [...] I loved her body. Not that, between ourselves, it's one way or another of any importance. My spasms could have been your spasms.[5]

This sexual binary is paralleled in the man's recollection of how his friend should have been black, like the girl, in order to give an aesthetic purity to the image of him in his black motorcycle leathers and helmet. In bringing into operation these body/soul, black/white polarities in his memories, the unnamed character of Man reveals his need for the implied potential for amalgamation that they carry, that is his own full integration into the lives of both the girl and his friend. He embodies this integration in the fantasy of the mixed-race children that he would have loved, the fruits of the carnal/spiritual resolution he craves but so visibly lacks. This would now be the emphasis in Pinter's writing; more poignant warnings against emotional paralysis and isolation as opposed to the simple statement of stagnation and infestation that we have at the end of so many previous works.

The impossible family that the man in *Monologue* imagines, in which children might be loved and nurtured by three bonded parental figures, is activated again in *Betrayal* (1978) in a recurring motif in which Jerry recalls playfully throwing Emma and Robert's daughter Charlotte in the air and catching her. With this play, Pinter was finally to close his personal examination of the anatomy of the fraternal bond, in an arrangement that most closely resembled some parallel narrative to that in the Joyce play: the affair between Emma, wife of the publisher Robert, and his best friend, the literary agent Jerry. The play is constructed with a reverse chronology of events, and in the final scene (which is the first incident in the story), Robert's acceptance of his friend's behaviour – flattering his wife at a party in the marital bedroom – might be read as an act of condoning the liaison and potential affair in the same way Richard promoted Robert Hand's pursuit of Bertha in *Exiles*. But, taking from the germ of a failure to maintain a bond and profit on admiration and friendship, as demonstrated in *Monologue*, the mutual desire for a single woman in *Betrayal* is no longer the psychological location of a struggle for dominance, as it was in pre-*Exiles* Pinter (and the reverse chronology of the play works in some way towards ensuring this). Instead, a sexual bond between men through the intermediary of a shared woman is accentuated as characteristic of an emotional immaturity, and there is a compensatory emphasis on the will and need of the woman in the equation, and this places in strong relief the inefficiencies of the male manifestation and articulation of need.

The play opens with Jerry and Emma meeting in a pub. The year is given as spring 1977 in the script, that is to say more or less the 'present day' for when the play was written, published and first performed. As the scenes progress, each is given a year and season, and these are clearly expected to be conveyed to an audience in some manner. Most commonly, this occurs in a programme but productions of this play often signal this information before each scene, either by placard or media screen. This is the first time in which such contextual information for each scene is provided by Pinter in one of his plays and has the effect of making the play's unusual backward chronology clearly signalled. The effect has an important impact on how we read the three main characters, as it disallows the ordinary attachment to motivation, and to cause and effect, and there can be no tension about any ultimate dramatic outcome.

The opening scene offers some clear exposition. We learn that Jerry and Emma have had an affair in the past that ended two years previously, that they both have children, that Emma runs an art gallery and is now having an affair with a divorced writer called Roger Casey, for whom Jerry acts as literary agent. We discover that Jerry is a friend of Emma's husband, Robert, but he sees him much less frequently than he used to. By the end of the scene we learn that Emma and Robert are divorcing and the scene ends with Jerry being told that his friend is now aware of his past affair with his wife. This revelation provides the first dramatic momentum that pushes the play forward, and scene two follows the first chronologically, with Jerry meeting Robert to address this fresh knowledge of his behaviour. In this way the play's first two scenes follow each other in perfectly usual manner, but even before the backward step to 1975 in scene three, scene two begins to unfold in ways that an audience might not expect.

Robert has agreed to come to talk to Jerry at short notice. Jerry is clearly agitated, and speaks in fragmented sentences. He is deeply disturbed by his friend having found out about the affair he enjoyed with Emma, but Robert displays none of the indignant behaviour one might assume of someone who has recently discovered that his best friend had been sleeping with his wife, and we soon learn that this is because he had discovered the affair four years previously. Jerry's response to this is to express first annoyance at Emma, and then, remarkably, at Robert for not having told him that he had known. He even goes as far as to call him a 'bastard' for having kept silent on the matter. Given how casually he and Emma first discussed their affair, and the equally dispassionate manner in which Robert considers it here ('I don't give a shit about any of this', he states),[6] the agitation that Jerry manifests suggests that the biggest betrayal in this scenario is this deliberate failure of communication of knowledge between two friends, and Emma's deception to Jerry over when she told her husband of their illicit relationship. Robert's revelation of his knowledge is, of course, as much a surprise to us as audience as it is to Jerry and his calm perspective on matters, dismissive of any personal emotional concern for the affair (other than a terse 'don't call me a bastard, Jerry' (32)), causes us to have to recalibrate our expectations. If the drama is not going to progress with the men falling out over this transgression, then what is going to happen? The scene continues with a discussion about literary matters, and we learn that Robert is Roger Casey's publisher. In this way, Casey comes to represent another bond between the two men through their professional association of writer, agent and publisher. This triangular relationship adopts the same shape as the one between the two men and Emma, and when Robert confirms that Emma is now having an affair with Casey, we are introduced not only to a seemingly inevitable cycle of such marital infidelities, but also a consolidation of the structure of Robert and Jerry's relationship being formed and even defined by intermediaries. Casey, then, is being positioned as a nodal point that conjoins the structures of infidelity and the structures of homosocial engagement. In discussing him as a writer who is 'over the hill' and whose 'art does seem to be falling away' but who nonetheless 'sells very well indeed' (35–6), Robert and Jerry establish compromised behaviour in their professional dealings that places them at a distance from the artistic and aesthetic values that they might once have cherished, as exemplified in the reference to them both reading W. B. Yeats. In moving the conversation from the potentially emotionally strained to the casual, professional and amicable in this way, Pinter not only readily displaces any sense that the play is 'about' betrayal in the form of infidelity, but sets up expectations that we are to learn more of these two men's relationship to examine the disloyalty between them.

Scene three then takes the play's first step back in time, to the winter of 1975. The setting is Jerry and Emma's flat, which we learn they had bought together and furnished as a location for their afternoon trysts and quasi-domestic arrangement. We witness the point at which their affair comes to an end, as the two quibble over reasons why they have been unable to see each other often enough to sustain their relationship. The scene contains some exchanges that might serve as exposition if this were the opening scene: they both assert that they have children and Jerry reminds Emma that Robert is his oldest friend. Given that the audience already know these things, there is something surplus to requirements about such exposition, and perhaps it serves to emphasise for the audience the family structures that shape these characters' lives. Reference to the children, including their repeated names, has been a feature of the dialogue in all three scenes so far, and in this scene the presence of children is equated to stable domesticity, in Jerry's phrase 'There are no children here, so it's not the same kind of home' (44).

Scene four takes a further step back, to autumn 1974. It is a remarkably event-less scene and, unlike previous scenes, no new information is imparted to audience or between the characters. Set in the period between Robert's discovery of and the end of the affair, the scene seems to have been written deliberately to take pause and consider the states of tension between the three characters. Jerry has dropped in at Robert and Emma's house, and the scene opens with a protracted example of vacuous small talk between the two men, as they wait for Emma to join them. Following the information that Emma is busy putting their son Ned to bed, Robert makes a comment about boy babies crying more than girl babies and Jerry concurs, adding that boys are more anxious. Shrugging off any lack of evidence for their trite observations, the two allow the subject to wane with a non-committal 'something to do with the difference between the sexes' before Emma enters (52). The vacuity of this peculiar few minutes of conversation serves a number of purposes; it again foregrounds a concern for children, it suggests that these two friends are no longer close in any meaningful way, it presents Robert as being in command in a way that diminishes Jerry's contribution to the relationship, and it draws a distinction between the sexes based on subjective, self-indulgent lines. The suggestion that two men have drifted apart is later corroborated by the news that Casey has effectively replaced Jerry as Robert's regular squash partner, and the subjective distinction between the sexes (and Robert's commanding personality) is further highlighted in a cruel put-down he gives his wife when she suggests she might come to watch them both play squash.

> Well, to be brutally honest, we wouldn't actually want a woman around, would we, Jerry? I mean a game of squash isn't simply a game of squash, it's rather more than that. You see, first there's the game. And then there's the shower. And then there's the pint. And then there's lunch. After all, you've been at it. You've had your battle. What you want is your pint and your lunch. You really don't want a woman buying you lunch. You don't actually want a woman within a mile of the place, any of the places, really. You don't want her in the squash court, you don't want her in the shower, or the pub, or the restaurant. You see, at lunch you want to talk about squash, or cricket, or books, or even women, with your friend, and be able to warm to your theme without fear of improper interruption. That's what it's all about. (57)

Scene four seems to have been constructed around this outburst, in which Robert's current contempt for Emma is laid bare in an overt expression of misogyny. In the sequence of the play, we might read this as a self-justified indulgence in pique on the part of a cuckolded husband who has been prepared to compromise his marriage for undetermined and unarticulated reasons. Those reasons perhaps are to be found buried somewhere in this declaration of a preference for the company of men. Pinter's fascination with this real or supposed social phenomenon between men may have been augmented by his close work as director on Simon Gray's *Butley* in the summer of 1971 (and in 1974 on the filmed version). Gray's play, which charts the disintegration of the eponymous academic, provided a further focus on the homosocial aspects of Joyce's play that had attracted Pinter, who said of *Butley*:

> It seemed to me that Butley was a man living in a kind of no man's land – between women and between men. I understood

from the play that his sexual experience was with women but that he probably liked men better. In other words, I didn't see him as a homosexual [...] I think quite a number of men are in this position and it makes life very difficult for them.[7]

Certainly, Robert's anti-woman speech presents him as isolated, not just from his wife in the unloving manner in which he addresses and excludes her, but in effect from Jerry too, as we infer from the rest of the scene that not only has Jerry long failed to honour any supposedly regular squash date with Robert, but that his work trip abroad distances himself from that kind of arrangement (just as we have learned work is to be used as an excuse for the breakdown of his affair with Emma). Robert's over-emphasis on the value of his time spent with Jerry is effectively undermined by Jerry's deficient attitude to finding that time. The speech also isolates Robert from audience empathy. It hardly makes him likeable and, on the back of his scene two revelation that he is inclined to give Emma the occasional 'good bashing' (33), it further distances him from any sympathy we might have for him as wronged husband. The whole scene, in this way, completes the shift away from a focus on Emma and Jerry that the play began with, and presents us with Robert's isolated dilemma and bruised emotional paralysis. At the end of the scene all he is left with is a semblance of control, as he kisses and holds his wife, who cries on his shoulder. Her tears are articulate of the tension that the scene has generated, and of the subtextual anger that has been disguised in his contemptuous behaviour, a subtext shared between them and the audience, with Jerry leaving the stage oblivious to it. The following scene, in which we step back to the point in time when Robert discovers his wife's infidelity, exposes the root of that subtextual knot of emotion.

Planted in the middle of the play, scene five is set in the summer of 1973 in a Venice hotel room, where Robert and Emma are on holiday. As with the previous scene, it has a prelude of small talk, in which the two discuss a book that Emma is reading, which Jerry has recommended, and which Robert had once rejected as publisher on the grounds that the subject matter of the book merited no further attention. When asked what he thinks the subject matter might be, he states it to be 'betrayal', which Emma immediately dismisses. This brief conversation binds all three characters again around the concept of betrayal, but declares an almost self-conscious warning to the audience that there is more to the play than infidelity through this sly metatheatricality of uttering the play title. Then, rather than declare that he has discovered her affair, Robert takes a sideways route to that declaration, and in doing so creates a tension that tortures his wife and builds apprehension in the audience. By informing Emma that he was offered her mail at the American Express office the previous day, and embarking on a faintly xenophobic dismissal of the attitude of the employees who assumed his connection with her via a shared surname, he sets in motion a painful sequence that obliges her to confess, first that the letter was from Jerry and secondly that they are lovers. In this way, Robert manifests the same cool determination to have control of a situation and of people that we have seen previously, and to do so as a means of circumnavigating any instinctive emotional responses. Despite his circuitous avoidance of an actual accusation, or any outrage, he nonetheless betrays his own feelings with an italicised '*sorry?*' in response to the meagre, awkward apology which Emma offers as much to cover a tense silence as by way of regret (70). Pinter follows this with a silence, in which an audience might ingest Robert's suppressed indignation. This surfaces again a few moments later when he learns that the affair is established and has been going on for five years, and seeks to clarify his paternity of their baby son.

As an audience, we cannot help but feel sympathy for Robert as he struggles to maintain a dignified front in the face of learning of a five-year affair between his wife and his best friend. Pinter saves some of the detail of his and Jerry's friendship deliberately until this scene, when we hear that they had been friends since sharing a passion for poetry at Oxford and Cambridge, respectively, and would compose long letters to one another. We also learn that Jerry had been the best man at their wedding and these details add to the density of the betrayal exposed. In this way, the impact of the scene establishes the vital worth of the play's backward chronology; we have come to dislike Robert and are likely during scenes two and four to have formed a negative judgement of him. Our concern for him here disrupts that, and suggests a moral ambiguity at play in the drama. Had the scenes been written in a chronological sequence, the manner in which we would receive his dismissive squash speech would be in the light of this emotional scene, and be taken as a consequence of it, an emotional negotiation of it.

As if to profit from this moral question mark, Pinter temporarily stalls the reverse sequence and has scenes six and seven follow scene five chronologically, all three in the summer of 1973, with Jerry and Emma first meeting in their flat, after the Venice trip, and then Robert and Jerry meeting for lunch in an Italian restaurant. In doing so, Pinter draws the focus in on the aftermath of the Venice revelations in what effectively becomes the central three scenes in a triptych, preceded by the future and followed by the past. This sequence allows us to consider both Emma and Robert's commitments to their individual relationships with Jerry, and to see how the emotional compromises they each assimilate are manifest in their behaviour toward him. Emma has brought a tablecloth from Venice, and it underscores her proud adoption of the role of home-maker in the flat, in a scene in which she brings lunch, talks of hoovering and delights in being able to 'cook and slave' for Jerry (81). Evidently, the confrontation with her husband has not brought the affair to an end (and, importantly, we already knew that) but seems almost to have validated it. Nonetheless, her nervous questioning of Jerry over the reason why he and Robert have a lunch date indicates she fears that her husband might plan to confront him. In the restaurant, Robert's terse conversation as the scene begins might indicate he has this in mind, and his reference to a trip he took to Torcello without Emma seems almost to act as an overture to a confrontation, as we remember how in Venice both husband and wife had planned to visit that island. The writing of this scene is remarkably taut, and an actor playing Robert has to chart the flow of the character's emotions and the spontaneous decisions he seems to be making, all of which bubble beneath a seemingly banal everyday conversation. Moving on from recounting how he read Yeats on Torcello, Robert shifts from the poetry he loves to the modern prose he openly dislikes, and tells Jerry that Emma loved the novel he had lent her to read. By declaring his distaste for modern literature he distances himself from his wife and friend, whom he identifies as a unit. As before in the play, the two men's shared professional interests blend within conversation with the woman whose love they also share. The scene closes with him inviting Jerry to come around to see them, and here we recognise his effective condoning of their infidelities as a means of maintaining and sustaining their friendship.

The final two scenes take us back to the heady early days of Emma and Jerry's adultery, first to 1971 and their secret flat, and then to 1968 and Jerry's seduction of her. In the first, a cosy domestic scene with Emma in an apron cooking a stew and Jerry pouring wine, their homely arrangement is set in relief against Jerry's marriage, as we have the longest discussion of his wife in the play, after Emma states she had bumped into her at lunch. Jerry's expressed surprise that his wife Judith was having lunch with someone else leads to his confession of irritation at her having a male admirer. This can only come across as petty hypocrisy, but then leads to a bizarrely logical exchange between Jerry and Emma about whether they had ever been unfaithful to each other. This culminates in her confession that she is pregnant, by her husband. Coming after their mutual declarations of adoration, and capped with Jerry's 'I'm very happy for you' (111),[8] Jerry's acceptance of his lover's pregnancy becomes an articulation of the kind of impossible family, melding the children and even parentage of two households, that has previously been activated by the repeated motif of his recollection of throwing Charlotte in the air and catching her.

In Pinter's 1983 screenplay of the play, the presence of the children is more readily foregrounded, and is of course much more easily facilitated in that medium. So, for example, before scene four we see Emma giving Ned a bath and, after their mundane conversation downstairs, Jerry and Robert enter his bedroom to watch her putting him to sleep, the impossible family together around the cot. Before his post-Venice lunch meeting with Jerry, Robert picks Ned up from his cot, and this simple addition emphasises the family bonds that are in jeopardy. Between the penultimate and final scenes of the dramatic script, Pinter inserted three short extra scenes into the screenplay to capture the unstable but thrilling tensions at the onset of Emma and Jerry's affair. In one, Charlotte walks in on her mother putting the phone down on Jerry, after having arranged a clandestine meeting with him. She asks who her mother was talking to, and gets the reply that it was 'daddy' and that he sends his love. With this small detail, Pinter captures not only the ready duplicity of infidelity, but, by displacing Robert with Jerry as declared father, he also activates that positioning of the impossible family that was earlier brought about by the issue of Ned's paternity.

Other Places
Victoria Station, Family Voices, A Kind of Alaska, Moonlight

After *Betrayal*, two plays furthered the agenda of this concern for the enriching potential of family and the behaviours that jeopardise or unsettle the sought or promised harmony. *A Kind of Alaska* (1982) stages a woman/child in the shape of Deborah, brought out of a coma that has stifled her since she was a pubescent girl. The radio play *Family Voices* (1981) captures parallel families in the narratives woven by a son as he addresses his distanced mother in what seems like the verbal reciting of correspondence. Added to these, the short play *Victoria Station* (1982) imagines the union of marriage as a form of enriching escape. Together, these three plays were performed in triple bill for the first time in October 1982 at the National Theatre under the collective title 'Other Places'.[9]

In *Victoria Station* the driver of a taxi exasperates the controller who is looking to get a cab to meet a fare at Victoria Station, before eventually revealing that he has fallen in love with a female passenger who is asleep on his back seat. Coming on the back of pointing out he has a wife and daughter, this positions a movement of migration between family positions that Pinter first humorously suggests in the *double-entendre* 'cruising'.[10] Both Driver and Controller seem to be isolated, separated from the real world, as though occupying some form of limbo: Controller can get no signal from any other driver, and Driver claims no knowledge of Victoria Station, and that he has parked outside the inexistent Crystal Palace. Loneliness, stagnation and aimless mobility are triggered in the brief play, with falling in love given as an escape from torpor and duty. It is a short vehicle for comedy, and features the common Pinter motif of an errant dreamer being called back to responsibility.

Family Voices also depends on the interplay between an individual and those who would assimilate him. The play pitches independence from family with the bonds that such independence inevitably puts under tension. As with *Landscape* before it, the play is set between two voices (those of a mother and son) neither of who seem to hear the other. A third voice, that of the man's father, comes in at the end, declaring himself to be speaking from the grave. Voice 1 and Voice 2 quite clearly start as epistolary voices, as the son signs off 'I shall end this letter to you, my dear mother, with my love', only for the mother to respond with 'Why do you never write?'.[11] This establishes straight away the failure to connect that sits awkwardly at the centre of the dialogue between their two voices. The son speaks with affection of his mother and father, and his letters home are filled with the details of his new life in an 'enormous city' where he expects soon to make friends and find a girlfriend, and where he speaks reassuringly of being happy in his new lodgings. As such, his words capture all the wonder of a good son who has recently left home and is exploring his independence, all the while considerate of his mother's need for news. The manner in which he first declares he is drunk but later states he was joking, and later promises to bring any new girlfriend home to meet her, suggests someone who still hopes to avoid his mother's disapproval. Given this, Pinter sews in a fault line in the way that, as the son's voice remains bold, loving and uninhibited in the descriptions of his experiences, the mother becomes more and more reproving, shifting from emotional blackmail ('Sometimes I wonder if you remember that you have a mother' (136)) to despair, to bitter dismissal ('I wait for your letter begging me to come to you. I'll spit on it' (142)). We hear that the son was absent when his father died, and that his sister has tried to help his mother find him, but that eventually he has been reported to the police as missing. He continues oblivious to all this, and finishes by stating he is coming home.

Pinter suggests that the impediment that obstructs the correspondence between this mother and son is to be found in the son's new family structure, the group of people named Withers in whose house he resides. One of them, Riley, admits to having opened the front door to a mother and daughter who were looking for their lost son and brother, only to have sent them packing as impostors. In his lengthy accounts, the son explains that he is uncertain about most of the people in the house, apart from the landlady, Mrs Withers, with whom he spends evenings at the pub, and her granddaughter, Jane, who is presented as a Lolita-esque schoolgirl. The name of the pub – The Fishmongers Arms – is mentioned twice and in theatrical contexts the inference in that name is indubitably one that suggests temptation and corruption, and we learn that Lady Withers, who wears a red dress, receives numerous guests at night.[12] Though we are invited, in these ways, to conclude that this young man has fallen in with a bad crowd who are actively blocking communication between him and his family, the oneiric, symbolic nature of this household (supported by the medium of expression that Pinter chooses) interrupts any straightforwardly realistic reading of this story of fragmented family. The mother and son are effectively in dialogue, their words structured in passages one after the other, and some breach of the obstruction between them is permitted this way. This suggestion is augmented in the manner in which the father seems able to breach the finality of death to also speak to his son. Love and death are connected towards the end of the play (and the character Riley has prepared this in speaking of 'the death that is love') (144) and the play seems to wish to meditate on the occlusions that corrupt the expression of love between family members, presenting the cautionary that we should profit from our bonds while we can, as the father's voice makes clear in the closing words of the play: 'I have so much to say to you. But I am quite dead. What I have to say to you will never be said' (148).

If death is one of the 'other places' that Pinter was now folding into his aesthetic palette as a means to consider and qualify our interpersonal behaviours, then he found the perfect metaphor to expand this in the 'other place' detailed in the case studies presented in Oliver Sacks's 1973 book *Awakenings* of a debilitating 'living death' condition named encephalitis lethargica. Pinter acknowledged Dr Sacks's book as the source for his next stage play, *A Kind of Alaska*,[13] a poignant one-act play whose central character suffers the condition. Reading Sacks's case studies, and the accounts of the experiences of patients who were brought out of their long-standing comas with the assistance of a drug called L-DOPA, it is easy to understand the attraction to Pinter of how these people, brought back to full consciousness, might embody their own past and present at the same time. The value to a dramatist interested in the manner in which past and present interact is self-evident, but rather than construct a character from this real experience to act as a straightforward metaphor, Pinter writes the forty-something Deborah into a family that has disintegrated around her, and as such his artistic focus is acutely trained upon the structures of care and sustenance that a family both enacts and relies upon. This is emphasised all the more by the nature of an extreme medical condition that simultaneously embodies both life and death.

The play starts with Deborah, in a bed against high-banked pillows, waking from her sleeping sickness as Hornby, a dark-suited man in his early sixties, observes her. Hornby's status is at first unclear, though his formal attire and his calm and measured explanations to Deborah, clarifying that she has been asleep for a long time, that he has awoken her with an injection, and that she is 'still young, but older' (155), would indicate to an audience that he is a doctor or carer. In response to her memories of her father and her question 'why hasn't mummy woken me up?', his 'I have woken you up' immediately places him as having replaced or displaced the natural caring mechanism of family (157). Deborah's confused mixture of vulnerable child and assertive woman confirms but confuses this inference, as we wonder how she might now respond to the revelation that she is both old and young, that she has been 'asleep' for years, and how she will respond to the man who brings her back to the world. Pinter promotes the displacement of her family further with the appearance of her sister, Pauline, and the details of the state of the rest of the family. At first, Pauline tells a tale of the how these are away on a cruise ship in the Far East, but Hornby soon, rather firmly, gives Deborah the truth that her father is blind and looked after by her other sister Estelle, and that her mother is dead. Added to this, we learn that he married Pauline eight years after becoming Deborah's doctor, effectively folding him into this fragmented group of relations. Pinter clearly wanted to foreground the tensions of care-keeping between people, and the paralysis that can establish itself in living relationships; if the play were just concerned with Deborah's dilemma, he did not need to write in such detail about the plight of her family, including features such as her father's infirmity and blindness. Working together, these details and Deborah's condition between life and death, between the present and the past, establish the play as being concerned with the barriers to an enriched existence through and with one another. When Pauline refers to herself as a widow, an assertion that her husband confirms, we are invited quite overtly to reflect upon how a concern for Deborah has brought stagnation into all family relationships. Hornby is effectively dead to Pauline, and when he later points out to Deborah that 'It is we who have suffered' (184), we understand that the dysfunctional arrangement has taken its toll.

Hornby's is an extremely rare name, more or less obsolete as a choice for boys by the time the play was written.[14] Perhaps this decision on Pinter's part might simply have been intended to date the play, and therefore respect the historical nature of the central illness, which had all but disappeared by the time of writing. But the name is resonant in a number of ways, all of which might impact on our reading of the character. As an audience we cannot help but query Hornby's seeming obsession with Deborah's care, to the detriment of his marriage, and the 'horn' syllable in his name simultaneously signals libido, devilishness and even cuckoldry. Certainly, Deborah's confused sexuality leads her to make accusations of inappropriate touching, but there is no evidence that Hornby's attachment to Deborah is anything beyond that of a carer. He does demonstrate a certain jealous possessiveness of her that manifests itself in the ways he permits or instructs his wife to talk to her own sister. The cuckoldry implication certainly interacts with an infidelity of sorts that he has committed by neglecting his wife in favour of Deborah. Another inference, though, is embedded in that name, in the designation of a popular manufacturer of model trains, the playthings of children that also obsess many an adult collector. Deborah has become something of a hobby for Hornby, an obsession that sets him at one remove from 'real life', and from his familial and social responsibilities. If Deborah acts as a metaphor, rather than as a literal representative of a curious illness, then she might operate to represent all that arrests us, all that causes us to fail to engage with one another.

Pinter returned to these themes of stagnated emotional states within family in 1993, with *Moonlight*. In this play, a belligerent old man, Andy, self-pityingly mopes in his sick-bed, tolerated and humoured by his wife Bel. He bemoans his '[t]wo sons. Absent. Indifferent. Their father dying'.[15] In a separate section of stage space, his sons Fred and Jake play a series of garrulous verbal games, avoiding all contact with their parents. In a third designated playing area, his sixteen-year-old daughter Bridget appears at the beginning and end of the play, and participates in two other scenes. The very staging of the play describes a fragmented family, set apart from one another in their separate playing spaces, and as much as this establishes their isolation from one another it also provides opportunities for poignant meetings, when the closeted separations are breached. The migration between the spaces of two other characters, Maria and Ralph, also suggests the potential for reunification at the hands of such mediators.

The play opens with a considerate pronouncement of care and love from Bridget toward her parents. She is discovered 'in faint light' and talks of not being able to sleep and wanting to go downstairs to walk about. She expresses concern not to wake her mother and father:

They're so tired. They have given so much of their life for me and my brothers. All their life, in fact. All their energies and all their love. They need to sleep in peace and wake up rested. I must see that this happens. It is my task. (319)

This is the most overt and unambiguous declaration of selfless care for others in Pinter's oeuvre, and sets the play in motion with the promise of a functional, loving family. This gentle, softly lit first scene is rudely interrupted in both tone and content by Andy's barked first words in the next, demanding to know if his wife has managed to get in touch with their sons. In the third scene, we meet those two conversing in a form of witty, often irreverent, almost stream-of-conscious to and fro. The subject of their conversation sways around their father and his failure to hold on to money, and consequently to be able to pass any to them. At the end of their scene, Maria joins them, declaring herself to be their mother's best friend, and gives a speech in praise of their parents. The play operates at quite a pace, swapping from one set of testimonies to the next, but what is clear from these early scenes is that everyone is offering differing perspectives upon the same family unit.

Maria and Ralph offer some sense of positive human contact and success to the play. In some ways, they represent the possibility of unification through evoking the Pinter trope of the 'impossible family' that has been postulated through this chapter. We learn that not only was Maria Andy's mistress, but that she also had an affair with Bel, and this triangular arrangement takes the shape of the *Betrayal/Monologue* relationships, but with a man here shared by two women. In talking of when she first met her husband Ralph, who we also learn was Andy's best friend, Maria points out that Bel also admired him, and we might infer another shared relationship. When Andy points out that Ralph had once taken him aside and told him that 'men had something women simply didn't have' (376), echoing a statement Bel recalls Maria making, we might further infer the homosexual attraction was not active just between the women, making the possibility of six pairing interactions between the four people. The parallel and binding structure between the couples is further drawn by Ralph and Maria also having three children, and when we hear Ralph expressing a distinction between himself and Andy in terms of his physical and Andy's intellectual self (recalling the same distinction drawn in *Monologue*), we are offered further evidence of these two couples connecting in mutually complementary manners. As they weave in and out of the play, turning up in both Fred and Jake's and Andy and Bel's rooms, they take on a role of arbiters, stitching to the two sides of the stage together.

Within all this, Bridget's early appearance is curious. As audience, we usually expect to establish a bond with the first character who appears before us in a play, to be given some information about them and how they fit in the drama that is to follow. By introducing us only briefly to the young Bridget, speaking lovingly of her parents, and then moving into what becomes the drama proper, we might retrospectively acknowledge her opening statement as some form of prelude to the main act, but those tender words and the promise of unity they bring sit uncomfortably against what follows, and linger in us as some promise of salve to the dysfunction that we are presented with. When we meet her next, she speaks of having completed a long journey through harsh terrain into a welcoming, protective jungle. She talks of being lost, of being '[h]idden but free' and adds sensory details as though to conjure a real experience for us: 'A velvet odour, very deep, an echo like a bell' (337). If we have been confused at the pace of the play, and by the dense wordplay of some of the characters' banter, this can only perplex us further, and if the tone of her opening words set her apart from the obstructive, confrontational language of the rest of her family, this scene isolates her further from them, suggesting she inhabits some fantasy world beyond the stage realism of their rooms and beds. The symbolism of her words might also promote an interpretation of her as, in fact, dead: lost but safe, hidden but not imprisoned. Her subsequent appearances confirm this. First, she appears alongside her brothers in what comes across as a flashback scene in which they are ten years younger, but she is younger by only a couple of years. Then, later, when Andy leaves his bed in the middle of the night to enjoy an illicit swig of booze, he notices Bridget in her faint light. His exclamation 'Ah darling. Ah my darling' leaves little doubt that she is a lost daughter (360). His reaction sets all his other behaviour in relief: this is a fragmented, anger-fuelled and resentful family with the death of a young daughter at its centre.

Pinter, though, makes no direct reference to Bridget's death anywhere in the text; nobody speaks of it and nobody acknowledges it. What is more, Andy seems to operate in denial of it, calling upon her to visit him on his deathbed, and bring the three grandchildren she might have mothered had she survived. Whether her death is a motivating factor in the characters' behaviour or even a cause of the family break-up is ambiguous. It is a tone, a texture, in the writing. Like the Beethoven sonata with which it shares its title, *Moonlight* meditates on loss, and the theme and references to death are developed further once Bridget's other-worldly status is more or less established. In effect, Bridget's appearances offer something of a sonata structure,[16] presenting an exposition of a theme at the play's onset, a development of that theme with her reappearances, and a final recapitulation in the play's last scene, in which she recounts being invited to a party in a house at the end of a lane. The house, with no lights on, bathed in a sheer moonlight that she must wait to wane before she might enter, acts as another metaphor for death as solitary but homely, as an isolating comfort.

Andy asks again after Bridget in his final scene, in which he asks 'What is happening?', indicating that he is close to death (383). In the following, penultimate scene, before Bridget's final appearance, Fred and Jake talk about a memorial service for a man they refer to as d'Orangerie – a pseudonym for their father. Fred, who states he is 'confined to my bed with a mortal disease' (384), seems to be in perpetual contempt of his father and the irreverent tone of the conversation closes the play with a sense of failure. The sons are either mocking their father's funeral, or an imagined future ceremony, and giving them the last word in this way is a way of avoiding the overt tragedy of death, while emphasising the tragedy of a misconnection between family members, who choose to remain separate from stubbornness, pride or some insurmountable difference. When Bridget then closes the play, the separation of death puts such willed separation into perspective, leaving an audience to balance the tragedy of the two.

Earlier in the play, speaking of his father, Jake declares that 'one day I shall love him. I shall love him and be prepared to pay the full price of that love' (367). He and his brother then go on to debate that price, and include death in the currency. Given the brothers' refusal or inability to commit to mature conversation, it is impossible ever to tell how sincere such statements might be, but real emotion seems to be kept tightly bottled in by them both. When Bel rings them to put directly to them that their father is seriously ill, Fred replies by greeting her as the owner of a Chinese laundry. She seeks to dismiss this puerile behaviour, but when he persists she asks if they do dry cleaning. This punctures the posture and, caught off guard, Jake puts the phone down without replying. His angry retort, once the conversation is ended, exposes a well of emotion that would prefer to be capped by play and pretence: 'Of course we do dry cleaning! Of course we do dry cleaning! What kind of fucking laundry are you if you don't do dry cleaning?' (382). Fred and Jake's deferred emotions and Andy's denial and anger serve to keep real human contact at bay, and it is by foregrounding these behaviours that Pinter considers the failure to address authentic need in relation to death through human contact. Bridget's death operates, then, on similar terms to the 'other place' that Deborah suffers in *A Kind of Alaska*, as a family collapses around it, and her utterances operate with the poignancy of the voice of the dead father in *Family Voices* who has love to express that can no longer be communicated.

Family Under Threat
One for the Road, Mountain Language, Party Time, Celebration

Between *A Kind of Alaska* and *Moonlight*, Pinter wrote three short plays that came to represent his political period. *One for the Road* (1984), *Mountain Language* (1988) and *Party Time* (1991) are angry works that address the vulnerability of the weak in the face of unremitting state power, but can also be considered to present an extension of their author's concern for the structures of family. The political potency of these plays will be considered briefly in the following chapter, and in more depth in the contributions by Ann C. Hall and Basil Chiasson later in this volume. It is commonplace in Pinter criticism to consider Pinter's decision to write ideologically inflected work in the 1980s as something of a radical shift, a significant change of direction. However, while there is much to be said for considering the 'Other Places' trilogy as something of a transition period, the focus on family and the contemplation of the separation of death that they mobilise very much acts as preparation for the substance of the political plays that followed. With *One for the Road*, *Mountain Language* and *Party Time*, Pinter presents the vulnerability of family as being under pressure from the machinations of state control, and oppression is expressed through the deliberate fragmentation of family structures. If there was a noticeable movement in Pinter's dramas after *The Homecoming* to employ children or the potential for having children as a means of considering the value of family bonds in achieving elusive human contentedness, with and after *A Kind of Alaska* Pinter moves to consider the internal and external pressures that put such family units under threat.

In *One for the Road*, three members of a family unit are one by one interrogated by Nicolas, a representative of state power. Victor, his wife Gila and even their seven-year-old son Nicky are questioned by Nicolas in general terms about their allegiance to the state, though it is clear that it is Victor who is the key subject of the correction that Nicolas seeks to instil. As such, both Gila and Nicky become tools to that end, and both are dismissed effectively: Gila is treated as a plaything that might 'entertain' soldiers with multiple rape, and the son's fate is ambiguous, though a reference to him in the past tense as the play closes suggests he might have been killed.

Structures of family are deliberately embedded in the play in ways that might be superfluous if Pinter's ambition with it was purely political. For example, he makes the curious decision to reveal that Gila's father was an important man in the history of the state authority that Nicolas defends. In this way, he weds the structures of state power with a rigid form of patriarchy that demands obedience to its defined codes of behaviour, and sets Gila and her family as at odds with that obedience. In response to her reference to meeting her husband in her father's room, she elicits an angry reply, motivated by a disgust that this woman's personal history might intersect with the national narrative he defends:

> Are you prepared to defame, to debase, the memory of your father? Your father fought for his country. I knew him. I revered him. Everyone did. He believed in God. He didn't *think*, like you shitbags. He lived. He was iron and gold. He would die, he would die, he would die, for his country, for his God. And he did die, he died, he died, for his God. You turd. To spawn such a daughter. What a fate, oh, poor, perturbed spirit, to be haunted for ever by such scum and spittle. How do you dare speak of your father to me? I loved him, as if he were my own father.[17]

The reference to the ghost of Hamlet's father here, in 'poor, perturbed spirit', doubles the sense of treachery that is being implied. The distinction that is drawn between thinking and living, with a heavy prioritisation on the latter, recalls the distinction drawn in *The Dwarfs* and *The Homecoming* on operating 'on' or 'in' things, and the implied rejection of intellectualism is terrifying. In combining God and country with the symbol of the betrayed father, Nicolas is uniting and wielding standard nationalist discourses of loyalty to nationhood. In this way, Pinter clearly sets in operation two opposing systems of family: one in which we owe unquestioning allegiance to a state, personified as a father figure (which Nicolas renders as authentic family in his claim to have loved Gila's father as his own) and one in which a private, nuclear family are defined by their shared experience and affection. Nicolas's job, then, is to replace one system with another, to rend asunder the nuclear family and make them, as exposed individuals, more malleable members of the national family. When, in the final scene, he suggests that Victor might benefit from the services available at a brothel that forms part of the institutional building in which they are meeting, he not only triggers in us a sense of indignation that recalls the sexual abuse that Gila has endured, he also indicates that the collapse of the private family is actually a function of loyalty to the state. He indicates, in speaking of the women at work there, that '[t]heir daddies are in our business. Which is, I remind you, to keep the world clean for God' (246). The moral oxymoron of women enrolled or enslaved in sex work for global purification is one indicator of the corruption that the state maintains, but the suggestion that the girls work separated from fathers who are soldiers of the state implies an utter devastation of family, subservient to ideological objectives.

Mountain Language continues this assault on the private family, and again has a husband and wife couple separated by brutal authority, matched by a mother and son pairing. The play opens on a queue of women, waiting in the cold outside a detention facility to see their husbands, fathers and sons held there, and so immediately presents multiple fragmented families before concentrating on the fates of the key two synecdotal pairs in the subsequent three scenes. The brutality with which these women are treated, represented by the bloodied hand of one old woman who has been bitten by a Dobermann Pinscher, sets the tone of threat and powerless vulnerability that pervades the play. We hear that the incarcerated men are 'enemies of the State',[18] and the state manifests itself here only in the form of the soldiers and guards that are employed at the facility. If *One for the Road* presented the bureaucratic self-justification of a dictatorial state system, here we see the workaday cruelty of the means by which citizens deemed incompatible with the dominant state ideology are treated. We learn that there are at least two categories of state enemy at this facility, political prisoners such as Sara Johnson's husband, and those whose infraction seems to be that they speak the language of the mountains. Both categories are represented by male/female pairs rigidly separated by the codes of law that govern the men's internment.

Scenes two and four take place in a visitors' room, and involve an elderly woman visiting her imprisoned son. In the first of these, the elderly woman is abused verbally and jabbed with a stick for only being able to converse with her son using the forbidden mountain language, though all she is doing is offering bread and apples. The guard, who argues that he is only doing his job in treating her this way, demonstrates how dehumanising his programming has been by using family as argument: 'I've got a wife and three kids. And you're all a pile of shit', he shouts at the prisoner (260). It is a noteworthy statement, given all the alternatives that might have been available to the playwright to put into the mouth of this guard: the character justifies his behaviour toward these two related people by evoking his own flesh and blood, effectively shielding himself behind the sanctity of family union. Perhaps he means to imply that he has no choice but to follow orders, that he too is a victim of the structures that dominate all their lives, or perhaps he means to elevate himself above these two, as someone participating in society in an appropriately formulated way. The latter seems the most likely, given his indignant response when the prisoner points out that he, too, has a wife and three kids. Just as Gila in *One for the Road* was not permitted the accurate memory of meeting her husband in her father's room, because of how this reality involved the co-presence of two opposing ideological narratives, the soldier here is appalled that the prisoner claims equal human status through family structure. In the second scene between these characters, we see the consequence of this, as the trembling prisoner has blood on his face and the old woman has been rendered mute as a result of the distress of her treatment. When the guard points out that the rules have been relaxed and that she is now permitted to speak her native mountain language, the prisoner attempts to communicate this to her, but her trauma is so deep that she remains silent, and the prisoner collapses to the floor in desperation. Pinter's final image, then, is of the successful subjugation and fragmentation of family by state brutality.

In between these two scenes, we see Sara Johnson a second time, confronted by the image of her husband propped up by guards and with a bag over his head. She is patronised by the sergeant and advised to complain to a man called Joseph Dokes, which is to say nobody.[19] Set in the liminal space of a corridor, the scene is structured to hold the second of two fantasy sequences that Pinter inserts into the play. As the lights dim to half and the brutal image of the hooded man set across the stage from his terrified wife freezes still, we hear the two of them speak to each other in a voice-over. Their voices recall being out on a boat in spring, and the repeated, shared memory of her waking to see him watching her: 'You look up at me above you and smile', 'When my eyes open I see you above me and smile' (263). The previous fantasy sequence occurs in the first meeting between the prisoner and his mother. She repeats 'They are all waiting for you' and points out that '[t]he baby is waiting for you' (261). In both sequences, Pinter captures in few words the depths of intimacy and love that bind families, the very qualities of vital experience that are violently collapsed by the institutional correction that is erected around them. Theatrically, the sequences serve to illicit our sympathy in a quite blatant manner: they foreground the persecuted characters' humanity against a background of dehumanising suffering. The impossibility of these encounters foregrounds this further; they are aspirational in form as we know that they cannot happen but we might will them to be able to happen. They activate in us a desire for justice on the grounds of humanity and the recognition of family.

In *Party Time*, Pinter continued to employ family structures as symptomatic of authentic human interaction, though the play concentrates primarily on the autopoietic, constructed morals of a powerful elite in a way that has only been hinted at in his previous work. In the calm, mostly unresponsive figure of Gavin, the host of the party which is the play's setting, we are presented with someone seemingly further up the chain of command than any authority figure we have previously met. Throughout the play, the character of Dusty repeatedly asks questions about the whereabouts of her brother Jimmy, much to the annoyance of her husband Terry who firmly insists that her brother's disappearance is 'not on anyone's agenda',[20] employing a business-like language to dismiss her concerns. Pinter punctuates the polite (though loaded) chatter of these elite party-goers with a niggling concern that something untoward has happened to this woman's brother, and that people in the party are implicated in that something, emphasised further by their exemption from the curfew that is in force on the streets outside. When the host Gavin first hears Dusty's concern, he brushes it aside with 'Nothing's happened to Jimmy. And if you're not a good girl I'll spank you' (284). This dismissive infantilisation also articulates a ready ability to take possession of her bodily, and we later gain more clues as to the brutal potential that lies beneath the polite if sneering veneer that characterises the conversations at the party.

When asked about her husband, the character of Charlotte pauses before answering with a straightforward reply: 'he died' (300). Pinter follows this with another silence, to allow us as audience to consider what is not being articulated. When the subject is brought up again later, and the merits of a short or long illness are excruciatingly discussed, Charlotte tolerates the conversation before declaring 'Oh by the way, he wasn't ill' (306). Unlike Dusty, she has learned to avoid the overt questioning of the regime that might cause such disappearances (and that is the implication here), but she manages to unsettle the discourses of power without rendering herself too vulnerable to them. When Dusty persists in making very public enquiries about the whereabouts of Jimmy, her husband pulls her to one side to threaten her, concerned that she is interfering in his blatant networking of a room of powerful individuals. He adopts genocidal vocabulary, telling her 'you're all going to die together, you and all your lot'. One of the modes of mass extermination he proposes is the poisoning of 'all the mothers' milk in the world so that every baby would drop dead before it opened its perverted bloody mouth' (302), and this cuts to the very heart of family construction. That this is used as a form of sexual arousal is a most acute example of Pinter suggesting the corruption by power of authentic human familial interaction.

Twice during the play, the natural progression of scenes is interrupted by the dimming of the lights on the playing area and an intense light 'burning into the room' through a half-open door (313). When this occurs a third time, a thinly dressed man walks through the door, and declares himself to be Jimmy. With the partygoers still, and in silhouette, he utters a final monologue in which he catalogues his sensory disorientation in a darkened room. Both his own name and own heartbeat are displaced. 'What am I?', he asks, and claims to be in possession of nothing but the dark in which he miserably steeps: 'The dark is in my mouth and I suck it. It's the only thing I have. It's mine. It's my own. I suck it' (314). Ann C. Hall argues that this evokes breastfeeding, and suggests the brutal substitution of nourishing authentic family with the vacant, depersonalising provender of state authority.[21] In his final play *Celebration* (2000), Pinter seems to extend this depersonalisation further, to consider an infection in culture itself.

Set in an exclusive restaurant, *Celebration* has more references to family embedded in it than any other of Pinter's plays. Lambert and Prue are celebrating their wedding anniversary at table one with his brother Matt and her sister Julie. Russell and his partner Suki occupy table two, and eventually join the first group. Culture is seen as acquired by these affluent people, not experienced, and the frequent references to family seem to serve to highlight the distance they have from authentic bonds of affection. As a married couple, Lambert and Prue's interaction seems altogether lacking in sentiment and they are equally distant from their children, whose absence from the celebration is dismissed by a platitudinous 'Children. They have no memory. They remember nothing. They don't remember who their father was or who their mother was'.[22] And yet, the childhood memories they themselves offer are vivid recollections of abuse. Russell recalls wanting to become a poet, but that his father discouraged him, referring to his son as 'an arsehole' (465). Prue recalls how as babies she and Julie could hear their mother 'beating the shit' out of their father and then see blood on the sheets in the morning (457). This inversion of the usual target of domestic violence sits alongside a number of references to women and power, and the inverted Oedipal investments that mothers are said to have with their offspring participates in this ('All mothers want their sons to be fucked by themselves', 'all mothers want to be fucked by their mothers') (452–3). Through such brutal recollections, perverted assertions and crude language, the verbal disintegration of family structures adds to the obscenity of these objectionable characters.

By contrast, both the restaurant owner Richard and the *maîtresse d'hôtel* Sonia offer recollections of their parents that relate to issues of heritage and culture. Richard explains that his concept for the restaurant was inspired by his memories of a country pub he remembers being taken to by his father. By extrapolating from the cheese rolls and gherkins available in a traditional, oak-beamed pub in a rural village, to the duck in sauce and Osso Bucco provided now for wealthy and unappreciative clients, Pinter is signalling the contemporary appropriation of 'tradition' as a consumed, integrated simulacrum. Simultaneously, he suggests the loss or distancing of an authentic experience that, in itself, fails to meet the currency value that its simulacrum promises. Russell adds to this with his memories of his mother's bread and butter pudding, in anticipation of the restaurant's take on that traditional British dish. By accessing these things via references to family, that authenticity is consolidated and its loss is mourned all the more, and when Matt and Lambert laud the values of 'tradition and class' we recognise the distance between these values and their articulation of them (448). This theme is pursued in the play predominantly through the figure of the Waiter, and within the series of interjections he makes in the diners' conversations. These too are filtered through memories of family, in this case his grandfather, as he supplies comically preposterous inventory of almost seventy famous people his grandfather was acquainted with.

The inauthentic behaviour that is foregrounded by the corrupt family structures articulated in *Celebration*, and the loss of and nostalgia for genuine nurturing affection, as captured in the figure of the cultured grandfather, provide a framework for the critique of consumerism the play operates. There is a subtle link that Pinter activates here between consumerism and political expediency, and the next chapter examines correlations that Pinter deploys in his political writing between consumption and ideology.

CHAPTER 5
POLITICS AND THE ARTIST AS CITIZEN

Anger and All That
The Birthday Party, The Dumb Waiter, The Hothouse

When the theatre critic Irving Wardle first applied the term 'Comedy of Menace' to describe *The Birthday Party* and *The Dumb Waiter* in 1958 – inadvertently setting in motion a critical paradigm that would prioritise the 'menace' over the 'comedy' – he nonetheless was proposing something more ideologically applicable than a description of a dramatic mode of expression. In his article, he applied 'comedy of menace' to both Pinter's work and N. F. Simpson's recent *A Resounding Tinkle*, but drew a very clear line between the ambitions of the two writers, dismissing Simpson's play as a comedy of manners. Pinter's 'manufactured fictional device' of menace, he argued 'stands for something more substantial: destiny' and he goes on to consider the function of comedy as a means of domesticating, or deferring, attention from issues of social destiny. Pinter's work, he continued, demonstrated 'that people, the lower-middle classes in particular, get used to anything, and that this is dangerous'. He therefore saw in the play an alertness to the Cold War tensions that were a distinct feature of the political terrain of the late 1950s, concluding that '[d]estiny handled in this way [...] is an apt dramatic motif for an age of conditioned behaviour in which orthodox man is a willing collaborator in his own destruction'.[1] Pinter's attention to 'conditioned behaviour' and our potential to become a 'willing collaborator' is manifest in his oeuvre from his earliest plays to his later political output, and the latter more explicitly examines the linguistic operations that underpin such conditioning.

In 1962, John Russell Taylor described Pinter in his influential critical work *Anger and After* as a realist playwright and, acknowledging the menace established by Wardle, associated Pinter's work at that time alongside those of his contemporaries, the so-called 'kitchen sink' dramatists. The harsh critical response to Pinter's first full-length drama might best be understood in this context. Perhaps *The Birthday Party* was too readily seen and considered as an exponent of the new wave of writers and, in part, the critical treatment it received may have been in intolerant resistance to the young movement to which its author would have been perceived as subscribing. Conversely, and more likely, the play may have been considered to have failed to live up to the contours of the new paradigms, and dismissed as an oddball pretender to the throne, one that failed to fit a mould cast by other, already championed young writers such as John Arden, John Osborne and Arnold Wesker.

Dan Rebellato, in his revisionist review of mid-twentieth-century British Theatre, *1956 And All That*, questions the anger of the generation of playwrights who embraced the term 'angry young men'. He affirms that anger as being without palpable target, as indicative of a loss of confidence and sense of potency among socialist thinkers, and too readily dismissible as 'entirely in a prepolitical psychological realm'. Rebellato asks why plays by the likes of Arden, Osborne and Wesker 'should have been so applauded by the left, since they would seem [...] part of the problem, not part of the solution',[2] arguing that their works lacked the articulation of any theoretical or concrete responses to the social realities they addressed. While 'the left' nevertheless did applaud those playwrights, Rebellato's assessment might well explain why some of them might have chosen not to applaud *The Birthday Party*, a play that seemed constructed wilfully to embrace that 'prepolitical psychological realm'. Although the drama takes an unequivocal stand against authority, it does so without clarifying or precisely locating the social provenance of that authority and offers a seemingly defeatist conclusion, promoting resistance even while representing it as futile. As such, the play might have been perceived as flawed for falling between the two stools of either rallying oppositional anger against an identifiable social reality or offering a compelling poetic aesthetic as some form of metaphorical commentary on the human condition, in the manner of the then fashionable Samuel Beckett, Jean Genet or Eugène Ionesco play. Apparently having a foot in both camps but satisfying neither of George Devine's 'two lines',[3] as that significant contemporary director saw this opposition between social realism and poetic drama, Pinter's first full-length play must have seemed to have been out of tune with London's theatrical zeitgeist.

The enlightened ambitions of theatres (such as Devine's Royal Court) to maintain an artistic agenda that kept a thumb on the pulse of contemporary affairs and politics and the editorial emphases of journals such as *Encore* created an environment where it was convenient if artists would conform to or identify themselves readily with either the radicalised young theatre or with the more concept-driven material being imported from the continent. Pinter's earliest plays – *The Room, The Dumb Waiter, The Birthday Party* and *The Hothouse* – are clearly driven by questions about the relationship between the individual and power structures that would compromise and constrain the individual voice, but Pinter was not one to want to declare his political position and specify his class enemy as might an Osborne or a Wesker. 'There is a considerable body of people just now who are asking for some kind of clear and sensible engagement to be evidently disclosed in contemporary plays', he stated in 1962, confessing that for him, instead, writing a play involved his usually having 'found a couple of characters in a particular context, thrown them together and listened to what they said, keeping my nose to the ground'.[4] In other words, he positioned himself as simply pursuing free-wheeling artistic impulses, not writing from any preconceived position. One of the original reasons he gave for rejecting *The Hothouse* as 'quite useless' was precisely as a result of such rejection of having written from the perspective of a given moral standpoint, and how that risks quashing creativity:

> The characters were purely cardboard. I was intentionally –
> for the only time, I think – trying to make a point, an explicit
> point, that these were nasty people and I disapproved of
> them. And therefore they didn't begin to live.[5]

When Pinter declared in 1961 that he was 'not committed as a writer, in the usual sense of the term, either religiously or politically',[6] rather than take such statements at simple face value, we might best consider them in the context of a climate where dramatists were expected to declare their agendas openly. We might consider both what was understood at that time by 'in the usual sense of the term' and in what other sense Pinter might have then conceded he was a committed writer.[7] To speak of political drama and plays with a social conscience in the late 1950s and early 1960s indicated a specific set of dramatic discourses and subject matters. The impact of Bertolt Brecht and Helene Weigel's Berliner Ensemble appearance in London in 1956 and the growing popularity of Brecht's theoretical texts among theatre makers, coincided with the growth of those 'kitchen sink dramatists' who brought working-class subjects and concerns to the stage in the late 1950s, and this created a very specific intellectual and creative community of political dramaturgy to which Pinter simply did not belong and with which he absolutely did not want to be associated. When he insistently set himself apart from writers of such committed drama, Pinter was making a clear statement that his work had no ambition whatsoever to instruct people how to think, how to vote or how to behave, but this stance did not mean that no politics might be broached in his plays. *The Birthday Party*, *The Dumb Waiter* and *The Hothouse* were his first attempts to wield his pen in ways that addressed ideological issues without lecturing his audiences and, as has been postulated in Chapter 1, the manner in which he rejected the manuscript of *The Hothouse* and veered expressly away from issues of organisational control in 1958 (turning his creative attention in the first instance to revue sketch comedy, and to *A Slight Ache*, *A Night Out* and *The Caretaker*) inaugurated phases of his career in which he would be most compelled to write around interpersonal behaviour of varying sorts, consciously becoming, at that point, a non-political writer.

Harold Pinter's seemingly abrupt switch to writing political drama in the 1980s coincided with his entering a content period of domestic stability. His relationship with Lady Antonia Fraser was sealed formally by marriage in 1980 after five years of co-habitation.

Fraser relates in her published diaries how, by 1984, '[p]olitics began to feature increasingly in Harold's life now that he had become, in his oft-repeated words, "the luckiest man in the world"'.[8] One might speculate about the confidence that such resolved happiness can bring, and how Fraser's intellectual match for Pinter provided him with a robust and challenging sounding board for his social conscience. One certain trigger for his refreshed ambition to find artistic means to express political concerns might be found in his rediscovery of a palpable bridge back to his period of writing those early plays in which a fierce resistance to social conformity had been first expressed. During the activities of moving into Fraser's house in Campden Hill Square in the summer of 1977, Pinter might well have come across his old rejected script for *The Hothouse*, as he unpacked boxes and arranged his new working environment. Or perhaps the discovery was in 1979, when he was able to set up his studio in a small one-up, one-down building he bought on the adjacent street (connected to their home by a long garden) and finally find space for all his books and documents. He refers to re-reading it in 1979 in a brief note that prefaces the published edition in the *Plays 1* collection.[9] He did some cosmetic editing to the text and eventually directed it himself, in June 1980 at the Hampstead Theatre Club.

In inaugurating Pinter's political period, *The Hothouse* also connected his new artistic objectives to those of his first plays: the relationship between the individual and an organisational structure that demands his or her unquestioning obedience, the linguistic means by which control is formed and social 'reality' narrated, and, structurally, the theatrical opening up of an ethical gap that troubles an audience and might haunt them beyond the performance event. In 1958, he had been concerned that the exercise of writing *The Hothouse* had been a venting of anger at the representatives of institutional power who turn well-paid blind eyes to the suffering that their self-protectionism perpetuates. By 1979 an emboldened political philosophy from the right focussed its energies on undermining and dismantling the mixed economy model that had dominated throughout the period of the post-war consensus, and the socio-political consequences of these significant reforms were to colour much of the landscape of 1980s public affairs. The ascent of a neoliberal discourse of consumption and traditionalism heralded by the election of Margaret Thatcher could well have focussed Pinter's mind back onto the machinations of a powerful elite. In his Nobel lecture, twenty-five years after the eventual stage debut of that old play, he offered his most detailed and illustrated attack on what he considered the moral corruption of aspects of the Western political community, and this informs our understanding of the sort of establishment figures that populate much of the rest of his dramatic output.

Art, Truth and Politics
The Nobel Lecture, *Precisely, The New World Order, Press Conference, Celebration*

When, on 13 October 2005, Harold Pinter received news that he had been awarded the Nobel Prize for Literature, he had every intention of travelling to Stockholm to deliver the lecture that was expected of each new laureate. In the event, a debilitating illness – pemphigus vulgaris – arrested him, and he was hospitalised on 7 November and later transferred to intensive care. It became clear that a trip to Stockholm to accept the prize in person was out of the question, and he resolved instead to give his lecture by recording it for video in a Channel 4 studio and having this broadcast at the ceremony in place of his scheduled appearance on 7 December. The vision of him, with a face drawn pale and thin from his ongoing incapacitation, sitting in a wheelchair with a checked blanket across his lap, was an image of determined fragility embellished by a rasping quality that clung to the edges of his usually clean, deep baritone. In an ungracious act of political timidity, none of the five terrestrial British television channels broadcast his speech. UK viewers had to seek it out on More4 after midnight. Remarkably, the BBC did not even make mention of it on their news bulletins that day. This was an astonishing media response to a British Nobel laureate for literature,[10] and one could not help but speculate that a fear of broadcasting outspoken political commentary motivated this marginalisation of his lecture.[11] If such speculation holds water, this media effacement of the lecture articulates something of the reputation Pinter had accumulated for expressing anti-establishment sentiment in a manner that irritated or clashed with standard media corporations' agendas.

In that speech to the Nobel Academy, Pinter expanded on the issues in his writing that the Nobel committee had highlighted in justifying the award.[12] He was particularly keen to consider in depth the 'oppression' aspect of the committee's statement, as he had explained on the day of its announcement to Kirsty Wark on *Newsnight*, the BBC's flagship terrestrial news outlet. When she asked if he felt that the prize was politically motivated, he simply expressed a satisfaction in being given a platform to speak of 'the mendacity and the corruption and the injustice of so many of the actions taken by what are called the freedom-loving democracies'.[13] Pinter had used the term 'freedom-loving democracies' two years previously in a speech he delivered in the House of Commons in January 2003, as oppositional concern over the preparations for the US invasion of Iraq was building, and much of his public statements at this time were in relation to that conflict and its aftermath. In the House of Commons address, he spoke of detecting a 'stink of hypocrisy' that he believed was manifested by the use of words such as 'freedom', 'democracy' and 'just war' in the remarks of politicians who supported the proposed invasion.[14] His repeated assertions that the language of politics acts as a mask to political agendas was to be the central pillar of his Nobel Lecture, which gives us a means of appreciating his artistic objectives in the writing of his political dramas.

In a scheduled event to launch an updated edition of his *Various Voices* book at The Royal Court Theatre, on 20 October 2005, Pinter declared that his draft Nobel Lecture had the provisional title 'Art and Politics'. By the time it was complete, the word 'truth' had been inserted as a hinge between those two primary concepts, and the artistic means of formulating and communicating truth formed a central axis to what he sought to express. The 'Art' portion of Pinter's

Nobel Lecture takes up less than a quarter of the length of the speech and operates as something of a preface to the political lecture. In it, he consider how 'truth' in creative work is 'forever elusive',[15] multiple and contradictory and how, accordingly, 'language in art remains a highly ambiguous transaction, a quicksand' (287). In then speaking of his approach to writing political drama, his words in 2005 are consistent with his rejection of a certain type of polemic writing in 1962, when he bemoaned the 'writer who puts forward his concerns for you to embrace, who leaves you in no doubt of his worthiness, his usefulness, his altruism':[16]

> Sermonising has to be avoided at all cost. Objectivity is essential. The characters must be allowed to breathe their own air. The author cannot confine and constrict them to satisfy his own taste or disposition or prejudice. (287)

There is the trace here of his own self-remonstration for writing 'cardboard' characters who could not 'begin to live' in *The Hothouse*, though now he begins to position an understanding of the necessity of some character restriction in political satire, the 'proper function' of which, he states, does not always allow the author to follow the characters where they will. He gives two examples of that from his experience: *The Birthday Party* in which, after allowing 'a whole range of options to operate in a dense forest of possibility' he found himself 'finally focussing on an act of subjugation', and *Mountain Language* which 'pretends to no such range of operation. It remains brutal, short and ugly' (288). Having established a writerly territory in which truth might be examined through a juxtaposition of the oneiric and the brutally restrictive, he segues these creative operations into a reflection on political expression:

> Political language, as used by politicians, does not venture into any of this territory since the majority of politicians, on the evidence available to us, are interested not in truth but in power and in the maintenance of that power. To maintain that power it is essential that people remain in ignorance, that

they live in ignorance of the truth, even the truth of their own lives. What surrounds us therefore is a vast tapestry of lies, upon which we feed. (288)

At this point, the lecture shifts to a detailed critique of decades of US foreign policy, during which he provides a series of illustrations of the gap that is constructed between the experience of those suffering the consequences of political manoeuvres, and the diplomatic language that belies or occludes the expression or visibility of such suffering. It is at this nexus, between an authentic experience of pain and the linguistic manoeuvres that systematically blur that authenticity, that Pinter both locates his creative stance and the point at which the artist and the citizen become a conjoined entity. When the artist and the citizen had first come explicitly together in the mid-1980s, this recognised stalemate between lived reality and political expression had been expressed as a kind of despairing determination:

> [R]eason is not going to do anything. Me writing *One for the Road*, documentaries, articles, lucid analyses [...] Finally it's hopeless. There's nothing one can achieve. Because the modes of thinking of those in power are worn out, threadbare, atrophied. Their minds are a brick wall. But still one can't stop attempting to try to think and see things as clearly as possible. All we're talking about, finally is what is real? What is real? [...] thousands of people are being tortured to death at this very moment [...] It has to be faced.[17]

The frustration here reveals an artist in the process of seeking a mode of expression that will capture the undeniable reality of torture, and a temperament that seeks to insist that such reality be faced openly and honestly. That repeated 'What is real?' – an exasperated intellectual hesitation between an awareness of the elusiveness of reality and of the ineffable corporeality of human pain – is a precursor to his Nobel statement that 'the search for truth can never stop. It cannot be adjourned, it cannot be postponed' (287). This same relentless enquiry into the reality status of human suffering within political agendas was the cause of Pinter and Arthur Miller being asked to leave the US embassy in Ankara, Turkey, during their joint visit to the country in March 1985. They were there as representatives of PEN International to investigate allegations of the persecution of Turkish writers. After a dinner hosted by the US Ambassador to Turkey, during which the conversation had turned to the difficult issue of prisoners of conscience in the state's jails, the Ambassador approached Pinter to ask him to appreciate the delicacy of the geo-political context; 'the political reality, the diplomatic reality, the military reality'. Pinter retorted that for him the most important reality was 'that of electric current on your genitals'.[18] This outraged frankness is of a piece with a much earlier expression of contempt for politicians at the time of the Vietnam war:

> I'll tell you what I really think about politicians. The other night I watched some politicians on television talking about Vietnam. I wanted very much to burst through the screen with a flame-thrower and burn their eyes out and their balls off and then inquire from them how they would assess the action from a political point of view.[19]

What Pinter articulated here in both the mid-1960s and mid-1980s is a crude, unqualified anger that seems provoked by the same interconnected diplomatic behaviours that he later so precisely anatomises in his Nobel Lecture: programmatic violence towards people as a means of maintaining political and or economic advantage (war, torture) and a manipulation of language to cover up and re-define such behaviour as expedient, necessary or even just. His imagined intervention takes the form of an expressed desire to inflict upon politicians the kinds of violence and bodily mutilation that they so readily determine should be delivered to remote, anonymised others, and to do so explicitly on the terms of their polite discourse, of 'how they would assess the action from a political point of view'. Effectively, he imagines a double rupture being performed: a breaching of the media screens that distance the politicians from the people they govern, and a breaching of the language of obfuscation to approximate the language of gritty description, of actual experience. Here, in 1966, is the very kernel of the objectives of Pinter's 'political' plays as unwrapped in his Nobel Lecture some three decades later: a theatrical means of bringing an audience closer to a set of painful realisations that daily diets of political chatter render invisible, unheard, unthinkable. Pinter performs a very similar act of writing in his Nobel Lecture, when he imagines Tony Blair holding the wounded body of an infant, the victim of the bombing sorties he authorised during the 2003 invasion of Iraq. Basil Chiasson unpicks the function of that image in his chapter later in this volume, arguing that 'through this process of capture and re-inscription, Pinter prevents the sense of violence and human toll in Iraq from passing across the "lining or hem" of ascendant portrayals and framings of Blair which at the time rendered him a benign figure'.[20]

Michael Billington describes Pinter's 'belief that truth is indivisible'.[21] When Pinter spoke of 'truth' in the context of politics, then, he was not concerning himself with the interpretation of political history, philosophy or even motivation. To speak of 'truth' in these contexts would be problematic, naive even. But the moment of pain experienced by a suffering victim is indivisible: it is an authentic experience that defies interpretation, and it is this indivisible moment, this 'truth', that Pinter repeatedly presented as demanding an unrelenting human response. His 'staging' of Tony Blair holding a bloody child, or talk of an 'electric current on your genitals' or of taking a flame thrower to those same parts, are all modes of taking that indivisible, undeniable agony and placing it as an insolent intruder within the domain of a political language that would deny its presence on their platforms. In seeking to unpick and expose the duplicities of politic discourse in these ways, Pinter might be understood to be operating in the sorts of critical territories that George Orwell established in the 1930s and 1940s, in which the objectives of propagandist strategies were expressed as to achieve more than but the simple misrepresentation of facts, but to impose a willing acceptance of the dominant discourses of power. In his Nobel speech, Pinter effectively expands the slogan 'Ignorance is Strength' from George Orwell's *Nineteen Eighty-Four* (1949), to claim how in contemporary political address '[l]anguage is actually employed to keep thought at bay' (293).

We might detect Orwell in the background of the intertextual references activated in or by other aspects of the Nobel speech, most notably perhaps in Pinter's quotation from a Spanish Civil War poem by Pablo Neruda, 'I'm Explaining a Few Things' ('Explico Algunas Cosas'). 'I quote Neruda', he explains, 'because nowhere in contemporary poetry have I read such a powerful visceral description of the bombing of civilians' (297–8). The valuing of the term 'visceral' as an affect of art is key here to understanding Pinter's own artistic ambition with his political writing: to make a bodily connection with his audience, to do so via moments of indivisible agony, and in so doing, to physically adjust them temporarily so that a re-adjustment is required after the aesthetic experience in ways that activate awareness of an ethical issue. Working in the predominantly visual field of drama and addressing in his prose how the visual languages of contemporary news media (such as the Blair illustration above) participate in a process of keeping thought at bay, he extends Orwell's vision to survey the sorts of threats to the representation of authentic experience that come about in the age of 24-hour news channels and of social media. The concomitant growth of 'spin doctors' and 'consultants' populating the corridors of power has seen media corporations and political parties form and consolidate questionable alliances over the last three decades,[22] and Pinter's dramatis personae expanded in his political works to include such figures.

The sketch *Precisely* was first performed in December 1983 as part of 'The Big One: A Variety Show for Peace', a revue of music and performance organised by Susannah York in support of the Campaign for Nuclear Disarmament. With contributions from Elvis Costello, Ian Dury, U2 and Paul Weller's Style Council, the target audience was a predominantly young crowd. Offering his sketch to the evening, directing it and permitting its subsequent publication in an associated anthology, this 400-word dramatic piece represents the first example of Pinter making a deliberate contribution by way of his art to a political cause. In it, he satirises the two-facedness of political bureaucracies that engender 'public relation' approaches to managing politically inconvenient statistics. Sitting at a table and drinking, Stephen and his inferior Roger are revealed to be discussing a figure of twenty million as being in some way scientifically verified, and are decrying those who would argue that an accurate figure is higher, implying either a media or activist contradiction of their statistics. Stephen speaks in passing of having a committee set up to deal with the detractors, but when Roger asks if he might stretch to speaking of twenty-two million, it is made apparent that the twenty million in question is an agreed figure for public consumption and compliance; 'the citizens of this country are behind us. They're ready to go with us on the twenty million basis'.[23] It becomes clear that the numbers in question are human corpses, as Pinter has Stephen make a morbid pun about the accuracy of the figures: 'It's twenty million. Dead' (219). In applying the word 'dead' here to mean simultaneously an exact figure and the extinction of human lives, Pinter conflates his two lines of aesthetic enquiry: the use of language to evade reality, and the exposure of that reality which is the artist's obligation. The central engine of Pinter's dark satire here is the dehumanising distancing from the bodily reality of nuclear extinction achieved through having his characters speak of multiple simultaneous deaths in such inconceivable numbers, and by their rendering this plurality down to a singular figure with which to negotiate in comfortable, middle-class bargains ('Give me another two, Stephen [...] Another two for another drink') (219). In his acceptance speech for the 2004 Wilfred Owen prize, Pinter expresses a comparable distaste for the dismissal of the civilian dead by the US military:

An independent and totally objective account of the Iraqi civilian dead in the medical magazine *The Lancet* estimates that the figure approaches 100,000. But neither the US or the UK bother to count the Iraqi dead. As General Tommy Franks (US Central Command) memorably said: 'We don't do body counts'.[24]

If 1983's *Precisely* was a first, brief foray into overt political dramatic writing, Pinter was to consolidate that position the following year with *One for the Road*, and in 1988 with *Mountain Language*, the titles of which both foreground language in different ways. Both Chiasson and Ann C. Hall address the political thrust of these two plays and of *Party Time* (1991) in their following chapters. Hall considers the representation of women in these plays, and this neatly progresses the approach offered in Chapter 2 of this volume, but also complements the thoughts on how these plays employ family structures, as ventured in Chapter 4. Chiasson's work adds depth to these analyses in his appreciation of how Pinter might be understood to be responding to the neoliberal narratives that were slowly growing to dominance in British and US political discourses over the period of his writing after 1979.

The origins of *One for the Road* and *Mountain Language* are to be found in instances of Pinter's exposure to real political situations. Antonia Fraser recalls the genesis of the first play in May 1983, when her husband 'starts to talk about a play about imprisonment and torture' and quotes his stated objective: 'Nothing explicit. No blood, no torture scene'.[25] She recalls him quoting an incident recounted in Jacobo Timerman's *Prisoner Without a Name, Cell Without a Number* in which a female prisoner is verbally abused before being removed by the guards and subsequently disappearing. The concept, nonetheless, lay dormant and without a dramatic context into which it might grow from his pen, until he had one of his characteristically uninhibited rows with two Turkish girls at a family birthday event in January 1984. The disagreement had centred around sentences, including death sentences, handed down in the recent trials of militants in Turkey, which the girls had disinterestedly dismissed as 'probably deserved' on the spurious grounds that they were 'probably communists'.[26] He sat down to write the play in anger that evening, and had it more or less complete within twenty-four hours. The next year, during his visit to Turkey with Arthur Miller, the two men listen to the stories of those tortured and imprisoned for writing, and of their wives who travel great distances for brief interludes with their husbands, threatened by Doberman Pinschers as they wait.

Appalled by the decree that banned the use of the Kurdish language, the germ of *Mountain Language* is found in these testimonies and these circumstances.

Hardly a 'phase' in any substantial way, Pinter's political writing, then, comprised three short one-act plays and a couple of sketches, to which we might add the sketch *Press Conference* from 2002. The three plays, though not conceived as a connected trilogy, operate effectively as one, with clear thematic connections and reiterations between them. So effectively do they speak to one another, that French director Roger Planchon very effectively stitched them together in 2006 into a full-length drama, premièred in French and performed as a tribute to the author on the occasion of the presentation to him of the 10th European Theatre Prize in Turin. Entitled *Le Nouvel Ordre mondial*, the cycle began with that sketch, *The New World Order*, followed by *Press Conference*, *Precisely*, *Mountain Language*, and *One for the Road* before concluding with *Party Time*, all in French versions by Jean Pavans. The collated works were effectively expanded by this illuminating collage and the production keenly underlined the links between the dramas by imagining them populated by a coherent set of characters, effected by the arrangement of the cast. The hooded intellectual about to receive the violent attention of Des and Lionel in the opening *The New World Order* reappears later as the mute hooded husband in *Mountain Language* before being relieved of his hood and appearing as Victor in *One for the Road* and finally the defeated, isolated Jimmy in *Party Time*. The thuggish interrogators in the eponymous sketch reappear as the low-ranking officers in *Mountain Language* before returning in formal attire in *Party Time*. The actor playing Stephen who seeks to convince his colleague Roger of the value of accurate terminology when accounting for the dead in *Precisely* returns as the minister in *Press Conference* before revealing himself to be Nicolas in *One for the Road* and Gavin in *Party Time*. Planchon's production effectively collated all of Pinter's overtly political plays and presented them in a way that allowed them to express their common themes: the duplicitous abuse of language for ideological ends, the application of psychological torture to render subjects obedient and the potential for unquestioning submissiveness to (or interpellation by) ideological discourses that we might all manifest.

In *The New World Order*, the violence that is to be meted out on an unnamed, hooded prisoner is deferred until after the sketch is complete. This deliberately focusses the drama's attention on the verbal torture that is the preparation for the physical torture, the former even obviating the latter, or rendering the latter as simply something that both satiates and vindicates the aggressors. By deferring the violence, it is rendered a delight, an entertainment, a moment to savour and digest and, as such, a reward to be consumed by those who defend the values of the powerful. The choice of character names here must be pertinent to this as, to a British audience, the names Des and Lionel might bring to mind Des O'Connor and Lionel Blair, two light entertainment song and dance performers of long standing in British variety circuits. Roote in *The Hothouse* positions the rape of his institution's inmates in terms of a perk for the hard-working functionaries of the ministry, and Nicolas expresses the same terrifyingly to Gila: 'I should think you might entertain us all a little more before you go'.[27] In preparing for his violent reward, Lionel in *The New World Order* becomes emotional, declaiming 'I love it. I love it. I love it' and confesses how pure his position of power makes him feel. Des corroborates this, explaining that Lionel's sense of euphoria is justified because he is 'keeping the world clean for democracy'.[28] In this way, Pinter displays how the commodification of violence is elided into a moral world-view that validates and rewards the abuse of those whose actions or beliefs are deemed to contradict or be a threat to that world-view. By distinctly separating verbal violence from physical violence, the former is shown to be a politically functional instrument and the latter as a privilege of the powerful. Violence re-narrated in this way – not so much as a punishment for the disobedient, but perversely as a morally fitting consequence of behaviour deemed inappropriate by the state – can, once thus justified, be appropriated as sport, a pastime for the muscle of the state.

In the 2002 sketch *Press Conference*, Pinter resurrects a Nicolas type in the character of the Minister of Culture who, remarkably for a politician, speaks the truth. When asked about his attitude to women and children in his former role as chief of Secret Police, he points out that, 'as part of an educational process [...] a cultural process' the children of subversives would have their necks broken and the women raped.[29] By eliding the roles of state-sanctioned violence with those that promote an 'understanding of our cultural heritage and our cultural obligations' including 'loyalty to the free market' (11), Pinter suggests in this brief satire that our 'cultural heritage' is corrupted by the aspirations of global capitalism which can manoeuvre unremitting force to protect its objectives, and project them onto patriotism as irresistible moral emblems. In her essay, Hall points out that in *Mountain Language* we might understand 'the language of the capital' to mean 'the language of capital',[30] something that Chiasson expands to chart the traces of neoliberal critique through Pinter's work, and in both essays consumption and the discarding of the by-products of their behaviours – including human lives and the corpses that remain – play a role in illustrating those tendencies. Artistically, there is a distinct progression here from the manner in which consumption had been allied with violence in earlier plays where the experiences were positioned as analogous. So, for example, we learn in the final act of *The Birthday Party* that Goldberg and McCann have 'had the last of the fry'[31] and in *The Hothouse*, Roote proposes a toast to 'our glorious dead',[32] which activates for us a grim irony in the evident distinction between the mass sacrifice of life and the kind of institutionalism that both caused that sacrifice and might persist as a result of it. David Pattie points out how, in *The Birthday Party*, 'correct behaviour, and moral rectitude are linked inextricably to the consumption of food' and suggests that we might consider *The Dumb Waiter* 'a grotesque black comedy of consumption and liberation, in which the operation of power is displaced onto food, and to the needs of the body'.[33] In the later political plays, this operation becomes more overtly expressed through the synthesis of the vocabularies of consumption and power, rather than just correlations between the two. *Party Time* in particular has this matter at the heart of its aesthetic structuring, and is heavily set with the celebration of consumption. The numerous references to an exclusive health club operate both to indicate the sealed privilege of the elite, but also to foreground the consumerism that is at the centre of contemporary political discourse, a consumerism that becomes tightly bound to a moral code that these people champion. Robert Gordon points out how, in the expanded screenplay of *Party Time*, Pinter 'grimly exploits the motif of consumption'[34] with the phrase 'We've had him for breakfast', which is used to describe the fate of a musician who was deemed by the party guests to have been 'talking the most absolute bloody crap' in projecting 'his ideas of the world'.[35] The colloquialism used in this context serves Pinter's purpose well, in that (as with Stephen's 'twenty million. Dead' in *Precisely*) it neatly conflates two distinct ideas into one process. Another colloquial phrase, Nicolas's 'one for the road' in the play of that title has a similar function, but deferred to the final scene when we must imagine the excruciating agony that Victor must endure in drinking an obligatory whisky with a cut tongue. It is a precise and theatrical image: a searing punishment of the organ of speech (that is to say, the origins of any infraction) with a 'celebratory' drink that seals Nicolas's victory of subjugation. Consumption, then, becomes woven into Pinter's political vocabulary as a process of bodily relish that is bound to the suffering of the politically vanquished, through which 'disorder feeds on the belly of order / And order requires the blood of disorder'.[36] Pinter's 2002 poem 'After Lunch' projects a theatrical scene, not dissimilar to the setting of *Party Time*, in which the 'well-dressed creatures come / To sniff among the dead / And have their lunch', 'stir the minestrone with stray bones' and 'lounge about / Decanting claret in convenient skulls'.[37] Similarly offensive 'well-dressed creatures' populate Pinter's last stage play, *Celebration* (2000).

If consumption had become something of a trope in Pinter's political writing, it was to be put centre stage in *Celebration*. Here though, consumption as an overt correlative of political behaviours is absent, and though the play cannot straightforwardly be considered political, this shift signals a form of loathing that maintains a connection back to the technocratic elite of *Party Time*, and further to those of *The Hothouse*. In *Celebration*, the distance between the aesthetic values of cuisine, ballet and opera and their currency as vessels for the projection of wealth and status is foregrounded in the uncouth behaviour and language of the clients of Richard's restaurant who seek out 'the very highest fucking standards' as something to be bought, not savoured or displayed.[38] Lambert and Matt's personal subscription to culture is manifest in three drunken bursts of song, first in a crude permutation of the Tin Pan Alley classic 'Ain't She Sweet', which Matt renders as 'Ain't she neat? / As she's walking down the street / She's got a lovely bubbly pair of tits / And a soft leather seat', claiming his version to be a 'traditional folk song' (447). Later, he offers a few lines of 'Wash me in the Water / Where you washed your dirty daughter' (451), a soldier's song from the First World War that features in the play *Oh What a Lovely War* (1963), and 'Who's in front / Get out of the bloody way / you silly old cunt!' which has all the qualities of a rugby song (505–6). Regressing in this way through these three songs, Lambert and Matt's access to culture is expressed in terms of libidinous desire and self-regarding need.

The only hint that there is any political context alert in this play is when the Matt and Lambert characters discuss their profession in the 'strategic consultancy business' (498). Lambert explains only that this means they do not need to carry guns, which suggests a link to security and a power beyond scrutiny, one that guarantees their safety. If the hint points toward the arms industry, then there is an ominous ambiguity in their parting words. Leaving the restaurant, Matt assures their hosts they shall return because there will be 'plenty to celebrate' to which Lambert agrees with a simple 'Dead right' (505), which recalls the adjectival use of 'dead' to mean 'precisely' in the earlier sketch of that name. We learn that Russell is a banker, which consolidates the sense that the satire is targeting the opportunistic benefactors of neoliberal capitalism.

The restaurant owner Richard and his *maîtresse d'hôtel* Sonia demonstrate such polite and tolerant responses to the crude behaviour of their clients that this suggests the unquestioning acquiescence of service industries to the appetites of such people, that the restaurants (and health clubs) of Pinter's world recognise their function as unquestioning providers of status, not of food or health. The conversation that Richard and Sonia offer is vapid and unchallenging, a string of platitudes such as 'ambience is that intangible thing that can't be defined' (475) and 'We get so many different kinds of people in here' (482) and where we might expect some subtextual put-downs we get blank acceptance. This activates a certain frustration in an audience that nobody is disapproving of the diners' crude behaviour. Although we laugh, we find this amoral structure bewildering and this in turn causes us to invest in the character of the Waiter, who alone offers some alternative to the stifling bad manners in the idle chatter between tables. Through this character, and the bizarre accounts he presents of his grandfather's numerous acquaintances, Pinter offers us a refreshing link out of this culturally vacant space and back to the civilising memories of artistic engagement. Written at the end of the century and millennium, the play tapped into the frenzy of backward-looking journalism and *fin-de-siècle* nostalgia that was active across the globe. The Waiter's grandfather, we hear, 'stood four square in the centre of the intellectual and literary life of the tens, twenties and thirties' (468). He was close friends with numerous celebrated authors in both Britain and the United States and was familiar with Hollywood film stars of the MGM golden era, as well as composers, painters, comedians and popular singing groups. By juxtaposing so many references to predominantly inter-war artistic and cultural activity, Pinter mobilises his own nostalgia to suggest that our consumption of culture has altered beyond recognition in a world where consumerism controls the definitions of value.

Further memories associate the Waiter's grandfather with major conflict. He is remembered as being a close friend of Archduke Franz Ferdinand, whose assassination triggered the First World War, and played poker with Winston Churchill and Benito Mussolini, key politicians in the Second. We hear also that he led a battalion in the Spanish Civil War. Other references have oblique political resonances, such as 'Chicago gang' and 'Deep South conglomerate' (468) and the Waiter's reference to Jewish gangsters and the Irish Mafia provide an intertextual leap back to Goldberg and McCann.

The merging of such political references or inferences into a body of cultural output troubles the litany of artistic achievement, and the image of the Waiter's grandfather playing poker with the Archduke, Mussolini and Churchill mirrors the unquestioning neutrality of the restaurant environment. That troubling is captured in the concocted list of injuries the catalogue of artists supposedly suffered: 'vast wounds to their bodies, their bellies, their legs, their trunks, their eyes, their throats, their breasts, their balls' (502).

When the play closes, the last word is given to the Waiter. He recalls his grandfather once more, this time for giving him a telescope to look out to sea, and to boats in the distance. The image of the ocean is one of both escape and oblivion, and the Waiter speaks of being unable to get out of the mystery of life, as his grandfather succeeded in doing. His last words, 'And I'd like to make one further interjection' (508), end the play on a hiatus, and that sense of hopeless continuation that the character has activated.

The Fist and the Kiss
Ashes to Ashes

One particular form of consumption that Pinter addresses in his political writing is consensual sex as a form of empowering transaction. This is distinct from the rape and sexual opportunism or abuse that is applied as a means of control, torture or entertainment. Lulu's unhappy seduction at the hands of Goldberg in *The Birthday Party* – a depraved sexual encounter that involved the unmentionable contents of a briefcase – is an early example of the latter, and she reproaches him in terms of consumption for having 'quenched [his] ugly thirst' with her.[39] Gila's predicament is the clearest example in the later plays. Consensual sex, by contrast, becomes an index of appetite and conquest amongst Pinter's disagreeable elite, and it is associated with power explicitly in ways that are not evident in plays that consider sexual relations such as *The Lover*, *Old Times* or *Betrayal*. In *The Hothouse*, Miss Cutts transfers her sexual allegiance between Roote and Gibbs as though to predict and pursue the current of dominant power. Nicolas's institution, which shares the multi-storey dimensions of the one Roote commands, contains a brothel for the ready pleasure of the male protectors of state virtues. In *Party Time*, Pinter draws this alliance between power and consensual sex most prominently. With the exception of the Thatcheresque Dame Melissa,[40] the position of the women in the play is one of passive subservience; they are trophy wives and temporary lovers, and the manner in which they are addressed gives no indication of authentic affection. A brief scene between Charlotte and Liz, in which Liz bemoans how another woman has seduced a man she finds attractive, sees both women speak using viscous misogynistic putdowns such as 'nymphomaniac slut' and 'bigtitted tart'.[41] In this way, Pinter suggests how the language of ideology can even corrupt and absorb those who are the targeted victims of that same ideology and, just as these women learn to hate women, then it is implied that all victims of power learn to utter their own submission to power. Pinter constructs an even more compelling version of this phenomenon in the way he structures sex and power together, articulated in sado-masochistic terms. When Terry admonishes Dusty for asking about Jimmy's disappearance, and speaks in genocidal terms of how she and her 'lot' are all to be put to death by any of a number of means, he tells her 'I want you to look forward to whatever the means employed with a lot of sexual anticipation' (302). The foul-mouthed rejoicing of the voice in the poem 'American Football' (1992) concludes with the words 'Now I want you to come over here and kiss me on the mouth'[42] and in 'The "Special Relationship"' (2004), Pinter configures that same satiation in terms of an emboldening political alliance: 'A man bows down before another man / And sucks his lust'.[43] This alliance of sex and power, whether directly in references to rape or indirectly in the form of erotic expression or sado-masochistic compliance, channels discourses of pornography that promote the impression of control over a distant human rendered as submissive object for our consumption. Pinter does not wield these discourses neutrally, he certainly does not seek to permit us to indulge them, but binds them to the monstrous personalities he constructs in Nicolas, Terry, Des, Lionel and the military personnel of *Mountain Language*.

In *Ashes to Ashes* (1996), Pinter again mobilises a bond between eroticism, sado-masochism and power, but in more sophisticated ways, as part of a theatrical apparatus for addressing the Holocaust and, more broadly, our own implication in grievous acts of state brutality. The Holocaust has resonated in corners of Pinter's writing from the onset. Charles Grimes for example identifies how Pinter echoes Nazi vocabulary in Goldberg's talk of the 'special treatment' (79) that Stanley requires to be suitably 'integrated' (78),[44] and Pinter later acknowledged that 'the idea of two men coming into a room and subjecting a third man to what they subject him to I'm sure was affected by my knowledge of the Holocaust, as well as my knowledge of rigid religious and nationalistic [...] forces'.[45] The Third Reich appears numerous times in other aspects of Pinter's career, indicating it was never far from his artistic consideration. Two plays he directed, Robert Shaw's *The Man in the Glass Booth* (1967) and Ronald Harwood's *Taking Sides* (1995), address the trials of Nazis. His screenplays of *The Quiller Memorandum* (1965), *The Heat of the Day* (1989), *Reunion* (1990) and *The Remains of the Day* (1993) all refract features of Nazi Germany.[46] With *Ashes to Ashes*, Pinter constructed a means of addressing the Holocaust without the kind of easy moralising or indulgent emotionalism that were anathema to him, and he did this primarily by considering the fragmented, troubled way in which our culture articulates and sustains the memory of that grievous event.

In an arrangement that is reminiscent of *Landscape*, a man, Devlin, asks questions of a woman, Rebecca, who does not always acknowledge him. At first, Devlin comes across as a doctor or therapist, as he solicits details from Rebecca about a love-play ritual she enacted with a former lover in which she would kiss his clenched fist and request that he put his hand around her throat. An intrusive question about whether her legs opened as she was pushed backwards by that grasp establishes a tone of jealous enquiry, and it soon becomes clear that Devlin is Rebecca's partner or husband, and the conversation develops into the kind of probing enquiry about former lovers that torments insecure spouses. But just as the play seems to be settling into this pattern, Rebecca's memories take a disturbing turn as she talks of how her remembered lover ran a factory that 'wasn't the usual kind of factory': it was damp, had no toilet facilities and was populated by obedient workers that doffed their caps and sang for their boss.[47] Then, from out of the blue, she recalls how he would 'go to the local railway station and walk down the platform and tear all the babies from the arms of the screaming mothers' (406–7). This shocking revelation causes a shift in tactics from Devlin, as he moves to demand scrutiny of what is true and what is not.

> **Devlin** [...] you made a somewhat oblique reference to your bloke ... your lover? ... and babies and mothers, et cetera. And platforms. I inferred from this that you were talking about some kind of atrocity. Now let me ask you this. What authority do you think you yourself possess which would give you the right to discuss such an atrocity?
>
> **Rebecca** I have no such authority. Nothing has ever happened to me. Nothing ever happened to any of my friends. I have never suffered. Nor have my friends. (413)

Rebecca utterly repudiates any claim she might have to having taken part in the incidents she recounts, and by embedding such a repudiation in her lines, Pinter is drawing our attention to her bonded emotional association with the narratives she seems nonetheless to recall as events from her own past. He goes further and, as if to secure a firm understanding in directors and actors, he states clearly in the published text, that the play is set 'Now' (that is to say 1996 at the earliest, when the play was first published and performed) and that both characters are 'in their forties' (391) and therefore born after the end of the Second World War. And yet, not only does Rebecca continue to recall the details of associated atrocities (she soon talks of seeing a crowd of people being herded out to sea to drown) the sado-masochistic relationship she recalls adds both an authenticating granulation to the 'memories' and, importantly, configures her as complicit with them, guilty by association. The issue of guilt acquired at a distance has already been positioned in a comic exchange over a 'perfectly innocent pen' (410) which adumbrates the question of an 'authority' to discuss (or, in the case of the dramatist, write about) atrocity. The infectious, suffocating quality of that guilt is then captured in the fictitious condition, 'mental elephantiasis', that Rebecca describes as 'a vast sea of gravy' that swells from spilling an ounce. 'You are not the *victim* of it, you are the *cause* of it' (417), she emphasises, and she mysteriously equates spilling gravy with handing over a child on a railway platform. Rebecca, then, acts as the filter through which an awareness of human brutality invades and unsettles domestic complacency.

By presenting images that signal the Holocaust, and asking outright what right we have to do so, Pinter is addressing the ethics of representation in those cultural systems that keep such memories alive: fiction, film, poetry and theatre. The release of Steven Spielberg's *Schindler's List* (1993) was an important threshold in the public interaction with these memory discourses and we could even recognise that some of Rebecca's recollections might actually originate in such popular depictions of the Holocaust. Her recollection of singing factory workers, for example, seems to come straight from Spielberg's film, and the handing over of a child on a railway platform is reminiscent of a scene from *Sophie's Choice* (Alan Pakula, 1982). By denying Rebecca authentic access to memories of the Holocaust, and having her express genuine trauma from what seem to be prosthetic memories, Pinter activates our recognition that our own awareness of these events, and the moral perspectives that they activate, are broadly constructed from mediatised fictions. In no other work of his is the political so deftly woven into the personal, and the synapse between life and art breached to activate ethical enquiry.[48]

When none of Devlin's interrogative or condemnatory strategies discharges Rebecca's troubled demeanour, he attempts to bring her back to the present. He does this by reminding her of her love of gardening, and asking about her visit to see her sister Kim and her toddler and baby. Again, family is used by Pinter as an index of harmony and completion, but the author inserts a fracture here to disallow any effective tonic: Kim's partner has been unfaithful and they are separated, with him begging to return. Rebecca participates in the conversation, but slowly slips back towards her perturbed behaviour. She states that she went to the cinema alone after visiting her sister (hinting at the possibility that her 'memories' are harvested from such experiences) and, speaking of the film she saw, describes scenes that are reminiscent of Bernardo Bertolucci's solemn *The Sheltering Sky* (1990), though she recalls other members of the audience taking it to be a comedy.[49] Rebecca then pulls her mind's eye back from the cinema screen and recalls that there was a man in the auditorium who sat rigid like a corpse. Her recollection begins to sound like the memory of a dream, with the deathly presence acting as an emblem of guilt. Devlin's attempts to pull her out of this reverie again fail, and the play moves to close with a detailed account of that baby that was torn from the arms of its mother. This time, though, Rebecca tells the story from the perspective of herself as the mother, only to finish by denying ever having had a baby. Her final utterances are punctuated by an echo of each line, obliging an audience to absorb each excruciating detail.

The final moments of the play are compelling and absorbing, and Pinter scaffolds a particular theatrical mode of closing that binds the lyrical, the hallucinatory and the implacable imagery of implied infanticide. All of his late plays – *Party Time*, *Moonlight*, *Celebration* and *Ashes to Ashes* – conclude with an epilogue of this sort which, in each case, seems to take place in a dramatic space at one remove from the location in which the preceding drama has taken place. Each play ends with a monologue delivered as if from some enclosed, unreal space, one that both entraps and defines the person speaking, and foregrounds the gulf between them and the world to which they might functionally belong. This feature of these plays' closing moments serves a number of dramatic purposes in each manifestation. Most straightforwardly, as with the variations applied to a coda at the end of a piece of music, it signals the impending closure of the work. In so doing, it also affects a final call for an audience's concentration, promising impactful concluding material. In *Ashes to Ashes* this concentration is further prompted by a focus-inducing change of lighting. Pinter specifies that the 'room darkens during the course of the play' and that the 'lamplight intensifies' so that '[b]y the end of the play the room and the garden beyond are only dimly defined'. Added to this, the lamplight beside Rebecca, as she delivers her final confession or memory, has become 'very bright' but notably 'does not illuminate the room' (393).

These epilogues have their antecedents most notably in the 'Schrödinger's cat' endings of *The Dumb Waiter* and *The Homecoming*, in which characters might proceed in numerous different manners once the curtain falls on the action. The closing moments of *Old Times* and *A Kind of Alaska* offer perhaps the most clear genesis of this structure, and the Father's voice in *Family Voices* or the voice-over vehicle employed in *Mountain Language* also animate utterances that speak or meet in spaces beyond the physical world. Deeley's desperate ballet between Anna and Kate in *Old Times* is the realisation of the scenario Anna had described previously, just as Devlin in the closing moments of *Ashes to Ashes* attempts to embody or appropriate the throat-grasping sadistic intimacy of Rebecca's imagined or remembered lover. Such performances within performances indicate the slippage the characters experience between what is real and what is inexpressible, and present desperate attempts to escape narrative. Deborah's final words in *A Kind of Alaska* begin with a lengthy description of walls closing in on her, as she describes the process of her illness slowly once more taking control of her. The drip that she imagines she hears, like a tap having been left on, recurs in Voice 3's perception of a dog barking, in Bridget's echoing bell, and in Jimmy's de-centred, faint heartbeat. Such auditory hallucinations evoke the enclosure of these characters' conditions, but also suggest the distance that they experience from those with whom they might enjoy communication. This effect is directly enacted in *Ashes to Ashes* through the addition of the echoes that repeat the ends of each of Rebecca's lines. With Devlin marginalised into the darkness, Rebecca's isolation here becomes all the more stark as she recedes into the post-traumatic reliving of an incident that never happened, 'a woman unable to escape the doom that seemed to belong to others. But as they died, she must die too'.[50] It is an utterly theatrical manifestation of a truth that haunts our cultures, a shared memory that none of us have experienced, an impossible bridge between memory and artifice, the personal and the political, and the most complete example in Pinter's oeuvre of art meeting truth meeting politics.

CHAPTER 6
SOME CONCLUDING REMARKS

When Harold Pinter directed his latest play *Celebration* at the Almeida Theatre in March 2000, he decided to mount it in double-bill with his first, *The Room*. For many this seemed a gesture of closure, a public acknowledgement that he perhaps recognised, approaching the age of seventy, that his work as a playwright was complete.[1] The sense of a retrospective appreciation of his life's work that the double bill incidentally promoted was in part accelerated by the context of the threshold between two centuries, and the nostalgic and reflective glance back at the twentieth century that was a part of much cultural activity and discussion at the time (and indeed embedded in that latest play). Two other significant stagings added to that sense of a public appreciation and appraisal of his career and legacy: the National Theatre in November 2000 mounted a production of *Remembrance of Things Past*, adapted from Pinter's unfilmed 1972 *Proust Screenplay*, while, across town at the Comedy Theatre that same month, a fortieth anniversary production of *The Caretaker*, directed by Patrick Marber, was staged to widespread acclaim. The celebration of his life's work continued into 2001 in London with further high profile productions of key plays, including a staging in July of *One for the Road* at the New Ambassadors Theatre (in which Pinter played the role of Nicolas) and a December production of *No Man's Land* at the National Theatre (which he directed). That production of *One for the Road* was prepared for a festival of his writing that was hosted by the Lincoln Center in New York, which would include productions of eight other of his plays, the screening of ten of his films, and symposia of discussion panels populated by guests such as Edward Albee, Ian Holm, Arthur Miller and Karel Reisz. On both sides of the Atlantic, clearly, something of a Pinter revival was very much underway, and such sustained acknowledgement of his lifetime's achievement must have consolidated and even rejuvenated his sense of artistic purpose. It was with all the more force, then, that the brakes were applied to his immediate ambitions when he learned in December 2001 that he needed to be treated for cancer of the oesophagus.

Though *Celebration* became his last play, he did write two more sketches: *Press Conference* (2002) and *Apart from That* (2006). Despite his ongoing treatment, Pinter performed the role of the Minister in the former as part of a National Theatre festival of his sketches in February 2002 (the character soberly embellished by Pinter's chemotherapy-induced hair loss) and offered a reading of the latter as an adjunct to a June 2006 interview on BBC's *Newsnight*. In addition to his uninterrupted political activities, he continued a modest output of poetry and completed two final film screenplays. The first, commissioned by Tim Roth, was an adaptation of William Shakespeare's *King Lear*, which he accomplished in 2000 but which remains unfilmed. The second, an adaptation of Anthony Shaffer's *Sleuth* was shot and released in 2007, directed by Kenneth Branagh. He makes a brief cameo appearance in it, his last as an actor on screen. The year before, in October 2006, he made what would be his last appearance as an actor on stage, in the title role of a production of Samuel Beckett's *Krapp's Last Tape* at the Royal Court Theatre, directed by Ian Rickson. The coupling of Beckett and Pinter, in that play and at that time, brought out all sorts of resonances to the stage and auditorium that rendered the performance all the more poignant. Those few hundred people who witnessed the production were invited to engage with the character of an ageing writer surrounded by the darkness of his impending demise, performed by an ageing writer who had recently survived not only cancer but a near-lethal bout of pemphigus vulgaris, both of which had palpably taken their toll on his once hardy frame, and audibly on his voice.[2] When, as the performance drew to a close, Pinter uttered the lines 'Perhaps my best years are gone. But I wouldn't want them back. Not with the fire in me now'[3] there was a potent meeting of life and art, captured in a historic and unique theatrical moment.

What this book has aimed to offer is an appreciation of the connection between Pinter's writing and common lived experience, communicated through the present-tense phenomenon of the performance event. In his Nobel Lecture, Pinter himself articulated a clear distinction between his approaches to art and to politics and, in so doing, expressed how the two activities are intertwined both in him as an artist and citizen, but by implication in all of us who digest cultural expression and are affected by political contexts. The sense of moral obligation Pinter foregrounds in relation to our awareness of (or selective blindness to) state control and oppression is effectively present across his oeuvre, which concerns itself fundamentally with how we treat one another and with how we care for one another, and the behaviours and forces that interrupt, distort or place such activities in jeopardy. His writing is at its most impactful when he used his art to expose and scrutinise the ideological discourses that govern our lives, and at its most emotionally affective when he examined the networks of care and interdependence that structure our bonds and relationships. Rather than categorise the plays into specific groups, this book has attempted to chart the developments of his chief thematic ambitions across his work and examine the evolution of certain lines of enquiry that he pursued as a writer. In so doing, the significant influence that working in a variety of media has had on his manipulation and structuring of the dramatic contract between a group of actors and their audience has been acknowledged and foregrounded.

One of the subtexts of this book, so to call it, is the manner in which Pinter's approach to dramatic form is integral to the success of the experience of his work: we appreciate his plays better if we consider what they do to us rather than what they might have to say. The first essay in the collection of four that now follows addresses that more explicitly. Actor and director Harry Burton offers some reflections on how Pinter's plays are structured to make their impression, and warns against the dampening effect of a reverence for the 'classic' status the plays now attract. His contribution complements the argument made in Chapter 1 that Pinter's early plays were innovative and unusual in the manner in which they sought to betray the conventions of audience investment in chief characters. Chris Megson offers an essay that introduces a perspective on Pinter's middle period of writing that adds to the survey given in Chapter 3. By considering *Old Times, No Man's Land* and *Betrayal* in the context of developments in British theatre criticism and practice of the 1970s, Megson also underlines the importance of form, and in so doing considers the nature of the confrontation that an audience must negotiate in those plays of interpersonal arbitration. Ann C. Hall takes up the momentum from my Chapter 2 and, responding to some of that examination of the discourses of gender, she applies further enlightening reflection on gender representation within the abrupt landscapes of Pinter's political plays. Her argument also speaks to the representations of family structure explored in Chapter 4, as well as offering some further nuances and illustrations to the evaluation of Pinter's politics given in Chapter 5. Basil Chiasson surveys that political territory further in his essay, which closes the volume, and considers how Pinter's political dramas encourage a critical response to how state power expresses and exerts itself. Together, in expanding or responding to some of the material and arguments from within the body of this book, these contributed essays participate in defining the impact and influence that Harold Pinter's work had during his lifetime, and the legacy that he leaves behind.

Reflecting on that legacy, fellow playwright David Hare claimed that 'Pinter did what Auden said a poet should do. He cleaned the gutters of the English language, so that it ever afterwards flowed more easily and more cleanly'.[4] Theatre director Richard Eyre argued that Pinter had 'entered our cultural bloodstream', and stated that from his writing he had learned 'that theatre was as much about the spaces between the words as the words themselves, that what was left off the stage was as important as what was put on it.'[5] In 1954, before Pinter's work was performed or published, Samuel Beckett had asked, 'And then what about silence itself, is it not still waiting for its musician?'[6] The question was intellectually rhetorical, a provocation to encourage a re-think of the proper constitution of dramatic material. Of all playwrights of the late twentieth century, it is perhaps not too fanciful to claim that Harold Pinter is the one who made the most robust and lasting response to Beckett's challenge. His skilful and measured deployment of pauses and silences as scaffold to the verbal intricacies of his characters is but one aspect of his range of theatrical strategies. In expanding the palette of writing for the stage beyond character and narrative, merging or retooling comedy and tragedy, and composing dramatic form that unsettles its audience by denying the fulfilment of generic expectations, the success of his writing paved the way for further experimentation. If he did subsequently become part of 'our cultural bloodstream', it was for more than being the reluctant source of a new adjective – the ill-defined 'Pinteresque' – but for being one of the few important writers who caused a shift in our understanding of what makes for effective, powerful dramatic writing.

CHAPTER 7
CRITICAL AND PERFORMANCE PERSPECTIVES

THE CURSE OF PINTER

HARRY BURTON

'First and finally, and all along the line, you write because you
want to write, have to write. For yourself'.

(Harold Pinter)[1]

Over the last two decades of his life, I was privileged to collaborate
with Harold Pinter on a number of projects. These were consistently
formative, exciting creative experiences which continue to exert a
deep influence on me professionally and personally. We were good
friends for over twenty years. An unfeigned interest in his fellows, as
well as a gift for loyalty ingrained in his character, made friendship
with Pinter a great blessing. In contributing the following chapter, I
am writing from this perspective of my first-hand contact with the
subject of this book and, while my chapter is therefore intended
primarily to offer a practitioner's perspective, I hope it may also serve
a wider usefulness.

Towards the end of his life Harold declared that he no longer
had the energy to direct plays. Perhaps this was true, but I remained
convinced that he still had an enormous amount to offer. So I
invited him to join me and a group of actors for an acting-in-Pinter
workshop. The idea clearly intrigued him, but with typical candour

he felt obliged to ask, 'What's a workshop?' It surprised me to learn that throughout his fifty-year career no one had ever asked him. Generally speaking, I told him, workshops are about the process rather than results. Happily he was persuaded to join.

In the end Pinter relished that first workshop. We subsequently repeated the process for a film called *Working With Pinter*, made in 2007 for Channel 4. I believe this was the only occasion where he allowed himself to be filmed with actors rehearsing scenes from his own plays. Pinter relished with an excited curiosity actors and directors discovering his work, not least because their doing so somehow empowered him to discover the plays afresh himself, an experience mingling nostalgia and renewal that gave him considerable pleasure. He encouraged and corrected us in a wonderfully open and collaborative spirit. He never asserted his considerable authority gratuitously, and took care to ensure that his observations of other people's work promoted the unfolding flow of discovery characteristic of productive rehearsals. These workshops enabled him to share freely from the immense storehouse of his experience. Alongside the intense business of rehearsal there was always a good deal of laughter and fun.

According to the publisher's contract my topic here is 'Pinter's Early Drama'. This sounds more like a headline from the sports pages rather than a juicy chapter in an indispensable volume. But given his youthful passion for sport perhaps it's not so inappropriate. After all he was a brutally effective schoolboy centre-forward; also an explosive sprinter, very proud of breaking the Hackney Downs School record for the hundred yards. But his abiding passion, sporting or otherwise, was cricket. As he once declared on BBC Radio's Test Match Special: 'Cricket was very much part of my life from the day I was born'.[2]

Combat, sporting or otherwise, is one of Pinter's signature metaphors. Territorial battle of one sort or another is a given in his plays. He brought with him into the world a fierce desire to compete, and was possessed of a brooding, combative drive to overcome an opponent through the imposition of his will. For Pinter the batsman this often resulted in a rush of blood and the loss of his wicket. But at tennis if he lost the first set he'd win the second without fail. His plays are peppered with duels, verbal and physical, while his movie scripts are spattered with brutal encounters on various tennis courts, ping-pong tables and cricket fields (to say nothing of violent country house scrimmages or bouts of Etonian dodgeball between servants and masters). Directors inclined to shy away from intensity and conflict beware: resistance is futile! If you don't know how to empower your actors to play dirty when it's necessary then you don't stand a chance with Pinter. But I'm getting ahead of myself.

To inject a dram of Jacobean excess into proceedings I'm calling this chapter 'The Curse Of Pinter'. Under the guidance of an inspirational English master, Joe Brearley, the adolescent Pinter was intoxicated with literature and language. He had already responded to a precocious calling as an erotic poet: 'I fell in love. Unhappily. When I was thirteen. And I wrote unhappy love poems. I never looked back'.[3]

As a schoolboy actor he tasted both the erotic intoxication of Romeo, and the murderous tyranny of Macbeth, familiarising himself in the process with archetypes whose echoes would recur in later works such as *Betrayal* and *One for the Road*. Aroused by Shakespeare's poetic authority, he was nothing short of obsessed by John Webster's debauched, death-drenched dramatic language. Webster's influence on the three plays Pinter wrote in 1957 is pervasive (at the time of writing *The Room*, *The Dumb Waiter* and *The Birthday Party* he wrote to a friend that playwriting had him by the balls), with their fantastic eruptions into torture, rape and murder.

Harold Pinter was a sensitive only child. He turned thirteen as Second World War entered its fourth year. For children it was a terrifying period to live through, despite the thrills of witnessing Hurricanes and Spitfires in dogfights with the Luftwaffe. To a child's restricted understanding of space and time it must have seemed unlikely ever to end. Wartime guillotined any sense of carefree childhood for a generation. Pinter experienced evacuation and separation from his parents as extremely distressing. The palpable presence of death in daily life was inescapable. Harold and his schoolmates were scarred veterans of bombing, trauma and terror. During a break from evacuation he watched from the house one night as a Luftwaffe incendiary set his garden ablaze.

Sex, too, became real during the war for the young Pinter. Even as the Germans carpet-bombed the East End, Pinter savoured his first erotic frisson huddled up to an older girl in a bomb shelter (perhaps that was when the love poems began). These early experiences of life and death intensely magnified had an electrifying impact on Pinter's febrile imagination. His camera-like memory began photographing everything he encountered, forever intermingling terror, danger, darkness, sex, excitement, violence, death. Clearly Harold was a very early developer, and not merely in a bomb shelter breathing in the heady female scent of a tender-hearted neighbour. His appetite for literature was similarly voracious, devouring Kafka, Dostoevsky, Hemingway, James Joyce. He scandalised his friends with Henry Miller ('There's a lot of defecating!' remarked Henry Woolf, aged sixteen, when Harold asked him what he thought of *Black Spring*). He introduced his gang to poets such as Dylan Thomas and George Barker. Before seeing anything much in the way of theatre, Harold joined a film club and fell in love with cinema, relishing the creepy surrealism of Buñuel, and American gangster Noir.

Such rich influences would add salt to any young self-identified writer, but with Pinter there are further dimensions to pay attention to. He was Jewish, as were most of the tight circle of friends surrounding him in adolescence. By the end of the Second World War British Jews could not doubt the fate that would have befallen them had a German invasion become reality. That horror was compounded (thanks to the perverted fairness of British democracy) by the release from internment of home-grown fascists who promptly renewed their brutalisation of Jews on the streets of the East End. Refusing to be cowed, Pinter and his mates skirmished more than once with Blackshirt goon-squads.

In 1948, aged eighteen, Pinter received call-up papers for his mandatory two-year stint of National Service. He refused outright, opting for trial by a Conscientious Objectors Tribunal. He took his toothbrush with him to the court, convinced he'd lose the case and be sent to jail. A remarkable personal statement to the Tribunal asserts his conviction that:

> As human beings we are bound to bring forth and foster that inherent wisdom and goodness which is endowed in us, and replenish and illumine our fellows with this spiritual realisation. Each person is compelled by this moral responsibility to hold sacred human life, to cast out fear, and to fulfil this existence as a creation out of the immense order of things. The position in society for one who believes in his responsibility as a Man is simple. He shall with great sorrow and love defend the innocent with physical sacrifice and moral enlightenment. But on no account shall he be the arbiter of another human's existence by taking arms. Nor shall he tarnish his soul by joining such a stupid, sorrowful organisation as the army. With these beliefs, it is therefore quite impossible for me even to contemplate such an act.[4]

Pinter's refusal to serve in the armed forces was his first substantial act of political conscience: a principled stand for which he was willing to sacrifice his freedom. Somewhat bewildered, his mother and father nevertheless stood by him ('His parents must have been so wonderful to him', an early girlfriend recalled, 'because he has never ever really doubted himself').[5] The courtroom drama ended in fines rather than prison. But here was not only intimate personal experience of a Kafkaesque encounter with unaccountable political authority, but also, more significantly, Pinter's personal admission into the freedom and responsibility of independent moral sovereignty.

The Court's asinine judgement stands as a perfect symbol of the dead traditions and 'shit-stained strictures'[6] of the establishment against which Pinter now set himself for life: 'This applicant was dogmatic and his statements did not show any sign of careful and conscientious weighing of pros and cons'.[7]

Pinter's formative experience of the world had set him by the age of twenty on a philosophical course that would only strengthen, never change. Raging with appetites, his soul fired up by a wild entanglement with poetry and language, he was an exuberant citizen of the world, involved deeply in its suffering. He recognised his own temperament well enough to realise he could never work in an office. But Joe Brearley and William Shakespeare initiated him into a passion for acting that lasted a lifetime. It also won him a scholarship to study at RADA, but the Royal Academy's snobberies were intolerable to him. After a few weeks he feigned a nervous breakdown and escaped:

> One morning at drama school I pretended illness and, pale and shaky, walked into Gower Street. Once round the corner I jumped on a bus and ran into Lord's at the Nursery End to see through the terraces Washbrook late-cutting for four, the ball skidding towards me. That beautiful evening Compton made seventy.[8]

If Pinter lacked the brazen chutzpah to inform his parents directly of his altered circumstances, they can hardly have harboured illusions about their self-possessed son's attitude to what he regarded as dead tradition. He comprehensively rejected synagogue after his Bar Mitzvah.

In recapitulating some of his formative history here I want to pull into sharp focus the natural political intelligence, reckless spiritual courage, and (at least to his mates) alarming sexual precocity of the young actor–poet preparing to make his entrance as a dramatist. By the age of twenty-six Pinter was married, a published poet, embarked upon an uncertain acting career, and completely broke. Constantly writing poetry and letters (some of his best letters from the 1950s are poems in themselves), he'd also undertaken an experimental rites-of-passage novel *The Dwarfs*, which Mark Taylor-Batty discusses at length earlier in this volume.

Pinter's discovery (around 1949) of Samuel Beckett's novel *Murphy* compelled him to hunt down and follow the Irishman's trail. He loved Beckett's humorous horror in the teeth of the ghastly nausea of life lived on life's terms, admiring his refusal to push away existential actuality in favour of the fake. Beckett was the dark room in which Pinter developed his own fundamental literary principle: 'So often below the word spoken is the thing known and unspoken'.[9]

A few years later in *Waiting For Godot* Beckett showed Pinter what was possible theatrically. He had somehow tunnelled into the very mystery of life and was not only writing from that place but getting laughs while doing it. Pinter yearned to join him there: 'What his writing was doing was walking through a mirror into the other side of the world which was, in fact, the real world, a writer inhabiting his innermost self'.[10]

Long before writing his first plays in 1957, Pinter's poems and prose were in the grip of the dramatic idea of the invasion of a room by someone or something from outside; an 'other' whose unsought presence generates irrevocable change for the room's occupants. This singular dramatic concept of occupied rooms and threats to their owners from external, alien forces never fades in his playwriting, it simply fragments and reconstitutes itself as the omnipresent, de-stabilising threat of *other* in one form or another. It's an obsession that synthesises his personal experiences of being targeted by the Germans for being British, the Blackshirts for being Jewish and the Establishment for being possessed of a fierce conscience, to say nothing of his political questioning about personal responsibility in a heinous, indifferent, godless world.

It was his friend Henry Woolf who pushed the hesitating playwright Harold Pinter off the cliff. They'd already discussed the idea for the play that became *The Room*, so when Bristol University's drama department offered Woolf space to direct a play, he exhorted Harold to take the plunge and write one. In its origins, its theatrical nature and reception, *The Room* almost serves as a kind of micro-cosmic lens through which to glimpse Pinter's entire playwriting career. The startling creation myth of the play tells us it was written at breakneck speed – four days if you believe Pinter, a mere forty-eight hours according to Woolf, who says:

> It must have been tightly packed within him. All those extraordinary ingredients that are in so many of his later plays were there, ready to come roaring out of the gun muzzle.[11]

Some of those ingredients originated from an incident at a party in Earl's Court (in the mid-1950s) when Pinter was taken to a flat to meet someone who turned out to be the writer Quentin Crisp. On the threshold a strange and unfamiliar sight burned itself into his imagination: two men, one in a kimono or feminine dressing gown, talking incessantly and fussing around the other, a very big man in working clothes, seated at a table, drinking tea and devouring a plate of fry.

Pinter's photo-memory captured both the scene's distinct oddness and its unexceptional domesticity. Clearly something was happening in that room. But what was that something's precise nature? Being the intruder, Pinter also sensed his own presence as an observer influencing the tension between the two men. He was mesmerised by the dramatic possibilities contained in the friction arising from people with different agendas occupying the same room. The action of his plays is always rooted in the unfolding of that unbearable tension, be it erotic, comic, violent, tragic or combinations of all these.

Returning at Woolf's instigation to the original image, Pinter seemed instinctively to write the play direct from the unconscious, as though stepping out of the path of something already in him; something primed to burst out into its own life. Pinter found he possessed an innate ability to give a kind of overseeing containment to an essentially autonomous creative process. Living images stored in his memory could be expressed onstage in theatrical form, image begetting image:

> I started at the top and at a certain point there was a knock at the door and someone came in and I had absolutely no idea who he was, who he might be or what he might say. I let it run, let it happen, and found it was the landlord. And then two visitors arrived and I didn't know what they were on about really, what they wanted, but they were just part of the whole atmosphere.[12]

In his playwriting process, the potency of the initiating image (usually a memory) is, once activated, amplified by Pinter's intense loyalty to the original spark of life it contains, eternally present in imagination. By means of that loyalty a field of possibility opens up where virtually anything can happen, rooted in a grain of truth, possessing its own integrity, but not anchored in cement; not linear or rational 'Truth' but, more ambiguously, a particle of something true for Pinter, liberated and fired by his imagination into new, previously unimagined forms.

It's understandable that some people are challenged by the idea that a writer of drama could possibly work like this. They imagine a playwright fully to be in conscious control of the creative process, able to command his or her characters to behave in the correct way for the situation to play out according to a pre-conceived outline (or plot, to use an old-fashioned word). And of course they're right. Plenty of dramatists can and do work in this way. But Pinter, emboldened by his many unsatisfactory experiences in rep of acting in humdrum plays to snoozing audiences, refused to take a proprietorial view of his characters. Whatever happened on stage had to be what his characters wanted to happen. His unerring commitment was to follow the clues they gave him, honouring their presence while trusting his poetic instincts and dramatic intuition:

> The explicit form which is so often taken in twentieth-century drama is cheating. The playwright assumes that we have a great deal of information about all his characters, who explain themselves to the audience. In fact what they are doing most of the time is conforming to the authors' own ideology. They don't create themselves as they go along, they are being fixed on the stage for one purpose, to speak for the author who has a point of view to put over.[13]

Whether it took two or four days, there's no doubt that Pinter was forced by circumstances to write *The Room* at great speed and without interfering with what came naturally to him: the opening up of a very spontaneous and direct channel into imagination. Throughout Pinter's career he had to wait (often for much longer than was comfortable) for the entirely unpredictable moment when a line of dialogue or an image suddenly detonated in his head like a little creative aneurysm. Once he could feel an image or a line of dialogue coming, his non-negotiable duty was to get to pen and paper as swiftly as possible, then hang on for dear life while the play poured out of him. There were many false starts and no methodical daily writing practice (in the Pinter Archive at the British Library there's a fascinating folder of openings that peter out). When the spark of an opening caught fire, a first draft could develop rapidly. Once it was on the page a ruthless process of drafting, shaping, cutting followed, as well as, crucially, the extremely precise refining of poetic language and rhythm. Pinter the actor road-tested every line of Pinter the playwright. Consequently his plays are rigorously wrought, finished and complete. This economy is at the heart of his style. Pinter the poet could work no other way, and his process remained essentially the same over fifty years of playwriting.

Actors love Pinter; his stylistic rigours require them to play at nothing less than their absolute best. Because ambiguity is frequently involved, he makes tremendous demands on performers to concentrate, to listen acutely, to remain constantly watchful for minute shifts in tension and feeling. Sometimes – even with a director present – it's impossible for an actor to be absolutely certain that one meaning is more important in a line than any other. Then he or she must attempt at least to accommodate that possibility and say (or perhaps *float*) the line allowing consciously for secondary meanings, but without sacrificing spontaneity and conviction. It's tempting for performers to assert certainty, because doing so feels somehow powerful. But if Pinter's lines are spoken too knowingly they lose some of their human essence, their truthfulness. Pinter's theatrical dynamite is subtext. But for subtext to do its proper work it can only ever be *revealed*, rather than overtly played. One way an actor can help such revealing is to play a specific thought with great imagination, commitment, and on the front foot (to use a sporting image). Pinter's ambiguous, multi-layered meanings can then reverberate and shimmer beneath the strong surface, subverting certainty in the murky depths beneath the audience's delight (or indeed horror).

A director's job is often therefore to encourage actors in Pinter to think a little quicker than might feel safe, so that the lines follow swiftly one upon the other, just as our own thoughts do when we're under pressure. Then the sudden stillness of a pause or a silence can truly do its work, as the tension between people re-aligns itself in the light of what has just been said or done. Technically for this swiftness of thought to be sustainable and become not simply speed for its own sake (which never helps), an actor requires a nimble mind and lungs like bellows to provide bellyfuls of air in support of every new thought and utterance.

Breathing is the secret of good acting. Without an influx of fresh oxygen to infuse each line with mental energy, an actor will overcompensate. When we push we inevitably unbalance the sense, losing energy at the very point where a typical line of Pinter (just as with Shakespeare) requires the vocal energy to surge and generate meaning towards the end of the sentence. The poet in Pinter offers up forms of language chosen with infinite care for their ambiguity, deliciously combining the sacred and the profane for actors to relish and play their shots all around the wicket (as Pinter might have put it). The process in rehearsal is one of seeking out rhythms to find and repeat, combinations of sounds and silences that can be played with an almost infinite variety of dynamics. Pinter very often finds himself delightedly hypnotised by the sounds in language, repeating a word three, four, five or more times during an interchange. Here are Goldberg and McCann torturing Stanley in *The Birthday Party*.

Goldberg Webber, you're a fake. When did you last wash up a cup?
Stanley The Christmas before last.
Goldberg Where?
Stanley Lyons Corner House.
Goldberg Which one?
Stanley Marble Arch.
Goldberg Where was your wife?
Stanley In –

Goldberg Answer.
Stanley (*turned, crouched*) What wife?
Goldberg What have you done with your wife?
McCann He's killed his wife!
Goldberg Why did you kill your wife?
Stanley (*sitting, his back to the audience*) What wife?[14]

By the sixth repeat of 'wife' Stanley is beginning to gibber, unsure what the word means any more. Here's a sequence from *A Night Out* between two young men indulging in a bout of verbal gymnastics:

Kedge Of course, he don't let much slip, does he, old Albert?
Seeley No, not much.
Kedge He's a bit deep really, isn't he?
Seeley Yes, he's a bit deep.
[*Pause.*]
Kedge Secretive.
Seeley What do you mean, secretive? What are you talking about?
Kedge You said yourself he was deep.
Seeley I said he was deep. I didn't say he was secretive![15]

In seven lines Pinter gives us four 'deeps' and three 'secretives' but there's a lot going on besides. Each time a word or sound is repeated an actor is tasked to find a subtle but real development from its previous utterance, a new shade of meaning and nuance. Why, after all, would Pinter (or any other poet) want a word to sound precisely the same each time it is repeated? Shakespeare loves these games too – think of Hamlet thrice repeating the phrase 'Except my life!' or Lear's five inconsolable howls. In other words, wordplay (humorous or otherwise) releases subtlety and depth, and Pinter loves it. The best reading of a line is sometimes most accurately assessed from the pleasure yielded by saying it with a certain cadence or emphasis of thought, or the weight of pause that follows before the next.

In rehearsing Pinter actors feel themselves stretched and emboldened, baffled and constrained, liberated and maddened until, line by line, they work to eliminate all wasted energy, all slackening of tension, make their choice and say the line with total commitment. Rehearsing Pinter feels almost like a plate-spinning act in a variety show. Starting out it's a real task just to get one or two plates to stay up. But, with exploration and repetition, what at first seemed impossible or unnatural begins to feel like second nature. Slowly but surely new plates can be spun with increasing confidence. Naturally all this is true to a greater or lesser extent whenever actors rehearse a play. But in Pinter, perhaps because his plays and characters brim with universally recognisable but nevertheless disturbingly extreme human motivation, these truths are somehow more visible than usual.

We go to watch and hear a play to see our human weaknesses and complexes amplified and mirrored back to us, made larger than life by acting, but still compelling and 'real'. Perhaps in Pinter we stare at aspects of ourselves we wouldn't normally be keen to admit to. Uncomfortable though it is, the audience nevertheless wants the same ruthlessness that Pinter wants from his actors. When it's right he rewards everyone generously.

Good actors want to be challenged by a writer, to feel themselves expanding and learning in response to a dramatic situation. It's worth remembering that Pinter served his own actor's apprenticeship with Anew McMaster and Donald Wolfit, two Titans of the old school, vast of voice and physicality, yet capable of fantastic delicacy. A great tragedian, McMaster actually saw in Pinter a possible successor to lead his company, such was Harold's promise and intelligence. Later when he came to write plays, Pinter understood actors wonderfully well. Instinctively he wrote to the far edge of a good actor's capability. Working with Pinter we feel ourselves growing and improving.

It's hardly surprising, therefore, that playing Pinter's characters and language requires a quality of presence that is exciting and demanding in equal measure. For performers he is, in that respect, like Shakespeare. His exacting economy (i.e. what's *not* said) goes hand in hand with his refusal to indulge in neat explanations, so there's plenty of ambiguity in the meaning of the lines. Consequently people demand to know what is being withheld, asking, for example (as a student asked me recently): 'What's Pinter *really* saying when Rose goes blind in *The Room*?', as though her spontaneous loss of sight is not in itself credible, and the author must therefore be using it to represent something else. In actuality, however, trauma-induced blindness is relatively well-documented. Pinter puts things in his plays we'd prefer not to think about (Meg groping Stanley when she takes him his morning cuppa), or that we find excruciating to watch (Ben bracing himself at the end of *The Dumb Waiter* to pull the trigger on Gus). But he never puts things in his plays that aren't credible and authentic to the world as he witnesses it.

Where ambiguity pervades and definitive meanings are elusive, actors can be encouraged to work intuitively, feeling their way towards an accommodation of textual tensions. Pinter's lines can rarely be spoken unselfconsciously, and yet they mustn't be overloaded. There has to be a shape and a rhythm, or the crucial tension goes slack. Great technical awareness – breath, diction, precision and economy of movement – are vital components in generating the highest possible stakes always demanded by a Pinter play. In acting terms we're describing neither naturalism nor realism but rather a moment-by-moment heightening of reality where language is presented, lifted, inflated, stylised, relished, embodied and released. In *The Dumb Waiter*, for example, Gus is transfixed by the horror of the impact on a woman's body of his assassin's bullet:

> **Gus** I was just thinking about that girl, that's all. (*He sits*) She wasn't much to look at, I know, but still. It was a mess though, wasn't it? What a mess. Honest, I can't remember a mess like that one. They don't seem to hold together like men, women. A looser texture, like. Didn't she spread, eh? She didn't half spread. Kaw![16]

This speech is a key moment in the play. There is enormous tension building between the two killers, leading to the terrible climax where one must shoot his partner. Slowly through the play Gus wakes up to the reality of his blind subscription to a murderous, unaccountable corporation. For the first time in his career he is considering what it is that he and Ben actually *do*. His new-found powers of reflection will have catastrophic consequences. The actor playing Gus must balance so much: the delicate pacing of the speech and its touching banality; the seeing of the girl so that everyone in the theatre sees her too; the repetition of 'mess' and 'spread', each re-stated sound increasing and intensifying the obscenity of what it describes; the necessary time taken for the finding of the word 'texture'; and finally judging the delicate theatrical power required to share his horror, so that the audience is ashamed for Gus, ashamed of itself for knowing, for having seen and shared in the girl's death, somehow complicit in the whole terrible act.

But when we talk about Pinter's language, we must also talk about its absence. Pinter was proud of his work and detested its reduction to the cliché *Pinteresque*. He felt the word was a curse. But any associative exploration of what *Pinteresque* might usefully mean immediately brings us face to face with his innovative use of pauses and silences.

Prior to Pinter, general theatrical convention was that rhythms and dynamics were the domain of the actor and director. Pinter broke with this by specifying on the printed page where characters paused and where there was silence. Both poet and actor, he took precise care in the shaping of every line and its relationship to the whole, feeling for the spaces between words, lines and people. Where these tensions seemed unmistakeable, he notated the script with 'Pause' to indicate a moment's breath or thought, and 'Silence' to suggest some (potentially deep) uncertainty as how to deal with whatever has just happened. In the documentary *Working With Pinter* he seized with purposeful relish the opportunity to stress that productions of his plays where written pauses and silences are treated as mere absences of action – timed suspensions of vitality – are extremely depressing for their author:

> I think these terms 'silence' and 'pause' have been taken much too far, and my wife calls them 'The Curse Of Pinter'. And I quite agree with her. These damn silences and pauses are all to

do with what's going on, what's happening, and if they don't make any sense then I always say cut them. In fact, when I act myself in my own plays, which I have occasionally, I've cut half of them actually. I've said this doesn't mean anything to me.[17]

The often desperate interactions of characters (Mr Kidd pleading with Rose to see blind Riley in *The Room*, or Stanley begging McCann in *The Birthday Party* to go for a friendly pint of Guinness, or Ben viciously striking Gus to silence his relentless questioning in *The Dumb Waiter*), the changing rhythms, the flow and ebb of tension, the shocks, climaxes and dying falls – all these are equally vital components of an integrated unity, a vision requiring balance and precision, control and relaxation.

The team assembled by Henry Woolf for the original Bristol production of *The Room* was exhilarated by the experience of working with a first play so instinctive, generous and downright weird. Here was a completely new voice exploring how speech is deployed by people as a means of self-defence in the vast minefield of human relationship; a writer striving to make a vivid theatrical impact by charging the everyday language of the ordinary world with a poetic immediacy, purity and economy. Henry Woolf remembers:

> We were immensely lucky because it was terra incognita, so when we did it, it got lots of laughs. The funnier the play is the more menacing it is. We were in the Garden of Eden. This play arrived and we let it speak for itself. And because Harold speaks in such a potent voice, it fell into its own shape.[18]

But Woolf also recalls a disturbing development in the short time between *The Room*'s first outing and its second production soon afterwards:

> When we first did *The Room*, the bloody mudwash of theories by people who realised something brilliant was going on and wanted to grab it and say it was theirs – people who said you

have to take this seriously because it's art – all that crap hadn't arrived yet. But as soon as my production was over another director remounted the play. The difference was there wasn't one laugh. And why? The Grim Hand of Reverence. Because this was 'Art' and 'Culture'. I've seen a lot of Pinter productions since that are dead and bear no relevance to ordinary life, or anything else.[19]

In a curious echo of Newton's law that every action has an equal and opposite reaction, it seems that, in certain circumstances, a Pinter play as naturally exciting and funny as *The Room* can in the wrong hands be rendered *not* very exciting, not at all funny, and pretty unnatural.

Woolf's Grim Hand Of Reverence was actually the earliest manifestation of a phenomenon later observed by Pinter's second wife, Antonia Fraser. It was she who subsequently coined the 'Curse Of Pinter':

We were having a rather glum de-brief after the press night of *Betrayal*. I've always considered the play very funny, unlike the rest of the world who took time to wake up. But apart from the sound of my own laughter, the performance had been received in unbroken silence. Harold and I were discussing the phenomenon of people saying nervously to me: 'I wanted to laugh but as it was Pinter, I knew I shouldn't!' I said: It's the Curse of Pinter.[20]

This curse seems to comprise at least two facets. The first (as observed by Woolf) is a tendency for certain productions to give off an aura of smug self-awareness that tells the audience: 'This is holy to *us*, the select few, and we don't care whether you get it or not'. Pinter creates a world on the page that requires tremendous theatrical energy to realise in production. That energy is thrilling and dangerous. It defies fakery. But if for any reason the danger is sidestepped (as it often is because of over-reverence), the play can come across as portentous, empty ritual. This numbing effect renders Pinter dreary, baffling and repetitive and is generally blamed on actors. More often it is the consequence of directors feeling intimidated by his reputation, or ambitious to enhance their own by superimposing themselves on his work. Consequently they sometimes fail to empower their actors to generate the right level and quality of presence.

The director's task is to guide the actors into the eye of the storm sometimes known as Pinterland. But sooner or later in the course of rehearsal a moment invariably arrives when an actor knows whether or not a director can help them. Plenty can't, unfortunately. Once an actor wises up, he or she will in effect put together a performance (if they're sufficiently skilful) designed to conceal the fact that they weren't sufficiently helped. The play is then hobbled and can't do the work it was intended to do, leaving the audience bored, irritated and mystified.

Another way to invoke the curse of Pinter is to distrust the author's theatrical nous, and ignore his own very helpful statement: *Everything to do with the play is in the play*. A case in point: in *The Dumb Waiter*, when the restaurant elevator crashes without warning into Gus and Ben's lives, the text tells us it contains only a note, which they take out and read. In a recent production, however, as well as the note the lift also contained a prominently displayed foot-high teddy-bear Guardsman, of a type sold to tourists from stalls near Buckingham Palace. Gus and Ben seemed not to notice it. It wasn't acknowledged in any way. Clearly the text doesn't refer to it. Yet the audience (many of whom were new to Pinter) could plainly see it, and naturally wondered about its significance (I wondered too, and I know the play). Afterwards several patrons expressed their bewilderment, feeling certain they'd failed to grasp an important reference. Not only did they feel stupid, they were pretty sure Mr Pinter had made them feel stupid deliberately. For whatever reason, the director did not trust the play on the page. The unfortunate result was that he wasted everyone's time.

The professional task of actors in a run is repeatedly to enter the world of the play wholeheartedly, compellingly, and speak their characters' lines with the spontaneity of someone speaking their thoughts aloud as if for the first time. But are they to banish the fluctuations of their individual lives and transform themselves into performing robots, giving the precise same reactions and line-readings at each and every performance? Or are they somehow to manage a collision of the personal with the prepared work, trusting that their life's experience can profitably mingle with the journey of a character through a story?

Most practitioners and audiences agree the quality of a performer's acting is a matter of presence expertly brought to bear: the timing of a line, the listening to another's speech, the space allowed for thought, the pace and precision of a cue picked up. The desired effect of all this cumulative onstage blending of instinct and technique is to generate the overwhelming sense of *something happening.* Thrilling productions of very good plays seem to bring together both the right kind of story and the right kind of character material for actors so that, with appropriate preparation, the illusion can be created of *something happening.* But to tell the truth this is not an illusion at all: something vital and essential *is* happening; the audience's disbelief is willingly suspended, and the fact that the play has been running for over fifty performances is utterly forgotten. We participate willingly in the self-evident illusion that whatever it is that's happening has never happened before; yet what is happening seems also somehow to be a particle of eternity, unfolding inevitably and forever, on this stage, before these spectators, *now.*

Writing and putting on plays is a risky business – almost as risky as buying a ticket to watch one. Theatre's maddening ephemerality is also the source of its powerful ritual magic. Eight times a week the lights dim as the actors (supported, lest we forget, by a director, a designer and a team of technicians) create the illusion of an often familiar story being told for the very first time.

Pinter wrote for everyone, but he had a prickly relationship with audiences. His experience in acting taught him a lot about the tortured, triangulated relationship between writer, actor and spectator. His repertory appearances in so many potboiler plays and thrillers gave him a sense of an apathetic audience who wanted not to be challenged but eased by a background hubbub of dialogue and decor into untroubled slumber. Pinter the dramatist decided to startle them awake. A really good production of a Pinter play *makes something happen.* The pauses crackle and fizz, the silences hold their tension until they're unbearable and someone *must* speak; the changes of pace and direction come thick and fast and the balance of power seems to jag around viciously, never maintaining a straight course but continuously shimmering and shifting.

Each audience member comes into the theatre from a different world, a different day, to form a single listening body. The actors enter via the stage door to gel into a single storytelling unit. They are also subject to life's vacillations. But the agreement struck in the purchase of a ticket gives the audience the right to require that the actors embody in their acting the essence of humanness, true to life but also necessarily inflated and magnified to penetrate the audience's chest. I like David Mamet's remark that:

> [Pinter] understands the drama as a poem which [has] the capacity to move, as does a real poem, musically – to affect on a pre-rational level.[21]

Mamet's is a radical proposition: that Pinter's theatrical poetry, always probing man's moral responsibility to his fellow, is somehow capable of connecting with the audience on an instinctive level. If, through some freakish aspect of his instinctual nature, Pinter is able to write directly from the unconscious; and if, as Jung and others have proposed, there exists in the human psyche a mutual layer where the contents of humanity's accumulated mythic imagination are stored, then far from being unique to him, Pinter's characters are actually components of the universally shared contents of the Collective Unconscious. This suggests that despite often claiming not to understand what the play means, we, the audience, actually fully understand all that is happening in Pinter's plays *on a pre-rational level.*

This is problematic, since we civilised folk go to the theatre after a gruelling day teaching children, or grafting in an office or working in a hospital, in order to be entertained, delighted and taken out of ourselves. But *The Room* takes place on a freezing winter's afternoon in a depressing, sparsely furnished room heated by a single gas fire in a large, unprepossessing, not to say diseased house somewhere in London. The two bloodless killers in *The Dumb Waiter* are stuck in a godforsaken basement in darkest Birmingham, a city considered one of the most depressing in the known universe. In *The Birthday Party* Pinter's deeply unappealing crew of characters co-exist in a greasy, sexually deranged boarding house somewhere near the seaside. As for the décor in *The Caretaker* or *The Homecoming*, let's not even go there.

The unavoidable reality of these plays is that they take place in some of life's more sordid sewers inhabited by people we civilised theatre-goers would prefer to pretend did not exist. And yet we know they *do* exist, and Pinter knows we know. We recognise *on a pre-rational level*, furthermore, that we share the world and tube trains and pavements with these ghastly people, and yet here we are in the theatre being forced by an uppity existentialist poet-dramatist to spend our hard-earned money and leisure time in the company of these disgusting, disturbed and broken people whose lives are disintegrating before our disbelieving eyes. Are we supposed to be grateful? Is this what the world has come to? No wonder immaculately dressed audiences sit in reverent silence and refuse to laugh, believing themselves to be a privileged elite indulging their preferred art form. The laughter of a Pinter audience is more often than not (with these early plays anyway) the laughter of recognition. But if you can't bring yourself to look in the mirror, recognition and the opening to humanity it brings are off the menu.

Apart from the famous story of Pinter's career almost ending before it had begun (with the play's disastrous run at the Lyric Hammersmith), the curious thing about arrival of *The Birthday Party* is that the experience of *The Room* was reversed: this time the first production was a dud. (Pinter blamed the design which undermined the grimness of Meg and Petey's grotty boarding house by adding a spiffing conservatory. Director Peter Wood defended it saying every house on the south coast had one.) The play's second production was directed in the round at Scarborough (at the instigation of Stephen Joseph, Pinter's tutor from the Central School of Speech and Drama) by the author, who restored the play to its rightful blend of violent menace and nightmarish vaudevillian comedy.

Pinter cast a young actor called Alan Ayckbourn in the role of Stanley Webber. In his delicious account, Ayckbourn tells how one rehearsal lunchtime the cast took Pinter to a pub to pump him about the play's deeper meaning. But before they could get going on Harold and his play, a wild-eyed man tore into the bar in a state of high agitation and appealed to the group for help. Pinter enquired what was up. The man told how, having found his mother-in-law searching for his hidden wage packet in the fireplace, he had flown into a rage and stuffed her up the chimney before fleeing the house in fear. Pinter, always a gifted listener, sympathised with the chap, but advised him quickly to go and retrieve the woman, or face a possible murder charge. Suddenly awakened to what he'd done, the man ran out. The silence that followed his exit was broken by someone saying: 'What an extraordinary bloke!' Pinter's reply: 'Was he?'

Maybe Ayckbourn's anecdote is the best available answer to the many questions posed by actors and audience about the meaning of Pinter's characters and dramas, especially regarding the early work. With their mystery and menacing poetics, it's natural for such questions to arise around these plays. But although Pinter obviously wrote from a remarkable and singular imagination, deeply penetrated by the influences of Webster, Dostoevsky, Kafka, Henry Miller, Hemingway, Joyce, Buñuel and Beckett, he also wrote direct from life. So while we may feel we *need* definitive answers and concrete conclusions, it's as well to remember that, in life, our turbulent disturbances often resist rationalisation and refuse to be explained away. In the years between his release from school and beginning life as an actor, Pinter was a rogue poet-prince of the bombed-out city, roaming hungrily about London's rubble, rubbing up against raw humanity in its dark, ruined places. Disturbed and disturbing characters populate the plays not least because in life he attracted them to him, just as something in them pulled him in.

So the Curse of Pinter is also modernity's curse, namely our collective abandonment of metaphor and mythic imagination, overwhelmed by an unconscious urge to conform to standardised ways of seeing, triggered into our terrified reflex to concretise the imaginal world. Responsibility for answering the question so often directed at the Pinter – 'What does it mean?' – is in fact our own. How do *we* cope when disturbed by encounters with unsettling people? What questions, emotions and meaning are we left with? What if we ourselves are the disturbed, unsettling people we fear so much? Renewed conscience, and conscious acceptance of our responsibility for one another, is Harold Pinter's living legacy. His absence leaves a deep space proportionate to his presence. But death can never diminish the marvellous vitality of his greatest poems: his plays.

'WHO THE HELL'S THAT?': PINTER'S MEMORY PLAYS OF THE 1970s

CHRIS MEGSON

'Apart from any other consideration, we are faced with the immense difficulty, if not the impossibility, of verifying the past. I don't mean merely years ago, but yesterday, this morning ...'.

(Pinter, 1962)[1]

Pinter's playwriting of the 1970s is celebrated for its vertiginous treatment of time and memory, and its evocation of the enigma of identity. The decade saw a consolidation of Pinter's reputation, in part due to his association with Peter Hall who took over the artistic directorship of the National Theatre in 1974. By the turn of the 1970s, Hall was already an experienced director of Pinter's work: he had staged *The Homecoming* (in 1965), *Landscape* (1969) and *Silence* (1969), and had also collaborated with Pinter on the stage adaptation of *The Collection* (1962). Hall's approach to the directing of Pinter's plays – described retrospectively by one critic as 'an austere, difficult, at times almost self-reflexive modernist refinement' – reached its apotheosis during the 1970s in response to new departures in Pinter's dramatic writing.[2] In an interview published in 1971, Pinter explained the nature of his intensifying preoccupations: 'What it all comes down to is time. [...] The whole question of time and all its reverberations and possible meanings really does seem to absorb me more and more'.[3] This chapter explores Pinter's absorption with time in three of his landmark plays of the decade which together anatomise 'the whole question of time' through different kinds of dramaturgical innovation. These are *Old Times* (RSC, Aldwych Theatre, 1971), *No Man's Land* (National Theatre,

Old Vic, 1975) and *Betrayal* (National Theatre, Lyttelton, 1978), all of them directed by Hall and all of them revived frequently.[4] In spite of their formal variances, these plays throw into question the premises of identity and locate memory as a dynamic process implicated in subtle or overt claims to power.

Old Times, No Man's Land and *Betrayal* might at first appear to be entirely sequestered from the large-scale, left-leaning playwriting ascendant in subsidised theatres during the 1970s. When Pinter began, in the 1980s, to assert that many of his earlier plays were in fact political – insofar as they engaged with forms of authority and violence – it is notable that he excluded his so-called 'memory plays' from this categorisation.[5] Given their focus on existential unease, interior life and the fraught territories of the domestic, his equivocation in this respect is understandable but the memory plays are in fact deeply implicated in their socio-political context in ways that have been largely unacknowledged to date. Ian Smith rightly observes that Pinter's writing of the 1970s 'examines images of English cultural life and identity which are viewed often through an acute sense of personal loss and a troubling, retrospective uncertainty'.[6] Indeed, it is the tropes of 'loss' and 'uncertainty' about the past that bring Pinter's playwriting of this period into correspondence, albeit obliquely so, with that of his younger contemporaries such as David Hare and Howard Brenton. As Hall put it in an interview in 1974, '[Pinter] is a very pessimistic dramatist but I don't really understand how anybody could honestly be writing in the 1960s or 1970s and be particularly sunny'.[7]

Aside from the plays' contribution to the pessimistic undertows of 1970s theatre, their focus on memory and its impact on character carries special import at this historical juncture. In the early 1970s, the word 'identity' was charged with specific kinds of political resonance due, principally, to the impact of feminism, the nascent campaign for lesbian and gay liberation, the anti-colonial movements, and the proliferation of class- and student-based activism. In his assessment of Pinter's early work, John Stokes offers the following perceptive observation:

> The current orthodoxy which insists that what we call 'identity' is exclusively determined neither by social nor by

biological pressures (nor even by a combination of both), but is actively constructed out of ideas – of class, or race, of gender, and of sexuality in particular – has led to a concern with the power of language that has made us at the millennium even more sensitive to the ways in which political power operates, at every level and in every sphere.[8]

From the early 1970s, the upsurge of identity politics in Britain – with its clarion call of 'the personal is political' – was important in enabling (often) minority groups to increase their visibility in the public sphere and, through forms of collective affiliation, protest and awareness-raising activity, to confront the historical roots of injustice on the grounds of class, race, gender and sexuality. The central claim of identity politics – that no vector of experience, including domestic or sexual experience, exists outside the operations of power or is immune from the determining influence of social structures – inspired many of the young theatre workers emerging from the counterculture and Civil Rights movements of the 1960s. This resulted in the creation of a number of 'alternative' theatre companies with a commitment to feminist and/or gay activism early in the decade. Moreover, by the mid-1970s, one of the principal vehicles for the articulation of identity politics in British subsidised theatres was the 'state of the nation' play, exemplified by large-scale dramas such as David Edgar's *Destiny* (1976) and David Hare's *Plenty* (1978). These plays offer a panoramic perspective on Britain's post-war history and an analytic scrutiny of that history – usually channeled through the experience of a protagonist or small group of representative characters – within a broadly social realist aesthetic frame. At a time when personal identity was being increasingly figured as a locus for class and sexual politics, Pinter's playwriting, while continuing to spotlight the shifting transactions of power and desire in domestic space, was becoming more attuned to what Austin Quigley calls 'the precarious status of the self'.[9] This point is critical: in challenging stable, continuous or essentialised notions of self – that is, in staging the self's 'precarity' – Pinter's theatre of the 1970s unsettles the shibboleths of identity politics even as it reinforces the perception (borrowing from Stokes) that 'political power operates [through language] at every level and in every sphere'. In Pinter's plays, and most forcefully in his memory plays, identity is not the aggregation of various social or biological determinants or traceable causalities, nor is it the marker of an 'authentic' self struggling into public visibility. Rather, identity is performative, constituted in shadowy processes of interlocution. Intrinsic to this fluid notion of identity is memory, which is conceived as a complex mode of self-presentation where emotions and expedients intersect, moment by moment, to exert control of the present.

'When the curtain goes up on one of my plays', remarked Pinter in 1960, 'you are faced with a situation, a particular situation, two people sitting in a room, which hasn't happened before, and is just happening at this moment, and we know no more about them than I know about you, sitting at this table'.[10] This comment is notable for its sense of character rooted in momentary time and devoid of verifiable history. The idea of theatrical performance as reducible to an encounter between enquiring spectators and unknowable strangers on stage finds acute expression in a number of Pinter's short but influential plays from the late 1960s; these pieces are significant because they foreshadow in structure and tone Pinter's major works of the following decade. In the revue sketch *Night*, for example, first presented as part of *Mixed Doubles* (a collection of eight plays) at the Comedy Theatre in 1969, a man and a woman attempt to reconstruct their memory of an earlier rendezvous but find it impossible to reach consensus about the events that may or may not have taken place. The piece gathers sustenance, not from the event in the past it ostensibly seeks to reconstruct, but from the erotic impulses that suture the duo's exchange in the present, especially in its poignant closing stages when both speakers unite in an intimate profession of lyric sensuality. A more substantial play is the one-act *Landscape*, directed by Guy Vaesen for BBC Radio in 1968 and then by Hall for the RSC at the Aldwych Theatre in 1969. Here, two speakers, Beth and Duff, sit on either side of a kitchen table against a 'dim' evening light.[11] Pinter's note on the play specifies that, although Duff speaks about Beth, he *'does not appear to hear her voice*' while Beth '*never looks at Duff, and does not appear to hear his voice*' (166). The stage image infers a level of dialogic correspondence between the two speakers but the visual composition of the scene quarantines each individual in the stage space and, for the most part, both engage in introspective recollections. In the opening speech of *Landscape*, past and present tenses coalesce in Beth's memory narrative dispersing her commentary inside and outside of the experience that is recounted. The image structure, which embraces sea, sand, rain, trees, ducks, dogs and butterflies, posits a notion of self bound inextricably to landscape, which itself is a resource for the artistic imagination. Beth:

> I drew a face in the sand, then a body. The body of a woman.
> Then the body of a man, close to her, not touching. But they
> didn't look like anything. They didn't look like human figures.
> The sand kept on slipping, mixing the contours. (178)

The making of art in *Landscape* becomes a metaphor for the alchemical processes of memory which 'mix the contours' of past and present. In *Silence*, the companion piece to *Landscape* and directed by Hall alongside it, one of the trio of speakers, Rumsey, parses his encounter with strangers in a way that recalls Beth's commentary:

> So many ways to lose sight of them, then to recapture sight of
> them. They are sharp at first sight ... then smudged ... then
> lost ... then glimpsed again ... then gone.[12]

The word 'smudged' echoes Beth's 'mixing the contours': in both instances, the human figure is rendered fleeting and blurred, resistant to recuperation through the labyrinthine workings of memory or the imaginative distillations of art. When Beth in *Landscape* describes the relationship between light and shadow in her artwork, she claims that '[s]ometimes the cause of the shadow cannot be found' (186): her observation, of course, points to the nebulous causality in the play as a whole where the numerous pauses that punctuate the spoken dialogue (the linguistic corollary of shadows in painting) mark particular intensities of feeling beyond words. The textual fragments at the end of *Silence* – a collation of snippets from earlier in the play – create a kaleidoscope of recollection or, as the critic John Barber describes the scene in performance, '[a] muted reverie, scored from themes stored in the rag-and-bone shop of memory'.[13]

The speakers in *Night, Landscape* and *Silence* occupy a liminal space between here and elsewhere, past and present, memory and imagination, where impulses to speak arise from uncertain histories and motivations. In Chapter 3 of this volume, Mark Taylor-Batty comments that, in the 1960s, 'Pinter's [...] experience in writing for the cinema was to offer him renewed creative avenues of exploration for his writing for the stage'.[14] This point is vital to an appreciation of the wider cultural topography in which Pinter's memory plays are situated. It is clear, for example, that *Landscape, Silence* and *Old Times* share thematic, philosophical and stylistic correspondences with New Wave cinema of the 1960s, perhaps especially the work of the French art house film director Alain Resnais. Resnais's *L'Année dernière à Marienbad* (*Last Year in Marienbad,* 1961) is a monumental intertext and key point of reference for students of Pinter's theatre of the 1960s and 1970s: set in an exquisite baroque hotel, the film is startling in its ambiguous treatment of time and depiction of the inscrutable relations between three characters (a woman and two men) who seem marooned in different versions of a shared past. Joseph Losey, who directed Pinter's screenplays *The Servant* (1963), *Accident* (1967) and *The Go-Between* (1971), and also collaborated with Pinter on *The Proust Screenplay* (published 1978), is the artist who connects Resnais to Pinter: Losey's films, at least in part, are indebted to the former's innovative filmic explorations of time and memory.[15] Pinter's achievement in his memory plays is to create recognisable but de-naturalised theatrical worlds, compelling in their structural ingenuity and emotional depth, which arbitrate similar preoccupations.

Old Times is set on an autumn evening in a remote, converted farmhouse. Two sequential lighting states open the play: the first – '*Light dim*' – brings into view an emblematic tableau of three figures on stage; the second – '*Lights up* [...]' – signals the start of the action proper.[16] In the opening moments, Anna stands upstage by the window but the ensuing dialogue between the husband and wife, Deeley and Kate, implies that she is at this point physically absent from the scene. As Taylor-Batty observes in Chapter 3, the ontological status of Anna in *Old Times* is by no means secure: 'Is she actually there, in the room with them [...] or does she occupy some liminal, theatrical space, presenting only symbolic value, on stage but not quite in the scene?'[17] Anna might be regarded as an incarnated memory or revenant – a view favoured by Peter Hall who argues that '[Anna's] not there, in actual, naturalistic terms, but she is there because she's been there for twenty years in each of their heads' – or else a projection from the unconscious of one or both of the married couple.[18] Act Two moves further into the interior of the house (the bedroom) but the spatial layout of doors and furniture remains the same as in the previous act, except that the sofas have been replaced by divans, and the divans and armchair are '*in reversed positions*' to the sofas and armchair in Act One (285). The near-identical configuration of theatrical space across the play, along with the similar arrangement of furniture, infuses the setting with a Sartrean air of entrapment and claustrophobia. This sense of indeterminacy in place and time in *Old Times* is also present in *No Man's Land*. In regard to the latter play, Peter Raby draws attention to 'the metaphorical everywhere and nowhere suggested by the title':[19] from the start, Hirst's room is hermetically sealed off from the outside world with its '[h]eavy curtains across the window'[20] and the stage directions for Act One give minimal information about time ('Summer. / Night') (319); Act Two, meanwhile, takes place the following morning yet Spooner's cryptic opening lines draw attention not only to his sense of *déjà vu* but also – in a reflexive theatrical flourish – to the atmosphere of menace that is a renowned feature of Pinter's work: 'I have known this before. Morning. A locked door. A house of silence and strangers [...] I have known this before. The door unlocked. The entrance of a stranger. The offer of alms. The shark in the harbour' (363–4). The motif of circularity, of a merry-go-round of emotions and repeated patterns of behaviour, was also inscribed in John Bury's design for the original production of *Betrayal*, which took place on a revolving stage.[21] In all three plays, then, theatrical space is denuded of naturalistic detail and the audience's experience of time is dislocated. Within this pared-down stage environment, intimate relationships are fissured by confrontation.

Old Times stages a contest between Anna and Deeley to appropriate Kate, to fix her identity through their apparently whimsical and sometimes contradictory recollections. In the end, this contest affirms Kate's status as the centrifugal force in the play: as the actor Barry Foster notes, '[t]he part of [Kate] becomes central, her intelligence, her beauty … She's a magnet. They're revolving around her, and she just *is*. She is ontological! She's *it*'.[22] Foster's point is that, unlike Anna, Kate's presence in the play is ontologically inviolable but his remarks overlook that fact that the audience's perception of Kate is filtered through the febrile interactions of Anna and Deeley. When Anna begins to speak, the tension between her and Deeley is palpable as each struggles to define Kate in their own terms:

> **Deeley** It's nice I know for Katey to see you. She hasn't many friends.
> **Anna** She has you.
> **Deeley** She hasn't made many friends, although there's been every opportunity for her to do so.
> **Anna** Perhaps she has all she wants.
> **Deeley** She lacks curiosity.
> **Anna** Perhaps she's happy.
> *Pause.* (261)

Early on, Deeley describes Kate as a woman who, in the past, 'lacked any sense of fixedness, any sense of decisiveness, but was compliant only to the shifting winds, with which she went' (273). Deeley's reminiscence about Kate's lack of fixity, her languid fusion with nature, echoes Beth's mixing of the contours of sand in *Landscape*. Kate's remarks shortly afterwards, which are bedded into one of the longest speeches in the play, express a similar sensibility:

> That's one reason I like living in the country. Everything's softer. […] There aren't such edges here. And living close

to the sea too. You can't say where it begins or ends. That appeals to me. I don't care for harsh lines. I deplore that kind of urgency. [...] The only nice thing about a big city is that when it rains it blurs everything, and it blurs the lights from cars, doesn't it, and blurs your eyes, and you have rain on your lashes. That's the only nice thing about a big city. (297)

Kate finds refuge in blurred perspectives, specifically the myopic vistas induced by rain, and her impressionistic imagination encapsulates the condition of memory dramatised in the play. The act of remembering, the transposition of lived experience into historicised personal narrative, is an intervention in reality that can serve expedient purposes in the here and now: to remember is to embark on a drama of self-presentation that is responsive to present priorities. Memory also, of course, carries an affective force whether or not it is submissible to evidential verification. As Anna puts it, '[t]here are some things one remembers even though they may never have happened. There are things I remember which may never have happened but as I recall them so they take place' (269–70). In this respect, the act of recollection is invested with world-creating properties inflected by desire and imagination. Anna's comment also exemplifies one of the distinctive features of Pinter's dramaturgy: memories are weaponised, they are the artillery of relentless interpersonal combat. This point is illustrated towards the end of *Old Times* when Kate, in her final speech to Anna, mobilises the rhetorical apparatus of remembrance to 'kill off' the latter:

But I remember you. I remember you dead.
Pause
I remember you lying dead. You didn't know I was watching you. I leaned over you. Your face was dirty. You lay dead, your face scrawled with dirt, all kinds of earnest inscriptions, but unblotted, so that they had run, all over your face, down to your throat. (309–10)

What is envisioned here is both a literal and figurative commemoration of Anna: 'literal' because the speech instantiates Kate's split with her former flatmate and seems to consign their intimacy to history – her words, as it were, cement their relationship in the past tense; 'figurative' because her testimony takes the form of an extended metaphor of abjection. Following her apparent demise, Anna's presence in Kate's memory narrative is supplanted by that of a man (perhaps Deeley). Kate describes him lying in Anna's bed and her subsequent attempt to smear his face with soil from the window box:

> He was bemused, aghast, resisted, resisted with force. He would not let me dirty his face, or smudge it, he wouldn't let me. He suggested a wedding instead, and a change of environment. (311)

Kate's wording – 'scrawled', 'unblotted', 'smudge' – reinforces her dislike of edges and lines but also evokes art, particularly writing: the speech registers her accession to power as the author of her own fantastical memory narrative. In its aftermath, a symphony in gradations of silence is played out through wordless choreography, quiet sobbing, stillness and a series of tableaux (311–13). In his review of the first production of the play, J. W. Lambert focuses on this final sequence: 'Alone, pulsing with merciless white calm, Kate remains, expressionless at the centre of perhaps the most piercing stage picture I have ever seen, creator and destroyer in one'.[23] The final stage direction – '*Lights up full sharply. Very bright*' (313) – is reminiscent of a camera flash: an indelible experience frozen at the point of its recession into history. The minimalism and intensity of the play led some critics to interpret the characters in terms of archetypal masculine and feminine forces, a perception endorsed by Hall's remarks in an interview of 1974: 'I must emphasise that most of what I'm talking about is making shapes out of instincts'.[24] John Simon, in similar vein, describes the characters as 'shadowboxing shadows'.[25] However, other commentators found *Old Times* too rarefied in style to be convincing as a viable portrait of human relationships, with

T. E. Kalem arguing that '[o]ne could scarcely care less about this flaccid trio. The blood of life does not pump through them. They are reveries and idle speculations posing as people'.[26]

No Man's Land also gains traction from its inquisitions on identity but, in this play, the inaccessibility of the past produces a haunting oscillation between memory and death, particularly from within the marinated reveries of alcohol-fuelled nostalgia. The initial exchanges of Spooner and Hirst are dominated by the former's garrulous articulations that seek to gain a foothold on the latter's identity: 'I haven't sufficient evidence to go on yet', Spooner concedes early on when commenting on Hirst's facility with the English language (325). The struggle to acquire a perspective on strangers, to rupture the carapace of anonymity, is further emphasised when Spooner talks in florid terms about his voyeuristic activities on Hampstead Heath:

> you can't keep the proper distance between yourself and others, when you can no longer maintain an objective relation to matter, the game's not worth the candle, so forget it and remember that what is obligatory to keep in your vision is space, space in moonlight particularly, and lots of it. (325)

In Spooner's terms, lived experience, especially in its recollection, is inescapably subjective. As the conversation proceeds, helped along by seemingly inexhaustible amounts of liquor, Spooner seizes on the moment when Hirst appears to disclose information about his own past since this opens up the prospect of intimacy on the grounds of shared experience:

> **Spooner** I am enraptured. Tell me more. Tell me more about the quaint little perversions of your life and times. Tell me more, with the authority and brilliance you can muster, about the socio-politico-economic structure of the environment in which you attained to the age of reason. Tell me more.
> *Pause.*
> **Hirst** There is no more. (336)

The patter 'about the socio-politico-economic structure of the environment' gestures sardonically towards the sociological dispositions of identity politics but Hirst blocks the invitation to elaborate further detail. At this point, Spooner changes tack and makes another attempt to open up Hirst's past life, this time by focusing on his wife: 'I begin to wonder whether you do in fact truly remember her, whether you truly did love her, truly caressed her, truly did cradle her, truly did husband her, falsely dreamed or did truly adore her' (337). Spooner's rhapsodic imaginings, accentuated in baroque prose, fortify his confidence to the degree that he is able, finally, to cast himself in a role that seems to guarantee future congeniality with Hirst: 'I offer myself to you as a friend' (339). Despite his symptoms of amnesia, and after returning from a temporary paralytic exit, Hirst proclaims the integrity and 'solidity' of memory by citing as proof the photographs in his precious album:

> My true friends look out at me from my album. I had my world. I have it. Don't think now that it's gone I'll choose to sneer at it, to cast doubt on it, to wonder if it properly existed. No. We're talking of my youth, which can never leave me. No. It existed. It was solid [...]. (351)

The photograph album extends the promise of an authentic past but can never wholly satisfy the nostalgic desire to recover history. The text of the play shuttles between images and tropes of liquidity and ossification, movement and paralysis, transformation and stagnation: memory is a 'no man's land', actualised in the present as both dead weight and galvanizing force. There is a comic sequence in Act Two when Hirst and Spooner appear to improvise their youthful memories of women with names such as Stella Winstanley ('Bunty Winstanley's sister') (377) and Arabella Hinscott in the clipped, Wodehousian language of old-school aristocrats ('I wrote my homage to Wessex in the summerhouse at West Upfield') (381). Gradually, however, Hirst's ruminations about the past and the fixed identities he associates with youth ('In my day, nobody changed. A man was') (382) direct attention once again towards the deceased people pictured in his photograph album. For Hirst, photography is a repository and preservative of memory, an intimation of mortality and, above all, a means of communion with the dead. The atmosphere in this scene darkens, in spite of the presence of Hirst's bullish 'helper' Briggs, and the language itself appears to frost over ('Allow the love of a good ghost. They possess all that emotion … trapped') (383). Briggs's response to the images of the dead is more prosaic: 'They're blank, mate, blank. The blank dead' (383).

As the play moves to its conclusion, Spooner uses the personal pronoun to assert his individuality and solicit employment as Hirst's secretary: 'I ask', 'I remain', 'I admit', 'I mean', 'I shall', 'I will' (392–5). However, Hirst subtly unsettles this grasp at autonomy by claiming to have seen a body floating in water only to discover that, after all, the body was not there (Spooner identified himself previously as the body in Hirst's dream). The ending of the play amplifies the eponymous motif of living death: 'No. You are in no man's land. Which never moves, which never changes, which never grows older, but which remains forever, icy and silent' (399). As Craig Raine puts it in his review for the *New Statesman*: '*No Man's Land*, it seems to me, is the inner landscape of the old – when life has stopped but existence goes on'.[27]

Betrayal constructs an altogether different framework for animating the relationship between past and present. The play up-ends conventional dramatic structure by reversing chronology and, in so doing, tracks the interactions of three characters backwards in time over nine years to the foundational moment of causality – namely, the start of the affair between Emma and her husband's friend, Jerry.[28] The play's procedure is thus archaeological: the trajectory into the past excavates the history of the relationships, re-framing our understanding of earlier scenes, and this palimpsest structure creates an emotive context for audience engagement. As Anthony Roche explains:

> The audience are the ones who most fully occupy the role of revenant, witnessing each scene of the 'unwinding' of the dramatic event in its intensity, bringing the knowledge of

future events to a reading of each scene's 'present' which – far from conferring a detached god-like perspective – enforces a great empathy with what is gone through.[29]

The skein of 'betrayal' ensnares all of the characters in the play. In scene one, which takes place in 1977, Emma tells her ex-lover Jerry that Robert, her husband, has been sexually unfaithful to her for years. On hearing this news, Jerry also feels betrayed by Robert's adultery: 'through all those years, all the drinks, all the lunches … we had together, I never even gleaned … I never suspected … that there was anyone else … in his life but you. Never'.[30] Emma also informs Jerry that she told her husband about her infidelity the night before – 'I had to' (22) – but the audience, later in the play, realises this is a lie since Robert learned about the affair while in Venice years before. Deception is thus established as a principal ingredient of the triangulated relationships in the play. From scene three, which elaborates the disintegration of Jerry and Emma's relationship in 1975, *Betrayal* moves backwards in time: scene five, for example, is set in 1973 when Robert discovers his wife's affair by reading a letter intended for Emma, and it is at this point that he recognises he is both husband and 'total stranger' to his wife (65). In performance, the play works an extremely intense effect as the audience extends its awareness of previous interactions in the light of successive incidents that are uncovered in the past. In the final scene of the play, set in 1968, Jerry confesses his love for Emma for the first time and his speech is worth quoting at length:

You're lovely. I'm crazy about you. All these words I'm using, don't you see, they've never been said before. Can't you see? I'm crazy about you. It's a whirlwind. Have you ever been to the Sahara Desert? Listen to me. It's true. Listen. You overwhelm me. You're so lovely. […] Look at the way you're looking at me. I can't wait for you, I'm bowled over, I'm totally knocked out, you dazzle me, you jewel, my jewel, I can't ever sleep again, no, listen, it's the truth, I won't walk, I'll be a cripple, I'll descend, I'll diminish, into total paralysis,

my life is in your hands, that's what you're banishing me to, a
state of catatonia, do you know the state of catatonia? do you?
do you? the stage of … where the reigning prince is the prince
of emptiness, the prince of absence, the prince of desolation.
I love you. (115)

As befits its title, the text of *Betrayal* is constituted in linguistic
repression, indirections, freighted subtext and double meanings but
this aria of romantic longing is one of the most emotionally raw
and spellbinding declarations of love in post-war British drama.[31]
Crucially, however, the audience hears Jerry's speech aware of what
the future has in store and so these sentiments appear earnest but
ultimately transitory (indeed, Jerry's words in this scene contrast
starkly with the somewhat clinical double negative he uses to end the
affair in scene three – 'I don't think we don't love each other') (44).
Emma's immediate reaction to Jerry's passionate oration is to deflate
it – 'My husband is at the other side of that door' (115) – and the
play concludes on an indeterminate note:

> *Emma moves towards the door. Jerry grasps her arm.*
> *She stops still.*
> *They stand still, looking at each other.* (117)

Betrayal thus winnows the audience's attention to this point of singu-
larity, to the germinal moment from which all of the action hitherto
staged in the play has flowed. In respect of its unusual structure,
there are correspondences between this play and David Hare's
Plenty, which premiered in the same year as *Betrayal* (1978). *Plenty*
also disrupts linear chronology, concluding with a scene that takes
the audience back in time to liberated France in 1944 – a moment
which, for the protagonist Susan Traherne, was characterised by
possibility and hope. Most of the preceding scenes of *Plenty* take
place chronologically after the final scene and the audience therefore
knows that Susan's life from this point on will slide ineluctably
towards disillusionment. But whereas Susan's despair is played out
against the major socio-political transformations of post-war Britain,

including the Festival of Britain and the Suez Crisis, *Betrayal* keeps its forensic focus on the private sphere: both plays are important examples of the turn towards disillusionment in British playwriting in the second half of the 1970s. Indeed, in his review of a revival of *Betrayal* in 1991, John Peter makes a comment that applies to both plays: '[t]he final effect is nightmarish: as if you realised with a shudder that what you have just been through were only about to begin'.[32]

Reflecting on Pinter's playwriting of the 1970s, Peter Hall observes that 'staccato contests between two characters scoring off each other have given way to very involved, long prose passages [and] sustained poetic writing'.[33] Richard Allen Cave also lauds the ambitious architecture of the plays, their 'structures of an almost symphonic complexity'.[34] While some critics recognised the increasing virtuosity in Pinter's work, others felt bewildered: although earlier plays such as *The Birthday Party* (1958) and *The Homecoming* (1965) raise questions about the mysterious identities of new arrivals, the elusive subject matter of the 1970s plays, along with Hall's punctilious direction and Bury's sophisticated design, led some critics to accuse Pinter of withdrawing from social reality into existential abstraction. For example, Steve Grant, in his review of *No Man's Land* for *Time Out* in 1975, argued that Pinter's 'technique [is] the technique of someone finding better ways of burying himself'.[35] Two years later, Bernard Levin published a caustic review of a revival of *The Caretaker* titled provocatively 'The Hollow Art of Harold Pinter', in which he wrote 'The truth remains that Mr Pinter has nothing to say, and that a drum makes a noise when you hit it because it is empty [...]. We come out exactly the same people as we were when we entered'.[36] Both critics contend that Pinter's aesthetic effaces or 'buries' his authorial identity, leaving the meaning of his plays smudged like Beth's drawing in the sand, or blurred like Kate's vision in the rainy city, or rendered 'blank' as in one of Hirst's photographs. Underlying these comments is the anxiety that Pinter's writing runs counter to the social realist drama then in vogue in British theatre and that his plays indulge obscurity at the expense of clarity ('Mr Pinter has nothing to say [...]'). Such criticisms, predisposed towards a drama defined by content and 'message', overlook the formal ambition of Pinter's plays in their anatomisation of the vortex of memory.

It is fitting to conclude with a typically pugnacious observation made by Pinter in an interview from 1966, which offers a sort of pre-emptive riposte to Levin:

> I had – I have – nothing to say about myself, directly. I wouldn't know where to begin. Particularly since I often look at myself in the mirror and say, 'Who the hell's that?'[37]

Pinter's response to the primal scene of encounter with his own reflection is, as we have seen, identical to the response he expects from an audience when encountering his characters at the start of a performance. As well as being a retort to his own mirrored image, 'Who the hell's that?' is the hermeneutic code, the abiding and irresolvable question, which extends from Pinter's memory plays.

REVISITING PINTER'S WOMEN: *ONE FOR THE ROAD* (1984), *MOUNTAIN LANGUAGE* (1988) AND *PARTY TIME* (1991)

ANN C. HALL

While Pinter was directing David Mamet's *Oleanna* in London in 1993, Mel Gussow conducted a brief interview with him. He observed that the writer had had a dry spell '[b]etween *A Kind of Alaska* and *One for the Road*', a period of about three years. Pinter admitted that he was at a loss. He was interested in politics, but he admitted, 'I didn't know how to do it [write political plays]'. The hiatus, however, launched some of Pinter's most explicitly political plays: *One for the Road* (1984), *Mountain Language* (1988) and *Party Time* (1991), all of which he says he had 'written out of anger [...] a very cold anger. Icy'. He later partially clarifies his motivation, saying, 'These plays, all of them, are to do not with ambiguities of power, but actual power [...] It's crude; that's the whole point'.[1] Pinter, of course, is being coy here. He has always written about power. His earlier works, we are commonly reminded, are often referred to as 'comedies of menace'. But these three plays marked his foray into explicitly political drama, a shift that sent Pinter scholars scrambling to re-examine his first plays, which he suddenly declared were political, contradicting earlier statements that his writing was apolitical and that he was not a political dramatist.[2] As the interview with Nicholas Hern illustrates, *One for the Road* inaugurates Pinter's entrance into political theatre. From that play onwards, he interrogated not only politics and power, but the tendency on the part of the culture and critics to separate art and politics, an interrogation that culminated, if such a static word can ever be applied to Pinter, in his Nobel Prize speech of 2005 during which he dissected the language of art and the language of politics for the entire world.

Pinter's political emphasis has been the subject of many fine studies including Charles Grimes's *Harold Pinter's Politics* and Austin Quigley's 'Pinter, Politics, and Postmodernism', as well as numerous essays in the *Pinter Review* and throughout this volume. What has not been addressed, however, is the representation of women in these three explicitly political plays. By examining the three plays and their women, it becomes clear that Pinter's female representation undergoes a shift within this political milieu. Unlike his earlier plays in which women represent an alternative to the patriarchal models of power and oppression, as Mark Taylor-Batty examines earlier in this volume, here, particularly in *Party Time*, his female characters become not only part of the political problem but also participants in oppressive political structures.

From *The Room* (1957) to *A Kind of Alaska* (1982), women in Pinter's plays represent a difference, an alternative perhaps to the dominant male cultures. Sometimes literally and sometimes metaphorically the women question and interrogate, while the men declare and conclude. In *The Dumb Waiter* (1960), for example, even an absent female prompts Gus to question his life, work, and the organisation that gives him his orders. In a short speech, we see the effect the feminine has upon him. He begins with declarative sentences, and then ends with questions. The woman has prompted him to rethink his life and work: 'I was just thinking about that girl, that's all. She wasn't much to look at, I know, but still [...] They don't seem to hold together like men, women. A looser texture, like. Didn't she spread, eh? [...] I've been meaning to ask you [...] Who cleans up after we've gone? I'm curious about that. Who does the clearing up?'[3] Gus is no longer a 'made' man. He is coming into his own as a result of this female intervention and we infer that he will no longer obey and play by the organisation's rules, a decision that may cost him his life.

In the famous scene in Pinter's classic, *The Homecoming* (1965), Ruth interrupts not only the world of men in their London home, but she also interrupts a philosophical discussion between Teddy, the doctor of philosophy, and his brother, Lenny, perhaps undermining western philosophical inquiry:

You've forgotten something. Look at me. I … move my leg. That's all it is. But I wear … underwear … which moves with me … it captures your attention. Perhaps you misinterpret. The action is simple. It's a leg … moving. My lips move. Why don't you restrict … your observations to that? Perhaps the fact that they move is more significant … that the words which come through them. You must bear that … possibility … in mind.[4]

The ellipsis, the questions, as well as the content serves to challenge male authority, certitude, and even philosophical debate.[5]

One for the Road is political patriarchy on steroids. As Pinter notes, power relations were always present in his plays, but with *One for the Road*, as Hern succinctly points out, 'these things that you wrote about then as metaphors have become facts now'.[6] Pinter responds with a caution perhaps, reminding Hern and readers that he is keenly aware of his anti-agit-prop stance, keenly aware that he may fall victim to political propagandising, something he loathes and loathed as a young writer when he 'walked out of Peter Brook's *US*' because it was too overtly political.[7] But Pinter's decision to address the political issue through the torture of an ordinary, nuclear family makes his plays much more accessible and effective. As Michael Billington notes, 'the play's horrific irony is that Nicolas tears asunder an individual family in the name of patriarchal values'.[8] And at the heart of the play and the family is Gila, the sole woman in this patriarchal house of horrors.

The play opens with the well-dressed Nicolas interrogating the abused and exhausted Victor. Nicolas is strikingly frightening because he is so well-mannered. He embodies not the comedy of menace but the terror of etiquette: he is well-groomed, well-educated, efficient and religious, the model of a successful man in this culture. The only idiosyncrasy here, of course, is the fact that this bureaucrat has a tortured man in his otherwise ordinary office. During the interview with Hern, Pinter tells an interesting story about a cricket game he played at Great Hampden. Through the course of the story, we learn that Pinter discovered that beneath the

pitch the Americans had constructed the 'centre of nuclear operations in Europe'.[9] The image resonates with the opening scene of
One for the Road – underneath the seemingly normal façade lies
torture and violence.

One of the problems with Nicolas is that he is so compelling.
Drew Milne notes that 'Pinter's representation of male power games
risks celebrating misogynistic wit, offering a train school in forms
of every authoritarianism that defeats the imagination. Greater
dramatic resourcefulness is given to those who abuse power. The
devil's party seems stronger and more compelling'.[10] Milne argues
for a postmodern investigation of Pinter's political metonyms, but
by examining Gila in the midst of this patriarchal structure the
limits of patriarchy are illustrated just as effectively.

In short order, Nicolas brings up Victor's wife: 'You're probably
wondering where your wife is. She's in another room [...] Good
looking woman. *He drinks.* God, that was good'.[11] Clearly, Gila is
being used as a pawn in this patriarchal game. She is, like the drink,
under Nicolas's control. In the words of feminist trailblazer Mary
Wollstonecraft, Gila is a 'cipher', a zero that merely adds value to
the numeric value of men.

But one of the most arresting aspects of this 'interrogation' is
the fact that Nicolas does not interrogate Victor at all. Michael
Billington, who may be under the very spell Milne cautions against,
argues that Nicolas's use of questions reflects his insecurity despite his
power. Billington and others view the play as about the victims but
also about the 'tortured nature of the torturer'.[12] But a close examination of Nicolas's use of questions (questions that Billington asserts
reflect Nicolas's insecurities and need for companionship) reveals
that they are rhetorical traps set to capture Victor in error or torture
him further. Nicolas, for example, repeatedly asks Victor about his
son and his wife. These questions do not require that Victor provide
information because he knows and we know that Nicolas has all
the answers he requires. Instead, the questions enable him to assert
control over these absent characters. In what could possibly be one
of the darkest comic moments in modern theatre, Nicolas explains
a joke to Victor: 'I'm talking about your wife. Your wife. You know

the old joke? Does she fuck? ... Does she fuck! ... It's ambiguous, of course. It could mean she fucks like a rabbit or she fucks not at all' (230). The joke not only demonstrates Nicolas's control over everything in the play, from characters to the interpretation of jokes, but it also illustrates the way that he uses his questions: they are another form of torture.

Through his sadistic sleight-of-hand, Nicolas conjures up Gila's presence in order to excoriate Victor. For example, he tells Victor that he and many other men have fallen in love with his wife. He then invites Victor to be his friend, to enjoy his company, and to fall in love with death as much as he does, asserting that death is more beautiful than 'sexual intercourse' (229). He repeatedly proclaims that 'Everyone else knows the voice of God speaks through me' (227) and, by the end of the scene, it appears that he has converted his victim to his gospel of death, as Victor responds 'kill me' (232). But Nicolas, the voice of God, is not ready to let Victor go. He admonishes Victor not to despair, and mentions how much he loathes despair: 'It should be castrated. Indeed I've often found that that works. Chop the balls off and despair goes out the window. You're left with a happy man. Or a happy woman' (233). Gender, life, death, Victor's family, interpretation; all are in Nicolas's power.

In a short but powerful scene that follows, Nicolas toys with Victor's son, ironically named Nicky. Here, Nicolas interrogates, but again, it is not an interrogation which is driven by any need for information. He asks Nicky rhetorical questions about the kind of toys he likes, for example. To some extent, the scene reads like Goldberg and McCann's interrogation of Stanley in *The Birthday Party*: a series of seemingly innocent questions creates terror. The fact that Nicky answers the questions honestly reflects his naïvety, and unwittingly seals his fate. The boy, for example, confesses that he did not care for the soldiers who came to his house and this is perhaps the answer Nicolas was looking for and it is no stretch of the imagination to conclude that he interprets this innocent proclamation as a threat against the state. He responds, saying, 'they don't like you either, my darling' (237) and we understand that Nicky is doomed.

By having Gila appear after the two male victims, the play emphasises her difference. Unlike the males, of course, she has been gang
raped. Like her son, she, too, is interrogated by Nicolas, but the
questions put to her are not innocent; instead, they establish her
relationship to the male characters in her life, demonstrating that
she is nothing without men. The first set of questions establishes her
relationship with Victor, but during one response she mentions that
she met Victor in her father's room. This detail leads to identifying
her through her relationship with her father, a man whom she has
betrayed, according to Nicolas: 'Are you prepared to defame, debase
the memory of your father? Your father fought for his country. I
knew him. I revered him. Everyone did. He believed in God. He
didn't think, like you shitbags. He lived' (240). Nicolas's attack
virtually erases her personal history.

When Nicolas questions her again on her first meeting with
Victor, Gila changes her story, saying that she met him in the street,
not through her father. She has absolutely no power here, and
Nicolas consistently attacks her on the basis of her relationship to
patriarchy. When he mentions her son and his behaviour, he blames
Gila for raising him incorrectly: 'He's a little prick. You made him so'
(244). Gila is only defined by her relationship to men and her fate
is to literally disappear when Nicolas says she will disappear. For the
moment, though, he will return her to his men because she 'might
entertain us all a little more before you go' (244). Wife, mother,
harlot. Gila is imprisoned by these patriarchal definitions. She is
only what they say she is.

Victor returns in the final scene, and though he now cannot speak,
he is not defined by social stereotypes as Gila is. Gila is neutralised
by gender roles and rape, while Victor is neutralised by violence. In a
sadistic attempt to celebrate Victor's imminent release, Nicolas offers
him the opportunity to go 'upstairs' to a 'high-class brothel', and we
know that it is the same place where Gila has been 'entertaining'
the troops. Nicolas explains that the women are brought in by 'their
daddies' who are in 'our business. Which is, I remind you, to keep
the world clean for God' (246). It is doubtful that any statement
has so succinctly summarised the ironies of patriarchy: there is the

absolute disregard for women, the link between oppression and sexuality, and the sense of moral certitude and superiority. The play concludes with Nicky's death confirmed: 'Oh, don't worry about him. He was a little prick' (247). At this moment, the title cannot be ignored. Not only has Nicolas had 'one for the road', in terms of booze, but he has his sacrificial victim, a young, innocent child sacrificed on the road to political and religious extremism.

While both men and women are victimised here, Gila's abuse is rooted in her femininity and feminine roles in patriarchy. She is a wife, mother, whore, and she is punished for both upholding and rejecting these various stereotypes. Through her, more than the other characters, *One for the Road* highlights the absurdities of political oppression. Nothing makes sense. She can never win. No matter what they ask of her, she is always in the wrong. Her son must be destroyed to prevent future retaliation and her husband, who apparently spoke out against the oppression, has been silenced. But given that Pinter's previously powerful women have resisted and spoken out, despite patriarchal structures and limitations, this play appears all the more frightening.

Perhaps as an antidote to the extreme oppression in *One for the Road*, *Mountain Language* presents a more typical representation not only of power but of women in oppressive patriarchal situations. Anthony Roche, who sees a connection between *Mountain Language* and Lady Gregory's *The Gaol Gate* (1906), observes that 'the chief brunt of the encounter is between women and prison authorities'[13] and these women, as in earlier Pinter plays, appear to offer something different, a difference that offers comfort and solace in this violent patriarchal culture.

The play quickly links speech, defiance, and political change in the opening scene during which the question of names, power and language is explored. When the guards ask that the women give their names, they respond saying that they have already given them. The women do not understand the rule of the game. They have no power and they have nothing to withhold. An officer instructs them on their new reality when he asks for the name of the dog that bit the elderly woman, and, in feigning cooperation, clarifies the reality for these women. They have no power; they have no control over language. To underscore the conclusion, the officer has the guard tell the women:

> Now hear this. You are mountain people. You hear me? Your language is dead. It is forbidden. It is not permitted to speak your mountain language in this place. You cannot speak your language to your men. It is not permitted. Do you understand? You may not speak it. It is outlawed. You may only speak the language of the capital. That is the only language permitted in this place [...] Any questions?[14]

The Kafkaesque logic of the prison is established. The women may not speak their language, and may only minimally understand the language of the capital, but if they do have any questions they are unable to raise them because, once again, they are not permitted to speak their own language. Political oppressors appear accommodating, upholding the rules and regulations of human rights, but they are ultimately tyrants.

Pinter's cast of characters, which provides no personal names, highlights the gulag's power over language. Men are defined by their relationship to the power: 'prisoner', 'guard', or 'officer', for example. The women, however, are defined by their gender, and this difference will be highlighted through the play. The young woman, for example, offers her name, Sara Johnson. She understands both the mountain language and the language of the state, but this dexterity will not help her. Her linguistic prowess means nothing in a world in which language is used to obfuscate, not illustrate. She discovers that her husband has been erroneously imprisoned, and that she, too, is in the 'wrong batch'. But given the linguistic gulag, truth is meaningless here. She is by the end of the scene a sex object, an intellectual with an arse that 'wobble[s] the best' (257).

According to Michael Billington, that line elicited criticism from some women who not only found it offensive but also misinterpreted the remark as a representation of Pinter's true feelings about women. Pinter defended the line and the play succinctly: the critics 'seem to me to have omitted one thing. It is the Sergeant talking. As a dramatist, I create characters. A female writer who was creating this Sergeant could equally well have written the same line'.[15] True enough, but the critics also miss the transformation of the woman in the scene, as well. She opens the scene having a great deal of power. She is representing the mountain language to the capital. She speaks both, and she seeks justice and fairness. But through a matter of lines, she is reduced to nothing more than a piece of ass. The decline is as terrifying as the imprisonment of her husband, if not more so, because we see her fall here and throughout the play.

The visiting room brings more challenges. The elderly woman has come to visit, but every time she speaks, she is poked or jabbed by the guard. Though the prisoner attempts to explain that she is old and cannot speak the language of the capital, the guard refuses to understand. The prisoner tries to make a connection with the guard: 'I've got a wife and three kids'. The guard, however, refuses to understand, 'You've got what?' and proceeds to contact his superior, saying, 'I think we've got a joker in here' (260). The prisoner, of course, 'has' nothing, but he must also be separated from the guard. There must be nothing in common between the two.

The elderly woman, too, is 'other', outside. Her language and her being must be kept outside, away from the cells. The two, however, manage to communicate through a voice-over. Pinter's choice here, an unusual one for the theatre, reflects his work in film, and through the scene we learn that the elderly woman is the prisoner's mother, and she offers him comfort. The scene suggests that there is more than language that connects us, particularly in a world where certain languages are denied. But the fact that Pinter must resort to voice-over indicates that as comforting as the idea of a world without language is, we must still rely on it.

In the next scene, 'voices in the darkness', the play highlights the position of women in the patriarchal prison. We hear the sergeant's voice off stage at the scene's opening. His language is ridiculous, perhaps indicating a deterioration of the very language the tormentors are attempting to uphold. 'What's this, a reception for Lady Duck Muck?' (262). The woman's presence may also reduce the oppressors to infantile verbiage. As he rants, once again, however, the prisoner and a woman are only able to speak via the voice-over. The voice-over is at once diegetic, representing the language the prisoners could speak if they were allowed, but also non-diegetic, representing their relationship that is removed, above and beyond the prison.

During their conversation, they recall good times together, and then the man collapses. At that moment, she calls out his name, 'Charley!' (263). Her presence has made him a person. He is no longer 'prisoner'. She offers an alternative to the oppression and violence of the prison. But the prison persists and she is asked to leave. There has been some mistake. She should not have been allowed to see the prisoner.

The sergeant tells the woman that to find out about the status of the prisoner and 'any aspect of life in this place' she can contact Joseph Dokes, an anonymous prison official who is 'right on top of his chosen subject' (264). The woman has learned the language of the capital and the prison and responds aggressively, asking 'Can I fuck him? If I fuck him, will everything be alright?' (264). In contrast to her logical approach in the first scene, she now behaves in the way that the oppressors have cast her. When the guard answers affirmatively, she even thanks him for his response. She, too, has begun to understand the language of the capital, which in this and most cases is the language of capital, the exchange of services and goods, nothing more. Her degradation from woman to object makes the scene and the situation all the more terrifying.[16]

In the final scene, the prisoner is badly beaten and bleeding, and sits with his elderly mother. As in *One for the Road*, men are abused physically, while women are abused both physically and in much more subtle and profound ways. Here, for example, the guard tells the prisoner that his mother may now speak her mountain language, that there are new rules, at least for the moment. The mother, however, does not or cannot speak. Whether it is because she no longer can or is unwilling is left unresolved, but the image of a silent woman cannot but help conjure up the image of Philomela, the Greek woman who was raped. She then tells her tale through art, in a tapestry. Like Philomela, the women in *Mountain Language* may be silenced, but as Max says in *The Homecoming*, in what has become an apt phrase to define Pinter's style, 'you never heard such silence'. The elderly woman's silence affects her son who also becomes mute. He is left trembling on the floor as she sits silently, while the guard scoffs: 'You go out of your way to give them a helping hand and they fuck it up' (267), dismissing their pain and their very existence. They are merely annoyances. But through Pinter's representation, we cannot dismiss these situations or these women.

Though the women do little to change the political prison of *Mountain Language*, they do offer an alternative. They enter the world of the prison, and try to play by the rules the prison world appears to support: logic, generosity and justice. These are the rules of the capital, the rules that make them feel good and pure, but the realities of the prison world are much crueller. And perhaps because of the disconnect between the manifest content of the prison verbiage and the latent realities, the world seems all more terrifying by the contrast. The women attempt to master the manifest content, but realise there is no winning at this game. They realise that there is no winning at all, particularly when one is a woman. In the end, there is only silence.

Party Time offers a marked shift in Pinter's female representation. Rather than being one of the victims as in *One for the Road* or a call to change as in *Mountain Language*, *Party Time* presents women as part of the oppressive power. They are not just the outsiders, and they are not just the beneficiaries of power by dint of their relationships to men. They play active and important roles in the oppressive political machine. There is an exception, Dusty, and it is through her that the play interrogates the apparently seamless narrative of oppression.

Gavin, a wealthy and apparently omnipotent power broker, hosts a cocktail party. In the opening scene, Terry, a sycophantic guest, describes the luxuries of his private club. We are clearly 'above and beyond' the rank and file. We are in the upper stratospheres of wealth and power. In the middle of Gavin and Terry's discussion, Dusty arrives and inquires about her missing brother. The question disturbs the comfortable and casual small talk. Her husband, Terry, makes it clear that she must remain silent on this matter. At this point, he quietens her by benignly changing the subject, distracting her with talk of the club and how wonderful it is. She, too, then discusses the 'alcoves', and the lovely surroundings. Here it is the trappings of capitalism, not Doberman-wielding guards, who silence a questioning woman, at least momentarily.

Melissa, another guest, also arrives bringing news of the city. She says 'it's like the Black Death [...] The town's dead. There's nobody on the streets, there's not a soul in sight, apart from some … soldiers'.[17] Once again, Terry stifles her discussion through luxury by offering her a glass of champagne. Dusty, however, will not relent, and she wonders out loud if she can believe anything she hears. Terry again asserts his patriarchal power: 'You don't have to believe anything. You just have to shut up and mind your own business, how many times do I have to tell you?' (287–8). Given the previous plays, Terry's behaviour is much more menacing than that of a man trying to keep the cocktail talk light and small.

In the expanded screenplay, the next couple we meet, Sam and Pamela, discuss moral superiority in cryptic terms: 'What are the values we choose to protect and why?', asks Pamela, but there is no answer from Sam. He responds, in the affirmative, 'Quite'.[18] Through her interrogation and his declarations, the Pinter gender divide is reflected linguistically. The women ask and enquire, the men declare and make statements even if they do not make any sense.

But in the next scene, the women are not represented so positively. Instead, we see two women creating a romance out of a virtual chance encounter and a glance. Given the situation and the surroundings, it is difficult not to assume that Pinter indicts this kind of discussion and behaviour. In the scene, Liz tells Charlotte of her new love, a man she saw at a party with another woman. As the other couple depart for further amorous adventures, Liz reveals the 'truth' of the encounter: 'As he was being lugged out he looked back, he looked back, I swear, at me, like a wounded deer' (289). The addition of the 'I swear' suggests that even she is not sure of his intentions, but she concludes that the entire scene results in the 'rape' of the man she loves. Of course, it is clear that these are Liz's fantasies. Illusions are all these women have, and given the treatment they receive by the other men in the room, it is no wonder. Rather than being abused physically, they are treated to luxury, champagne and fantasy, the opium of the modern, ruling class.

In contrast to such female fantasies, the next scene offers the male version. Fred and Douglas discuss the future of their country and the means to achieve those ends, illustrated succinctly by Douglas's clenched fist (292). If the two women represented romantic illusion, the two men represent the illusion fostered and promised by violence, and there is great reward to these illusions, as the following scene between Suki and Emily illustrates. They discuss their weekend plans, and it is clear that Emily's husband, a great horse jumper, is unavailable because he is working in the city, the city that is the 'black death', that is the site for the violence. And what is Emily's husband working toward? According to Fred and Douglas, who return in the next scene, they are working toward not just 'peace,' but 'a cast-iron peace' (292). Violence, oppression and force uphold this city of dreams.

During a jocular discussion among Melissa, Gavin, Terry and Dusty, Terry's hostilities break through. Melissa is clearly interested in Gavin, and she attempts to bring him out by discussing his hobbies, as well as the club. Terry and Dusty participate, but as they discuss boats, Terry attacks Dusty for disliking 'being fucked on boats'. The detail pierces through the small talk, and though Melissa covers by saying, 'That's funny. I thought everyone liked that' (296), Dusty takes the bait and returns to the taboo subject – her brother. Infuriated, Terry lashes out even more: 'I don't know what it is. Perhaps she's deaf or perhaps my voice isn't strong enough or distinct enough. What do you think folks? Perhaps there's something faulty with my diction' (296). Dusty will not remain quiet, and persists. Gavin assesses the situation saying from the ruling class perspective, '[s]o odd, the number of men who can't control their wives' (297). Though the setting has changed, the party is still a gulag, and Pinter uses the oppression and silencing of women to illustrate the far-reaching effects of political oppression. On the one hand, Terry and Dusty's strife illustrates that the political unrest affects the personal lives of the people trying so desperately to ignore that violence. On the other hand, the couple's conflict illustrates the fact that no matter how strong, no matter how far-reaching, there will always be someone who questions authority, but any hope this offers is quickly tempered. Gavin, of course, is part of the problem, the patriarchal tyrant, but then Melissa agrees with him:

Gavin It's the root of so many ills, you know. Uncontrollable wives.
Melissa Yes, I know what you mean. (297)

Dusty's attempts to question authority appear wiped away in a brief sentence. Melissa is a woman who upholds patriarchal power for one of the first times in Pinter's political plays. She, too, is part of the problem.

As the play progresses, the apparently stable marital relationships, however, begin to falter. Liz, who had the fantasy earlier, is actually married. And Charlotte, her friend, appears to know her husband very well: the words 'He gave me a leg up in life', has more resonance than getting a helping hand in business. As Charlotte says, 'Oh, yes. I'm still trembling' (299). Not only is the ruling class not what it appears to be, the women are in competition with the men. They are not banding together as they did in *Mountain Language* to help one another; they are vying for relationship with the men. To underscore this destructive behaviour, the play ironically presents Liz discussing how proud she is to be part of this world: 'I mean to be part of the society of beautifully dressed people' (299). Amidst this shimmering pronouncement, Charlotte reveals that her husband is dead, but the party moves on. There is no explanation, only an invitation to further distraction from Douglas who invites her to his summer island home.

Any matters for concern are quickly dispelled. Women are invited to summer retreats, and the truly great warrant speeches on their greatness as mothers. There may be flirtations, affairs, but all is well in this world. These are the chosen people, people who retain their good figures by living 'clean' lives. They are not like the other people, the people in the streets. But in the midst of the wave of wealth and champagne, Terry and Dusty argue brutally. Terry is so taken aback by Dusty's behaviour, he threatens to kill her. Rather than being intimidated, Dusty confronts him with his own violence, violating the rules of engagement by asking whether or not she will enjoy her manner of death. Once again, she challenges him, and once again she asks about her brother.

As the party comes to a close, Terry once more sings the praises of their club. This time Melissa, not Dusty, concurs. She admits that she has belonged to a number of clubs, but all of them have closed and many members have died: 'But *our* club, *our* club – is a club which is activated, which is inspired by a moral sense, a moral awareness, a set of moral values which is – I have to say – unshakeable, rigorous, fundamental, constant. Thank you' (311). Given the earlier scenes of flirtatious relationships among the guests, the moral code of the club is clearly in question. The moral code of the club is the fact that they are in the club and the other people 'down there' are not. What is more disturbing, too, is the fact that Pinter gives this speech – which in some ways reflects Nicolas's in *One for the Road* – to a woman. The women in Pinter's political plays generally question the authority, but here, the woman upholds the authority. She is part of the game, part of the political tyranny.

Pinter compounds the disturbing speech with another by Gavin who mentions that there has been a 'round up' that evening in order to return to 'normal service' for 'ordinary' citizens (313). The play concludes with Jimmy's appearance, in which he describes what life is for the 'other', the people who are not invited to the party, who have been rounded up. He describes life 'under' the party, and once again, as in *Mountain Language*, he loses his name and his identity. He has nothing but darkness, darkness to 'suck' (314). Given the representation of women in this play, the sucking image suggests the breast, a breast that once provided sustenance, but now provides only darkness. It is a grim depiction of the changing role of women in patriarchy, and it begs the question, what causes Pinter to change his representation of women in these political plays?

One possible answer is Margaret Thatcher's stint as the United Kingdom's first woman Prime Minister and the longest serving of the twentieth century. Billington succinctly describes Pinter's attitude towards Thatcher as follows:

> Ironically, Pinter, like Peter Hall, had voted Tory in that election [1979], inspired partly by his disgust with the National Theatre's wave of wildcat strikes. Pinter now says, 'I look back on that vote with disbelief. I in fact realised within weeks that it was a stupid, totally irresponsible and shameful act.' One can easily see why. On her election to power, Mrs Thatcher abandoned one-nation Toryism, unstitched the post-war consensus on a whole range of issues from the Welfare State to education, introduced anti-union legislation, set about the privatisation of national utilities and turned a belief in the free market into a form of secular religion.[19]

The political environment of Thatcherism certainly encouraged Pinter and Lady Antonia to become more politically active, inspiring them to 'host a private discussion group' of left-leaning writers in 1988.[20] Though there is no evidence that he had Thatcher's gender in mind as he wrote *Party Time*, it is clear that her politics are 'in the air' and, according to Billington, the wonderful speech Pinter added to the screenplay of *The Comfort of Strangers* (1990) was inspired by Thatcher's own inordinate attachment to her father.[21]

What is interesting to note, however, is the context of the interview with Gussow that linked the three Pinter political plays. Though David Mamet took Pinter on as an inspiration and a kind of mentor, he was frequently criticised by feminists at this time for his misogynistic representation of women. *Oleanna* (1992), particularly the New York production, was one of the most controversial. A young student accuses her professor of sexual harassment. Gussow conducted the interview during a break while Pinter was directing Mamet's play. As Billington recalls, the American production was 'loaded' against the woman and prompted audience members to encourage the professor to 'Hit the Bitch'. Pinter presented a more balanced case and ran into a 'head-on conflict with Mamet'.[22] For the New York production, Mamet had changed his ending, and it tipped the scales in favour of the professor. Pinter demanded that the original ending be retained in the London production and won. The story highlights Pinter's awareness of feminist matters, as well as the role of women in patriarchy.

The context, albeit coincidental, underscores the role of women in Pinter's canon and in these three plays. For the most part, the female characters serve as victims and as representations of what is lost in closed political systems. Women, who are bright, smart, intelligent and independent, are forced into constraints, sometime more terrifying than their male counterparts. With *Party Time*, Pinter presents a brave new world, a world in which a woman is just as tyrannical and oppressive as the men. She, too, participates in patriarchal oppression. And this shift is also terrifying. Who will remind the men that they have 'forgotten something', that there is more to life than their patriarchal philosophies? And now that Pinter is gone, who will interrogate us?

PINTER'S POLITICAL DRAMAS: STAGING NEOLIBERAL DISCOURSE AND AUTHORITARIANISM

BASIL CHIASSON

Pinter's overtly political dramas emerged in tandem with Margaret Thatcher's eleven-year tenure as Prime Minister of the United Kingdom. Thatcher's policies facilitated free-market capitalism, and her political rhetoric animated ways of thinking, speaking and behaving which not only ratified the market but made it the ballast of reason itself. The former Prime Minister re-coded extant social welfare state ideology through privatisation, a discourse of individualism and competition, economic liberalisation programmes and even shocks to the physical body in the form of police state intervention into resistance to austerity measures; all of which she regarded as changing the soul by means of economics.[1] Her orientations were, and still are, instrumental to a swelling western-led project (namely by Germany, the United States, the United Kingdom) of economic positivism, the aim of which is to redraw the social architecture in the post-war era chiefly by extending the market and market logics into every sphere of life.[2]

A number of Pinter's contemporaries wrote head on into Thatcherism and the political and social changes transpiring in Britain under her: Howard Brenton with *The Romans in Britain* (1980), Sarah Daniels with *Masterpieces* (1983), David Hare and Howard Brenton with *Pravda* (1985), Steven Berkoff with *Sink the Belgrano!* (1986), Kay Adshead with *Thatcher's Women* (1987), Caryl Churchill with *Serious Money* (1987), and Doug Lucie with *Fashion* (1987). In this same period, Pinter dramas such as *Precisely* (1983), *One for the Road* (1984) and *Mountain Language* (1988) do not confront Thatcherism but instead take up the issues of nuclear armament in Britain and abroad, the torture and disappearing of political dissenters in the Southern Cone and the politically inspired suppression of the Kurdish language in Turkey. In fact, in Pinter's political dramas there is a lack of focus on economic and market-related subject matter which at first glance suggests that these dramas are not at all concerned with Thatcher's neoliberal programme.[3]

In Pinter's early and mid-career dramas, issues of class, gender and sexuality predominate. Economics and party politics do not, in any formal sense, appear. Neither his dramas, nor Pinter's discourse as an activist from the 1980s onwards, address economics or the market, except for occasional references in speeches to inequality, social disenfranchisement and structural poverty and, more frequently, the notable sums the American Government has devoted to paramilitary activity, coups and the support of jingoistic dictators abroad. In the 1990s, however, the plays *Party Time* and *Celebration* suddenly begin to gloss realties and issues related to Thatcherism insofar as they feature characters who stress their upper-class privilege and the money and class power they enjoy. Still, the style of representation has not prompted readings which understand the work to be concerned with economics, the market and capitalism.

Pinter's dramatic representation of the abuse of political power, 'repressive regimes, their operation, and their ideology'[4] and how force is used by apparently democratic societies 'to repress and exclude dissidents'[5] suggests a concern with socio-political realities far more general than economics and the market. But even in this apparently more general focus on the abuse of power and authoritarianism, I would argue that there are grounds for linking Pinter's work to neoliberalism, namely given how authoritarianism, totalitarianism and even fascism are increasingly being understood as necessary to realise the neoliberal project.[6]

In dramatising how violence and torture are being used in apparently foreign contexts to produce docile subjects and to maintain the status quo, Pinter's dramas speak to some of the technologies of power which are synechdocal of a much larger form of governmentality referred to as free-market liberalism and democracy, or advanced capitalism. Consider, for example, how Thatcher's imposition of neoliberalism entailed an invocation of the police state,[7] specifically in how the Prime Minister translated the unilateral approach taken in the Falklands War into local contexts, deploying police state force on coalminers' unions which posed a threat to the mandate for widespread privatisation and individualism.[8] Pinter's repeated dramatisation of authoritarian discourse, as well as of force and violence (in parallel with a staunch critique of both the American and British governments through the 1980s onwards), may not be a direct response to free-market liberalism, but it is indeed a response to the authoritarianism and violence which function to underpin neoliberal democracy and the ways of speaking which correlate to the rationality instrumental to the neoliberal project.

Just as Pinter's post-1983 political dramas appear to chart a general surge in post-war era authoritarianism, they can be seen, more specifically, to be sketching some of the contours of neoliberalism as it takes the form of an intertwined cultural and political project, from its instrumentalisation of life through discourse to the use of force to secure the status quo and legitimise specific ways of thinking, speaking and being. As much as his political corpus seems to gaze outward from Britain and towards international socio-political realities, the abundance of British tendencies and markers in the dramas, signifiers marking the principal villains as English, returns us to the neoliberal and democratic world Pinter himself inhabited.

Pinter's work from the 1980s onward is populated not by politicians and political leaders but by experts and functionaries – whether these be technocrats, soldiers, bureaucrats or consultants – whose ways of speaking are what arguably generate dramatic interest for spectators. In the sketch *Precisely* (1983), over drinks two technocrats named Roger and Stephen flout their specialised knowledge and mock the populace for misquantifying predicted death tolls resultant from what is implied to be some kind of nuclear strike:

Stephen I mean, we've said it time and again, haven't we?
Roger Of course we have.
Stephen Time and again. Twenty million. [...] It's a figure

supported by facts. We've done our homework. Twenty million is a fact. When these people say thirty I'll tell you exactly what they're doing – they're distorting the facts.
Roger Scandalous.
Stephen Quite. I mean, how the hell do they *know*? [...] We've done the *thinking*. [...] I'll tell you, neither I nor those above me are going to put up with it much longer. These people, Roger, these people are actively and wilfully deceiving the public. Do you take my point?[9]

Death and human carnage are sidelined by Roger and Stephen's specialist knowledge as the language of numbers from which it derives is invested with an incontestable truth value. Where an ethical discussion on the legitimacy of bombing civilians seems in order, the technocrats offer the audience instead a debate about whose system of quantification is truer: theirs or that of their detractors. As the sketch proceeds, the men's insistence on numerical accuracy and boasting of their abilities as experts imbues the posture with a kind of religious sanctity.

We might note the timely appearance of the technocrat in Pinter's oeuvre and how the playwright's linkage of instrumental reason to evil and 'criminality', as Charles Grimes observes,[10] indicates how attentive to and critical Pinter was of certain of the less visible yet instrumental forces that were shaping political developments in the late-Cold War era, while free-market capitalism was becoming hegemonic through the 1970s in parts of Europe and the Americas. Pinter endows Roger and Stephen with what Naomi Klein would call 'the carefully cultivated façade of scientific neutrality so central to the Chicago Boy identity':[11]

Chicago Boys and their professors, who provided advice and took up top posts in the military regimes of the Southern Cone, believed in a form of capitalism that is purist by its very nature. Theirs is a system based entirely on a belief in 'balance' and 'order' and the need to be free of interferences and 'distortions' in order to succeed. Because of these traits, a regime committed to the faithful application of this ideal cannot accept the presence of competing or tempering world views. In order for the ideal to be achieved, it requires a monopoly on ideology; otherwise, according to the central theory, the economic signals become distorted and the entire system is thrown out of balance.[12]

Klein's emphasis here finds overt expression in Roger and Stephen's discourse in *Precisely*, in particular Stephen who makes numerical accuracy and cold calculus an end in itself and thus a site of truth. Doing so, of course, suffocates the conditions for ethical or emotional concern for potential victims and makes human life expendable by reducing it to a cipher which is, arguably, not evocative of images that may affect one's subjectivity in any serious way.

Moreover, just as the language of numbers and an addiction to quantification through cold calculus refract the connection between Roger and Stephen and those on the receiving end of their war machine, the violence performed on human life is ethically and emotionally eased by money, the mention of which, curiously, marks a rare moment in Pinter's political corpus where economics figure. 'That's what we're paid for', Stephen asserts, to which Roger replies: 'Paid a bloody lot too'. 'Exactly', Stephen then adds, 'Good money for good brains' (216). To characterise as 'good' (i.e. positive and morally upright) money spent on the militaristic decimation of a population should make us laugh on the wrong side of our face, so to speak, and an attentive audience will likely discern immediately that by 'good brains' the men do not mean a capacity to produce scientific and 'objective' information but rather only those 'facts' which the elites who are paying these technocrats desire to see.

The sketch is dramatically potent for how the characters' concern does not rest with the material reality of death their weapon of mass destruction will bring about, but rather the accurate prediction of the number of casualties. Quantification rules here in a way that reminds us of the entrenchment of instrumental reason in the West across the latter half of the twentieth century[13] and its more local culmination in Britain in the targets and measures culture centralised by Tony Blair's New Labour government.[14]

The drama's second order of violence, following the discursive occlusion of civilians, surges up when Roger and Stephen provide detailed scenarios of what they will do to those who challenge their quantification of casualties: 'I'll put the bastards up against a wall and shoot them', Roger threatens, while Stephen proposes in response: 'I'm going to recommend that they be hung, drawn and quartered. I want to see the colour of their entrails'. 'Same colour as the Red Flag, old boy' (216–18), Roger says; his response an apparent branding of their victims as communists. Roger and Stephen's draconian reaction to the idea of communism may well estrange our comfortable notions of democratic political figures and complicates spectators' making any easy and comfortable invest-ments in the men's recognisably British, cosmopolitan urbanity. As the sketch enables spectators to move from the cold calculus of Roger and Stephen's discursive attenuation or occlusion of their victims towards what Pinter summarised as 'mess, pain, humiliation, vomit, excrement, blood',[15] the estrangement of the audience from the characters appears as a re-working of the technocrats' alienation of their victims through placing them at a distance by means of language.

Come the end of the sketch Roger and Stephen shift to a language which juxtaposes their euphemistic use of figures and the blunt word death, something kept at a distance until this point. Thus the ante is upped from the characters' will to quantification and the more general instrumentalisation of human life when their speech ceases to occlude death and brings it into plain view:

> **Stephen** Another two?
> **Roger** Another two million. And I'll buy you another drink. Another two for another drink.
> **Stephen** (*Slowly*) No, no, Roger. It's twenty million. Dead.
> **Roger** You mean precisely?
> **Stephen** I mean dead. Precisely. (*Pause.*) I want you to accept that figure. (*Pause.*) Accept the figure. (*They stare at each other.*)

Roger Twenty million dead, precisely?
Stephen Precisely. (219–20)

Stephen repeats the death toll in a way that urges his audience to register its magnitude and gravity. In doing so his identity as a hawkish functionary likely employed by a government with a jingoistic foreign policy fissures here, in the final moment, to become its opposite. Simultaneously, the audience becomes, by proxy, Stephen's interlocutor, Roger, as they are captured in the uncomfortable event of having to linger with Stephen and hold his stare, as it were, attempting to digest what 20 million deaths resulting from a nuclear strike actually entails.

The single word 'dead', exemplifying Pinter's familiar dramatic terseness, achieves great intensity by bearing the load of all prior instantiations of described violence. With it, Pinter forges dispassionate calculation ('dead' as in 'precisely') with grim reality, and throws that realisation at the audience in the repetition of the title of the piece. As death gets excavated from beneath the surface of the technocrats' discourse, this linguistic unit raises the material world up before us and thereby exploits the affective dimension of the drama. The move from cold calculus to offering vivid descriptions of corporeal discipline to uttering the word 'death' aloud establishes the conditions for spectators to think through the reality of politically orchestrated death. If delivered effectively in performance, the word will function to indict the technocrat figures, their logic and discourse *precisely* by insinuating, through dramatic means, the audience into a prolonged moment which demands that we confront the expansive, overwhelming and un-articulable reality that death is.

Precisely dramatises how the voice speaking from the centre of power diffuses socio-political realities but then re-inscribes the immediacy and experience which has been displaced by that same voice and its instrumentalising and rationalising forms of speech. Attending to this aesthetic feature permits us to overlay Pinter's representation and critique of the technocrat figure with a consideration of the ways in which the drama works to endow the characters' way of speaking and thinking with a violence and shock value congruent with the literally violent material consequences lurking beneath all the talk and the posturing.

As noteworthy and predictable as the subject matter of this sketch may be because of its emergence when '[t]he anti-nuclear debate [had] become the single most important feature of political life in Britain, and throughout Western Europe',[16] equally important is the dedicated dramatisation of how ways of speaking can be politically expeditious in making the irrational seem rational (i.e. the decimation of a population) and, moreover, in constructing common sense both *with* and *within* a language which is actually deployed to distort and attenuate thought. Roger and Stephen's insistence on their system of quantification is effectively an imposition of a language upon a people who speak, think and live otherwise; and the parallel use of force is also important to neoliberalism because, as a political and cultural project, it advocates and proscribes certain ways of speaking, and thus of thinking and acting, while exaggerating the elements of constraint which feature in classical liberalism during moments where opposition to the market presents itself.

In *Mountain Language* (1988), the freedom and control of the dominant group is achieved through the suppression of a minority language in a thoroughly bureaucratised process entailing internment, humiliation, torture and violence. This 'brutal, short and ugly'[17] drama carries on the obsession with linguistic precision we saw in *Precisely* as it features a number of situations where language itself seems to become the subject matter. In the play's earliest moments an armed representative of the State responds to a complaint that the Elderly Woman has been bitten by a military dog by obsessing over the animal's name and whether or not it stated its name before biting its victim:

> **Sergeant** [...] Every dog has a *name*! They answer to their name. They are given a name by their parents and that is their name, that is their *name*! Before they bite they *state* their name. It's a formal procedure. They state their name and then they bite. What was his name? If you tell me one of our dogs

bit this woman without giving his name I will have that dog shot![18]

At base, the absurdity of the remark opens a space for the audience to laugh at this political functionary, and thus foster a critical orientation towards him. Yet, the process also draws attention to the centrality of language and its use in the dramatic world as well as to how in a thoroughly bureaucratised military setting the obsession with protocol (correct usage of language in this instance) is destined to eclipse and displace concern for human well-being. In fact, the subscription to correct procedure is exemplified not by any reference to the Elderly Woman who was bitten but in the Sergeant's threat to shoot the dog, which thrusts the *human* civilian into the background only to place the animal and the character's duty to state-sanctioned procedure high on the list of priorities.

The drama of this early scene derives from both the absolute deferral to the authority of law and official language and the reality of state-sanctioned violence and physical harm, and indicates a great deal about Pinter's aesthetic composition: how the play employs an admixture of, first, performances which delineate the general value of language, and voice, 'to all forms of life and all scales of social organisation',[19] and how language is key to the oppression of a minority and less politically powerful group and, secondly, images and scenes which dramatise the reality of suffering – talk of the damage caused to the woman's hand by the dog bite is likely to make spectators bristle.

The dramatisation of language as a site of social and political contestation, including struggles over individual and group identity, culminates early in the play when the Officer refers to his as the 'language of the capital' and then forbids the mountain people's language – declaring by fiat that theirs is 'dead': 'It is not permitted to speak your mountain language in this place. [...] You may not speak it. It is outlawed. You may only speak the language of the capital. [...] This is a military decree. It is the law. Your language is forbidden. It is dead' (255). However, he then, arbitrarily and without warning or explanation, permits its use:

Guard Oh, I forgot to tell you. They've changed the rules. She can speak in her own language until further notice.
Prisoner She can speak?
Guard Yes. Until further notice. New rules. (265)

The performative nature of speech comes to the fore as the scene demonstrates how language is used to foment sudden and turbulent reversals of the situations lived out by those subjected to power. Language dramatised thus is, on the one hand, representing the social hegemony a group achieves when it gets control of or imposes the lingua franca by which all members of a community engage and, on the other, doing something, inserting itself into the bodies of speakers and interlocutors, as well as spectators, and not simply delivering meaning which is then either understood or not.

Although Pinter is writing in response to having met and heard the stories of the relatives of imprisoned writers in Turkey,[20] his engagement with language from this standpoint at this time in the 1980s is significant when neoliberalism, relates Nick Couldry, is taking on an express 'role in allowing the social world to become unnarratable from certain points of view' in a way that 'has major consequences for freedom'.[21] In this way, *Mountain Language*'s dramatisation of how powers coming to ascendancy will foster ways of thinking, behaving and being with others precisely by imposing a language both desired and ratified by the State translates well enough into the context of democracies: even Britain, for example, where the State can be vigorous in its use of discourse to promote and consolidate specific values, codes, conventions, habits and approaches to meaning-making in a way that migrates the populace towards desired socio-political and cultural shifts.

Normative readings of Pinter's work emphasise the dramatisation of the playwright's running 'obsession with the gulf between reality and fact'.[22] This obsession, I maintain, finds dramatic expression as *discourse*; by which I mean, following Michel Foucault, the production of specific orders of truth and what is accepted as 'reality' in any given society. Language usage and ways of speaking in the political oeuvre dramatise how reality is constituted on the basis of the authority of the speaker's discourse, of having said something is so. In some instances, this entails pushing standard meanings so far that they flip into their opposite.

One for the Road is a short work of four scenes whose central villain is an agent of discipline named Nicolas. As we discover, Nicolas's access to the soul is the first step in a project to refashion it:

> **Nicolas** Why am I so obsessed with eyes? Am I obsessed with eyes? Possibly. Not my eyes. Other people's eyes. The eyes of people who are brought to me here. They're so vulnerable. The soul shines through them.[23]

Nicolas strives to access the souls of his victims as a means to re-educate them, to bring them in line with the State, which means respecting it as an institution and therefore not turning against it. Yet the values perpetuated by the State which are to be respected and adopted are never mentioned in the play, just as the locale remains more or less blank.[24] Ultimately *One for the Road* is not about informing spectators what these values are so much as dramatising palpably the production of obedience through both discourse and marking the body. In general, language in Pinter is aestheticised in ways that demonstrate how speech is not about conveying information so much as giving shape to relationships and even compelling or manipulating.[25] And this is relevant to the discursive dimension of neoliberalism and democracy under contemporary capitalism. As a political and cultural rationality which foregrounds the market, neoliberalism advocates and prescribes, sometimes overtly and at other times tacitly, language usage which prompts a re-fashioning of the subject into an individual whose enjoyment of freedom happens to underwrite capital and render the market and its logic – cost-benefit analysis, instrumentality, efficiency, productivity – immanent to one's relations with oneself and with others.

Following spoken language as a means of disciplining subjects, the second pole of Pinter's dramatic aesthetic is corporeal and psychological punishment. The psychologically and physically disciplined body is the theme running through the political corpus. Despite prevalent claims that these dramas prompt spectators to understand and even identify with the villains featured,[26] what comes to the fore is how turbulent Pinter's stylisation can be for spectators and actors. As Mary Luckhurst notes of Pinter's first full-length political drama:

> *One for the Road* is relentless and harrowing, leaves its audiences silent and choked with horror, and caused the original actors such distress that they 'couldn't face the idea of doing the play again for anything but a very short run'.[27]

This passage prompts us to consider how Pinter's villains do not facilitate identification or recognition so much as break the circuit of investment between themselves and spectators, precisely by placing their victims at a distance in order to dehumanise them and/or by articulating, and thus mediating, their victims' voices, plight and even experiences. Thus the audience's estrangement from the villains doing myriad forms of violence to their victims ultimately brings near those subjected to abuse and violence, yet precisely in a way that makes difficult or even blocks easy, clichéd and thus problematic spectatorial connections (as these arguably invoke opinion and stymie real thinking). By folding together performances of language which place pain and suffering at a distance and instances where the suffering victim comes to the fore, Pinter's political dramas are not simply appealing to emotion or conjuring familiar feeling but engendering sensory experience which demands of spectators the kind of 'new standard of responsiveness to suffering' which Susan Sontag attributes to Goya's paintings about war.[28]

Pinter's aestheticisation of torture and disciplined bodies rapt in pain is timely for the 1980s, 1990s and the new millennium as it points obliquely to the fact that '[f]rom Chile to China to Iraq, torture has been a silent partner in the global free-market crusade'.[29] Yet while these forms of discipline are more readily associated with a foreign policy seeking to establish the conditions for market economies in 'foreign' territories, the State can also have, more locally, a 'monopoly of the means of violence' which will serve to 'protect corporate interests and, if necessary, to repress dissent'[30] and preserve, at all cost, the freedoms of 'strong individual private property rights, the rule of law, and the institutions of freely functioning markets and free trade'.[31] Without touching economics, Pinter's dramas do table the 'silent partner' in the free-market crusade as they urge spectators to witness the performance of pain by those in positions of power, of psychological and physical abuse and occasionally the suffering which results from them.

In scene two of *Mountain Language*, the Elderly Woman is jabbed 'with a stick' and told that her language is forbidden when she tells the Prisoner next to her that she has bread, and is jabbed a further two times as she looks at the guard and then indicates that 'I have apples' (258–9). The overt physical abuse is then bolstered with abuse in the form of shouting and dehumanising remarks:

> **Guard** Forbidden! Forbidden forbidden forbidden! Jesus Christ! (*To Prisoner*) Does she understand what I'm saying?
> **Prisoner** No. [...] She's old. She doesn't understand.
> **Guard** Whose fault is that? (*He laughs.*) Not mine, I can tell you. And I'll tell you another thing. I've got a wife and three kids. And you're all a pile of shit. (259–60)

Scene four opens in silence with an image of:

> *The* Prisoner *has blood on his face. He sits trembling. The* Woman *is still. The* Guard *is looking out of a window.* (265)

Following which the scene and play conclude with this image:

> *The* Prisoner's *trembling grows. He falls from the chair on to his knees, begins to gasp and shake violently. The* Sergeant *walks into the room and studies the* Prisoner *shaking on the floor.*
>
> **Sergeant** (*To* Guard) Look at this. You go out of your way to give them a helping hand and they fuck it up. (267)

The aesthetic intermingles speech which dehumanises, inflected with comedy as a means to animate the audience's revulsion, and physical regimes bearing the affective load of literal violence which spectators rarely if ever see inflicted. Political discourse staged thus folds together the registers of spoken word and the suffering body, forming a charged image which surges up and does violence to characters and moments in the work where rhetoric is employed to legitimate the realisation of contentious material realities.

Beyond his dramatic writing, we can plot the playwright's dramatisation of the voice speaking from the centre of power, its various discursive formations and the performance of ways in which the corporeal body gets disciplined, and thereby suffers. In his Nobel Lecture, *Art, Truth and Politics* (2005), Pinter relates an anecdote about mainstream media representation of Tony Blair and the 2003 invasion of Iraq, which ultimately functions to interrupt his audience's ability to take for granted Blair's legitimate status as a democratic leader who therefore has access to a language of democracy, peace and all related ways of speaking:

> Early in the invasion there was a photograph published on the front page of British newspapers of Tony Blair kissing the cheek of a little Iraqi boy. 'A grateful child,' said the caption. A few days later there was a story and photograph, on an inside page, of another four-year-old boy with no arms. His family had been blown up by a missile. He was the only survivor. 'When do I get my arms back?' he asked. The story was dropped. Well, Tony Blair wasn't holding him in his arms, nor the body of any other mutilated child, nor the body of any bloody corpse. Blood is dirty. It dirties your shirt and tie when you're making a sincere speech on television. (296)

Pinter's aestheticisation of the two images turns upon a form of dramatic apposition whereby the Prime Minister's photo opportunity – a 'plain folks' propaganda device invoking Blair's renowned 'capacity to, as it were, "anchor" the public politician in the "normal person"'[32] – is colonised by the distressing image of the child: a figure persisting under a discourse which occludes the fact that civilians make up a significant portion of war casualties.

Through this process of capture and re-inscription, Pinter prevents the sense of violence and human toll in Iraq from passing across the 'lining or hem'[33] of ascendant portrayals and framings of Blair which at the time rendered him a benign figure and, more to the point at hand, a democratic leader. As the image of the armless child cannibalises that of Blair, the 'drama' becomes ponderous with the sense that so often remains extrinsic to simple linguistic representation, namely in the form of clichéd constructions and familiar models of argumentation one finds in public and political debate, as well a great deal of mainstream journalism.

Pinter's discursive strategy in this instance of *Art, Truth and Politics* betrays a logic similar to *Party Time* (1991), arguably the most overt attack on the realities at the heart of the implementation of neoliberalism across the globe, namely the re-signification of liberal and utilitarian concepts. Observe Douglas's placement of the word 'peace' at the centre of his speech to Fred in the middle of the play:

> **Douglas** Look. Let me tell you something. We want peace. And we're going to get it.
> **Fred** Quite right.
> **Douglas** We want peace and we're going to get it. But we want that peace to be cast iron. No leaks. No draughts. Cast iron. Tight as a drum. That's the kind of peace we want. And that's the kind of peace we're going to get. A cast-iron peace. (*He clenches his fist.*) Like this.[34]

Calling something 'peace' or 'democracy' when the signified in fact involves realities antithetical to what those concepts denote and connote is not about the power of communicating standard meanings but rather the *authority* of the language and the speaker's power to decree. Speech in this mode is about the mere fact of having said something is so. Notice how this conjures earlier moments in the oeuvre, for example in *The Homecoming* (1964) when Lenny briefly controls the narrative and speaks reality into being when he assures Ruth that the 'certain lady [...] down by the docks' in his anecdote was in fact 'diseased' – simply because he 'decided she was'[35] and in *The Birthday Party*, which 'concludes with Meg and Petey beginning to readjust to a life without Stanley as if the events of the play [which consist in large part of invasion, manipulation, rape, physical assault, and psychological torture] had never happened'.[36]

Speech in this mode is actually integral to neoliberalism insofar as truth gets linked to the market by 'the regime of veridiction': 'not a law (*loi*) of truth, [but] the set of rules enabling one to establish which statements in a given discourse can be described as true or false'.[37] We need not see Douglas in *Party Time* as being wrong about what constitutes peace but rather appreciate how he forces an intimacy between the word 'peace' and protectionist policies and then invests that union with a truth value. His re-signification of peace conjures the language of liberalism and democracy, but only with a view to foreclosing ways of seeing and thinking democratically. In this way, Douglas and the play at large point to a contemporary reality whereby neoliberalism's 'most far-reaching legacy' is, arguably, the '*loss of a wider deliberative language for politics*'.[38] Just as Pinter's oeuvre has demonstrated the extent to which language creates reality, neoliberalism has fashioned a language which renders the market the dominant reality: freedom, for example, meaning chiefly the freedom to consume and buy and/or sell goods.

From an aesthetic standpoint, Douglas's sharpening of peace with descriptive phrases such as 'cast iron' and 'tight as a drum' folds the language of democracy into various moments in the play which dramatise violence, constraint and oppression, the repression of dissent, dehumanisation – many of the realities indexing police and authoritarian states. The immediately visible elite conditions of the party at Gavin's as well as the guest's overdetermined descriptions of the club and its various luxuries are progressively colonised by the more overt violence of images signalling what is transpiring in the police state outside the flat and, more seriously, of Jimmy's broken self, as that body and psyche literally appear and close the play.

The body of Jimmy rapt in pain appears only to speak of sometimes hearing voices and then quiet, of not hearing anything when terrible noises come, of not hearing, breathing, and of being blind, and then asking 'What am I?', only to have everything close and to suck on the dark (313–14). The dialogue and the visual form a complex image which, in bringing spectators near to the reality of Jimmy's punishment, calls out Douglas's euphemistic way of speaking about the police state being facilitated outside of this soirée for elites.

Across the political oeuvre one can discern the dramatisation of the material reality of a suffering victim in a way that unleashes the violence of that image on to parallel performances in the dramas where political discourse is employed to dehumanise the victims of power or to legitimate or refract their plight. In tandem with the subject matter and representational content relating to specific political realities, herein lies the politics of the work. In lifting 'the veil off sanctimonious language to reveal the profitable thuggery beneath it' and illustrating how the facts of suffering are smokescreened by political language,[39] Pinter's later dramas offer subject positions for spectators which can interrupt deferrals to easily digestible and manageable feelings and emotions. By inviting spectators to navigate the interplay between alienating performances of abuse and bodies rapt in suffering and traumatic postures, the dramas eclipse 'empathy or emotive identification, or any form of identification for that matter'[40] and are thereby capable of engendering affects which are closer to a total form of experience which produces a 'disruption, violence or dislocation of thinking'.[41]

Pinter's depiction of neoliberal political realities works simultaneously to challenge and dislodge neoliberal modes of thought by representing and then rendering their logic alien, as spoken through authority figures, precisely by linking neoliberal logics and discourses to their victims and social consequences. This dimension of Pinter's aesthetic, therefore, lifts the dramas out of their status as straightforward representations of synechdocal features of neoliberalism (Pinter's emphasis of torture and the police state as a monopoly of violence available to and used by the State being definitive of neoliberal democracy) and places them in a register whereby they become political by intervening at the level of the spectator's body, increasingly the terrain where capital has come to operate in recent decades as it formulates ever-complex means of resetting, even displacing, its own limits.

Harold Pinter's political plays are nonetheless not *about* neoliberalism or the neoliberalisation of Britain, as the phenomenon is not an 'automatic system', but rather an 'earthly process, realized through political action and institutional reinvention' across conjunctures and connections and through synechdochal moments and events and not through realties which are easily legible and relatable to some monolithic whole or totality.[42] By dismantling ways of speaking and of disciplining the body – behaviours which get legitimated by the powerful as a matter of political expediency – Pinter permits spectators to engage critically with types of agents, events and claims which emerge within 'the broader terrain of socioregulatory restructuring' under neoliberalism.[43] The sign systems in Pinter's dramas are predisposed to offer up subject positions which block routine and easy investment in the performance and which prompt spectators to think at the edge of, and even beyond, their habitual selves and quotidian subjectivities and on to new orientations towards political reality. Perhaps this will make Pinter's later dramas appear more complex than they have been taken to be, while suggesting how live theatre has at least some promise as an interruption to the ubiquitous market logics which instrumentalise life, route subjective and collective reality and experience through market-friendly paradigms of interpretation and understanding and, in the final analysis, 'offer precious little scope for the exercise of individual or collective voice'.[44]

CHRONOLOGY

1930	Harold Pinter is born in Hackney, East London.
1939	Evacuated to Cornwall during the Second World War.
1944–8	Attends the Hackney Downs Grammar School.
1948–9	Studies acting for two terms at RADA.
1949	*Kullus* written. He is tried as a conscientious objector.
1950	Two poems published in *Poetry London*.
1951–3	Studies for a term as the Central School of Speech & Drama.
	Works as an actor in Anew McMaster's company, including a tour of Ireland. Acts for one season in Donald Wolfit's company.
	The novel *The Dwarfs* is composed.
1954–7	Employed as an actor in regional repertory companies, using the name David Baron.
1956	Marries Vivien Merchant.
1957	15 May: His first play, *The Room*, is performed at the University of Bristol.
1958	28 February: First production of *The Dumb Waiter* in the Kleines Haus, Frankfurt.
	28 April: *The Birthday Party* is performed at the Lyric Opera House, Hammersmith.
	Daniel Brand (né Pinter) is born.
	The Hothouse is written, but remains unperformed and unpublished until 1980.
1959	9 July: *A Slight Ache* is broadcast on the BBC Third Programme. Contributes sketches to comedy revues.
1960	21 January: British premiere of *The Dumb Waiter*, in a double bill with *The Room* at the Hampstead Theatre Club.
	1 March: *A Night Out* broadcast on BBC radio.

24 April: *A Night Out* televised as part of ABC's *Armchair Theatre* series.

27 April: *The Caretaker* opens at the Arts Theatre.

27 July: *Night School* is broadcast by ARTV.

2 December: *The Dwarfs* is broadcast by the BBC Third Programme.

1961	11 May: *The Collection* is broadcast by ARTV.
1962	18 June: *The Collection* is staged by the Royal Shakespeare Company.
1963	28 March: *The Lover* is broadcast by ARTV.

June: The film of *The Caretaker* is released.

18 September: Stage versions of *The Lover* and *The Dwarfs* premiere together in a double-bill at the Arts Theatre.

14 November: *The Servant* is released.

1964	15 July: *The Pumpkin Eater* is released.

Performs the role of Garcin in a television production of Jean-Paul Sartre's *In Camera*, broadcast as part of the BBC's Wednesday Play series.

1965	25 March: *Tea Party* is broadcast by the BBC.

3 June: *The Homecoming* is premiered at the Aldwych Theatre.

1966	Appointed CBE.

9 February: *Accident* is released.

10 November: *The Quiller Memorandum* is released.

1967	20 February: *The Basement* is broadcast by BBC TV.

Directs Robert Shaw's *The Man in the Glass Booth*.

1968	Pinter's first collection of poems is published.

25 April: *Landscape* is broadcast on BBC radio.

1969	2 July: *Landscape* and *Silence* are performed together at the Aldwych Theatre.
1970	Directs James Joyce's *Exiles* at the Aldwych Theatre for the RSC.

Awarded the German Shakespeare Prize.

1971	1 June: *Old Times* premieres at the Aldwych Theatre.

29 July: *The Go-Between* is released.

Directs Simon Gray's *Butley*.

1972   Writes the *Proust Screenplay*, which is never filmed.

1973-83   Associate director of the National Theatre.

1973   13 April: *Monologue* is broadcast on BBC TV.

1975   23 April: *No Man's Land* premieres at the National Theatre.

1978   15 November: *Betrayal* premieres at the National Theatre.

1980   24 April: *The Hothouse* premieres at the Hampstead Theatre.

          Divorces Vivien Merchant.

          Marries Lady Antonia Fraser.

1981   22 January: *Family Voices* is broadcast by BBC radio.

          August: *The French Lieutenant's Woman* is released.

1982   14 October: *Other Places: A Kind of Alaska*, *Victoria Station* and *Family Voices* are produced together at the National Theatre.

1983   9 February: *Betrayal* is released, adapted from the 1978 play.

1984   13 March: *One for the Road* premieres at the Lyric, Hammersmith.

1988   20 October: *Mountain Language* premieres at the National Theatre.

1989   6 July: *Reunion* is released.

1990   The novel *The Dwarfs* is published.

          30 November: *The Comfort of Strangers* is released.

1991   31 October: *Party Time* premieres at the Almeida Theatre.

1992   24 November: *The Trial* is released.

1993   7 September: *Moonlight* premieres at the Almeida.

          Directs David Mamet's *Oleanna* for The Royal Court Theatre.

1995   Awarded the David Cohen British Literature Prize.

          Directs Ronald Harwood's *Taking Sides*.

1996   12 September: *Ashes to Ashes* premieres at the Almeida Theatre.

	Turns down a knighthood offered by Prime Minister John Major.
1997	Awarded a *Molière d'honneur* in Paris.
	Receives a BAFTA Fellowship.
1998	*Various Voices: Prose Poetry, Politics 1948–1998* is published. It subsequently recieves two updates, in 2005 and 2009.
	Awarded the title of Companion of Literature by the Royal Society of Literature.
2000	16 March: *Celebration* is performed in double bill with a revival of *The Room* at the Almeida Theatre.
	23 November: *Remembrance of Things Past* premieres at National Theatre, adapted by Di Trevis from Pinter's *Proust Screenplay*.
	Awarded the Critics' Circle Award for Distinguished Service to the Arts.
	Plays the role of the director in Samuel Beckett's *Catastrophe*, directed by David Mamet as part of the *Beckett on Film* project.
	Composes *The Tragedy of King Lear* screenplay, commissioned by Tim Roth. It is never filmed.
2001	Awarded The S. T. Dupont Golden Pen Award 2001 for a Lifetime's Distinguished Service to Literature.
	December: Diagnosed with cancer of the oesophagus.
2002	8 February: Performs in premiere of *Press Conference* at National Theatre.
	Made Companion of Honour.
2003	17 April: A staged version of *The Dwarfs*, adapted from the novel by Kerry Lee Crabbe, premieres at the Tricycle Theatre.
	War, a collection of poems, is published.
2004	Awarded the Wilfred Owen Prize for war poetry.
2005	Awarded the Nobel Prize for Literature. Pinter's Nobel Lecture is projected before the Nobel Academy in Stockholm on 7 December.
2006	Awarded the 10th European Theatre Prize.

Plays the title role in Samuel Beckett's *Krapp's Last Tape* at The Royal Court Theatre as part of their 50th anniversary celebrations.

2007   Awarded the Légion d'honneur by the French Prime Minister.

23 November: *Sleuth* is released.

2008   24 December: Harold Pinter dies, succumbing to cancer, and is buried on 31 December at the Kensal Green Cemetery, London.

NOTES

Introduction

1   'Video Player', Nobelprize.org. http://www.nobelprize.org/mediaplayer/index.
    php?id=21 (accessed 28 June 2011).
2   The original Swedish word 'avgrunden' might better be translated as 'chasm', though
    'precipice' captures the sense of risk that the word evokes.
3   Hare, David, 'In Pinter you find expressed the great struggle of the 20th century',
    The Guardian, 14 October 2005, G2, p. 8.
4   Albee, Edward, in Susan Hollis Merritt (ed.), 'Talking About Pinter', in Francis
    Gillen and Steven H. Gale (eds), *The Pinter Review: Collected Essays 2001 and 2002*
    (2002), p. 161 and p. 147.
5   Kane, Leslie (ed.), *David Mamet in Conversation*. Michigan: University of Michigan
    Press, 2001, p. 173.
6   Curtis, Nick, 'The Madness of Patrick Marber', *London Evening Standard*, 7
    November 2000, p. 23.
7   Dorfman, Ariel, 'The World That Harold Pinter Unlocked', *Washington Post*, 27
    December 2008, p. 15.
8   Sierz, Aleks, *In-Yer-Face Theatre: British Drama Today*. London: Faber and Faber,
    2001, p. 92.
9   Miller, Arthur, in Susan Hollis Merritt (ed.), 'Talking About Pinter', p. 66.
10 Billington, Michael, *Harold Pinter*, second edition. London: Faber and Faber, 2007,
    p. 15.
11 Pinter, Harold, *Monologue*, in *Plays Four*. London: Faber and Faber, 2011,
    pp. 122–3.
12 Pinter, Harold, 'On *Waiting for Godot*', in *Various Voices: Sixty Years of Prose, Poetry,
    Politics 1948–2008*, third edition. London: Faber and Faber, 2009, p. 17.
13 Billington, Michael, *Harold Pinter*, p. 11.
14 Pinter, Harold, 'Josepth Brearley 1909–1977', in *Various Voices*, p. 177.
15 Harwood, Ronald, *Sir Donald Wolfit: His Life and Work in the Unfashionable
    Theatre*. New York: St Martin's Press, 1971, p. 224.
16 Pinter, Harold, 'Mac', in *Various Voices*, p. 39.
17 Pinter, Harold, 'Writing for Myself', in *Plays Two*. London: Faber and Faber, 1996,
    p. vii.
18 This image has been uploaded on a website dedicated to the work of Ronald Searle
    at http://ronaldsearle.blogspot.co.uk/2010/10/searles-eye-view-imaginary-portraits.
    html (accessed 22 July 2013).
19 Trussler, Simon, *The Plays of Harold Pinter*. London: Victor Gollancz, 1973, p. 187.
20 Esslin, Martin, *Pinter the Playwright*. London: Methuen, 1982, p. 275.
21 Ibid., p. 262.
22 Published in 1970, it was revised and published under the title *Pinter: A Study of his
    Plays* in 1973, and as *Pinter the Playwright* in 1977 and 1982.

23 Esslin, Martin, *Pinter the Playwright*, p. 274.

24 Almansi, Guido and Simon Henderson, *Harold Pinter*. London; New York: Methuen, 1983, p. 18.

25 Susan Hollis Merritt mapped and scrutinised this undulating landscape of Pinter scholarship in her 1995 monograph, *Pinter in Play*. Since 1987, a great variety of Pinter scholarship has been collated in *The Pinter Review*, edited by Francis Gillen and Steven H. Gale and published by the University of Tampa Press.

Chapter 1: Invasions and Oppressions

1 Smith, Ian, *Pinter in the Theatre*. London: Nick Hern Books, 2005, p. 125.

2 Pinter, Harold, 'Writing for the Theatre', in *Plays One*. London: Faber and Faber, 1991, p. ix.

3 Pinter, Harold, *The Room*, in *Plays One*, p. 94. All subsequent references to this edition are given in parentheses.

4 Pinter, Harold, 'Writing for Myself', in *Plays Two*. London: Faber and Faber, 1996, p. viii.

5 In 1958, the Royal Court staged the first UK productions of plays written by black playwrights (Errol John's *Moon on a Rainbow Shawl* and Barry Reckord's *Flesh to a Tiger*). Sheila Delaney's *A Taste of Honey*, first performed in 1958, of course featured a black character. The first agency for black actors in Britain had been established in 1956 by Pearl Connor-Mogotsi and her husband Edric Connor and, in the same year, the West Indian Drama group was founded by Joan Clarke. In August 1956, John Elliot's *A Man from the Sun* starring Errol John, became the first television documentary drama to address the tensions experienced by Caribbean immigrant families in the UK, and it is not unlikely that Pinter saw or was aware of the broadcast. Stephen Bourne describes the cast list as reading 'like a directory of African and Caribbean actors and actresses then working in Britain' and lists seventeen names (113). Thomas Baptiste, who played Riley in the first professional production of *The Room* in 1960, went on to play the first black character in Granada TV's *Coronation Street* before a successful career in film.

6 Pinter, Harold, *The Birthday Party*, in *Plays One*, pp. 4–5. Subsequent references are in parentheses.

7 Fuller's teashops (and Lyon's Corner Houses, which Stanley refers to later) were sober, mature alternatives to public houses as places to meet socially over a beverage. Boots, the chain of chemists, offered a high-street lending library service in many branches until the 1960s. Goldberg also applies an association with both establishments as emblematic of a worthy, blameless existence (p. 50).

8 Pinter, Harold, interview with Brian Glanville, 'I am a Jew who Writes', *Jewish Chronicle*, 11 March 1960, p. 8.

9 Pinter, Harold, 'On *The Birthday Party* I', in *Various Voices: Sixty Years of Prose, Poetry, Politics 1948-2008*, third edition. London: Faber and Faber, 2009, pp. 22–3.

10 Pinter, Harold, *The Dumb Waiter*, in *Plays One*, p. 131. Subsequent references are in parentheses.

11 Pinter inserts two references to excellence in sporting teamwork to underscore the faltering teamwork on stage. Gus discovers a picture of a 'first eleven' of cricketers,

which is to say the top players on their team. There is also a reference to Aston Villa, who won the Football Association Challenge Cup against Manchester United in 1957.

12 Pinter, Harold, *The Hothouse*, in *Plays One*, p. 197. Subsequent references are in parentheses.

13 Wolf Cubs were established in 1916 to permit younger boys to participate in the Scouting community activities established by Robert Baden-Powell in 1907. Lamb accurately recites the 'law' as learned by boys between the ages of seven and eleven in such Cub Scout 'packs'. Lamb's name is deliberately ironic in this context.

14 Pinter, Harold, interview with Mark Batty, in Mark Batty, *About Pinter: The Playwright and the Work*. London: Faber and Faber, 2005, p. 82.

15 Pinter, Harold, 'The Art of Theatre', interview with Lawrence M. Bensky, in Ian Smith, *Pinter in the Theatre*, London: Nick Hern Books, 2005, p. 61.

16 The rental rates of £7 a week that Mick quotes to Davies in *The Caretaker* (in *Plays Two*, p. 33) are deliberately positioned at the high end of the market to make Davies wince at the possibility they might be demanded of him. They also contribute to the sense of unrealistic fantasy that surrounds Aston's ambitions to renovate the house.

17 Examining contemporary, comparable productions by the same producer, Donald McWhinnie, such as that of Samuel Beckett's *Embers*, broadcast in June 1959, or of Pinter's own *A Night Out*, broadcast in March 1960, a sonic landscape is present in both from the outset, supporting the notion that the omission of incidental, contextual sounds in the 1959 production *A Slight Ache* was a deliberate artistic decision.

18 Pinter, Harold, 'The Examination', in *Various Voices*, p. 99 and p. 103

19 Pinter, Harold, *A Slight Ache*, in *Plays One*, p. 167.

20 Pinter, Harold, *The Caretaker*, in *Plays Two*. London: Faber and Faber, 1996, p. 6, p. 17 and p. 22. Subsequent references are in parentheses.

21 Pinter, Harold, correspondence, in Mark Batty, *About Pinter*, p. 114.

22 These 'papers' might include the national identity card that was issued during the war. These were abolished in 1952, but the registration number became the National Health Service patient record number.

Chapter 2: The Company of Men and the Place of Women

1 Pinter, Harold, *The Dwarfs*. London: Faber and Faber, 1990, p. 56. All subsequent references to this edition are given in parentheses.

2 Wylie, Andrew, *Sex on Stage: Gender and Sexuality in Post-War British Theatre*. Bristol: Intellect, 2009, p. 53 and p. 72.

3 Pinter, Harold, *A Night Out*, in *Plays One*. London: Faber and Faber, 1991, p. 335. Subsequent references are in parentheses.

4 Milne, Drew, 'Pinter's Sexual Politics', in Peter Raby (ed.), *The Cambridge Companion to Harold Pinter*, second edition. Cambridge: Cambridge University Press, 2009, p. 239.

5 Pinter, Harold, 'Harold Pinter Replies', interview with Harry Thompson, in Ian Smith, *Pinter in the Theatre*, London: Nick Hern Books, 2005, p. 46.

6 Pinter, Harold, *Night School*, in *Plays Two*. London: Faber and Faber, 1996, p. 209.

7 Pinter, Harold, *The Collection*, in *Plays Two*, p. 131. Subsequent references are in parentheses.

8 Billington, Michael, *Harold Pinter*, second edition. London: Faber and Faber, 2007, p. 150.

9 Pinter, Harold, *The Tea Party*, in *Plays Three*. London: Faber and Faber, 1997, p. 125. Subsequent references are in parentheses.

10 Pinter, Harold, *The Lover*, in *Plays Two*, pp. 148-9. Subsequent references are in parentheses.

11 In the TV production, the two have separate single beds. No instruction is given in the script for this arrangement.

12 Peacock, D. Keith, *Harold Pinter and the New British Theatre*. London: Greenwood, 1997, p. 176.

13 Pinter, Harold, interview with Mel Gussow, 'Pinter on Pinter: The Lincoln Center Interview', in Francis Gillen and Steven H. Gale (eds), *The Pinter Review: Collected Essays 2001 and 2002*, Tampa: University of Tampa Press, 2002, p. 17.

14 The original manuscript is available in the Harold Pinter Archive at the British Library, under the catalogue number Add MS 88880/1/46.

15 At the time of writing, none of the original television plays are available for purchase on DVD, though unofficial publication of *The Lover* on sites such as YouTube does seem to have been tolerated. A 1976 Granada Television recording of *The Collection* was recently released on DVD (Apted, Michael (dir), *Laurence Olivier Presents Harold Pinter's 'The Collection'*, Network, 2009).

16 Pinter, Harold, *The Homecoming*, in *Plays Three*, pp. 60–1. Subsequent references are in parentheses.

17 Sakellaridou, Elizabeth, *Pinter's Female Portraits: A Study of Female Characters in the Plays of Harold Pinter*. London: Macmillan, 1988, p. 178.

18 Ibid., p. 107.

19 Pinter, Harold, *The Pumpkin Eater*, in *Collected Screenplays 1*. London: Faber and Faber, 2000, p. 131.

20 Pinter, Harold, *Accident*, in *Collected Screenplays 1*, pp. 420-1.

21 Original draft manuscripts are available in the Harold Pinter Archive at the British Library, under the catalogue number range Add MS 88880/1/21-24.

22 Milne, Drew, 'Pinter's Sexual Politics', p. 243.

Chapter 3: Present Continuous, Past Perfect

1 Bosworth, Patricia. 'Why Doesn't He Write More', *New York Times*, 27 October 1968, sec. V, p. 3.

2 Billington, Michael, *Harold Pinter*, second edition. London: Faber and Faber, 2007, p. 195.

3 Pinter, Harold, 'On Being Awarded the German Shakespeare Prize in Hamburg', in *Various Voices: Sixty Years of Prose, Poetry, Politics 1948–2008*, third edition. London: Faber and Faber, 2009, p. 52.

4 Knowles, Ronald, 'Joyce and Pinter: Exiles and Betrayal', *Barcelona English Language and Literature Studies*, No. 9 (1998), p. 186.

5   Pinter, Harold, *Landscape*, in *Plays Three*. London: Faber and Faber, 1997, p. 170.
    All subsequent references to this edition are given in parentheses.

6   Joyce, James, *Exiles*. London: Four Square, 1962, p. 36. Subsequent references are
    in parentheses.

7   Gussow, Mel, *Conversations with Harold Pinter*. London: Nick Hern Books, 1994,
    p. 38.

8   I consider the significance of Pinter's work on Joyce's play, and his correspondence
    with Samuel Beckett on the subject, in 'Joyce's Bridge to Late Twentieth-Century
    British Theater: Harold Pinter's Dialogue with *Exiles*', in Richard Brown (ed.), *A
    Companion to James Joyce*, London: Blackwell, 2008, pp. 300–17.

9   Pinter, Harold, *The Pumpkin Eater*, in *Collected Screenplays 1*. London: Faber and
    Faber: 2000, p. 95 and p. 98.

10 Pinter, Harold, *The Go-Between*, in *Collected Screenplays 2*. London: Faber and Faber,
    2000, p. 107.

11 Gale, Steven H. (ed.), *The Films of Harold Pinter*. New York: Albany, 2001, p. 83.

12 Pinter, Harold, *Silence*, in *Plays Three*, p. 190. Subsequent references are in
    parentheses.

13 Pinter, Harold, *Night*, in *Plays Three*, p. 219.

14 *Old Times* is the one of only two of his plays, the other being *A Kind of Alaska*, in
    which the women outnumber the men.

15 Pinter, Harold, *Old Times*, in *Plays Three*, p. 244. Subsequent references are in
    parentheses.

16 The word 'casserole' might also indicate better cuts of meat, and that the dish is
    cooked in the oven as opposed to on the hob which, historically, also denotes a class
    difference in affordability of produce and facilities for food preparation. Deeley later
    mentions how Kate would be happy to 'put the old pot on the old gas stove' (279),
    thereby implying that this casserole might more pedantically be called a stew.

17 'Lovely to Look at Delightful to Know' and 'Smoke Gets in your Eyes' were
    written by Jerome Kern, with lyrics by Otto A. Harbach and Dorothy Fields, for
    the 1935 musical film *Roberta*, which was remade by MGM as *Lovely to Look At*
    in 1952. 'Blue Moon', written by Richard Rodgers and Lorenz Hart in 1934, was
    covered by Elvis Presley in 1956. The Fred Astaire performances of Jerome Kern
    and Dorothy Fields' 'The Way You Look Tonight' and of George and Ira Gershwin's
    'They Can't Take That Away From Me' featured prominently in their respective
    films *Swing Time* (1936) and *Shall We Dance* (1937) and became hits in 1956 for,
    respectively, The Jaguars and Louis Armstrong. Frank Sinatra sang Eric Maschwitz
    and Jack Strachey's 1936 song 'These Foolish Things (Remind Me of You)' on one
    of his 1946 debut 78rpm releases, collated as his first long-player in 1955, and
    later sang Jerome Kern and Oscar Hammerstein II's 'All the Things You Are' and
    Cole Porter's 1934 song 'I Get a Kick Out of You', contributing these tunes to the
    popular soundscape of the 1950s. The exception here is the 1960 ballad 'Sixteen
    Reasons (Why I Love You)', written by Bill and Doree Post and made popular by
    Connie Stevens. Anna's sung line from this number, 'The way you comb your hair',
    fools Deeley into following with 'Oh no they can't take that away from me' from
    'These Foolish Things', due to the first song's lyrical similarity with the thematic
    development of that second song (Pinter, Harold, *Old Times*, p. 265). This is a small
    example of how Anna derails and undermines Deeley that might have been noted
    by some members of the play's first audiences, but is mostly imperceptible to today's
    theatre-goers.

18 Gale, Steven H., *Sharp Cut: Harold Pinter's Screenplays and the Artistic Process*. Lexington: University of Kentucky Press, 2003, p. 373.

19 Pinter, Harold, *The Go-Between*, p. 3.

20 Pinter, Harold, *Langrische, Go Down*, in *Collected Screenplays 1*, p. 194.

21 Pinter, Harold, 'Introduction', in *Collected Screenplays 2*, p. ix.

22 Ibid.

23 Pinter, Harold, *No Man's Land*, in *Plays Three*, p. 323. Subsequent references are in parentheses.

24 Billington, Michael, *Harold Pinter*, p. 244.

25 For London audiences, then as now, the notoriety of Hampstead Heath as a gay cruising ground is one inference activated by Pinter's choice of locations.

26 Gambon was at that time playing the role of Hirst in a production of *No Man's Land* at the Duke of York's Theatre, London.

Chapter 4: The Impossible Family

1 One way of rationalising Ruth and Teddy's behaviour is to postulate that Max hits the nail on the head when first meeting her: that she is an escort that Teddy has paid to play a role, but who finds a better prospect with his family as a result of that guise. Her reference to 'the children' might simply, in this interpretation, be of the same currency as Richard's evocation of fictional children in *The Lover*. There is no further textual evidence for this, but nor is there any for the existence of the children, and it is an interpretation that might be fruitful in the rehearsal room as actors attempt to inhabit their roles.

2 Pinter, Harold, *Night*, in *Plays Three*, London: Faber and Faber, 1997, p. 215.

3 Joyce, James, *Exiles*. London: Four Square, 1962, p. 158.

4 Gale, Steven H., *Sharp Cut: Harold Pinter's Screenplays and the Artistic Process*. Lexington: University of Kentucky Press, 2003, p. 193.

5 Pinter, Harold, *Monologue*, in *Plays Four*. London: Faber and Faber, 2011, p. 123.

6 Pinter, Harold, *Betrayal*, in *Plays Four*, p. 33. All subsequent references to this edition are given in parentheses.

7 Pinter, Harold, 'Butley', The American Film Theatre/Cinebill, January 1974, p. 33.

8 In translation, this line is often rendered with the word for 'you' in the plural, in languages where such an indication is unavoidable. The fecund ambiguity of the 'you' in English participates in the construction of the impossible family, in the manner in which it offers a hesitation of intended meaning that captures the tensions between Jerry, Emma and Robert.

9 *Family Voices* had received its first performance, in its intended medium as a radio play, on BBC Radio 3 on 22 January 1981.

10 Pinter, Harold, *Victoria Station*, in *Plays Four*, p. 194.

11 Pinter, Harold, *Family Voices*, in *Plays Four*, p. 133. Subsequent references are in parentheses.

12 In Act 2 Scene 2 of William Shakespeare's *Hamlet*, the eponymous hero refers to Polonius, Ophelia's father, as a fishmonger, which has commonly been understood to imply a bawd or a pimp.

13 Pinter, Harold, *A Kind of Alaska*, in *Plays Four*, p. 151. Subsequent references are in parentheses.

14 In the 1911 census of the UK population, the latest that is publicly available, there were only 35 males named Hornby.

15 Pinter, Harold, *Moonlight*, in *Plays Four*, p. 348. Subsequent references are in parentheses.

16 Extending this comparison further, we might note that, as with Beethoven's opus 27 no.2 C# minor sonata ('Moonlight'), Pinter opens with something of a gentle prelude rather than the allegro statement that was usual of the sonata form. Though there is no evidence that Beethoven's sonata was a meditation on death, it manifests and innovates musical mourning devices known as *Trauermusik*.

17. Pinter, Harold, *One for the Road*, in *Plays Four*, pp. 240–1. Subsequent references are in parentheses.

18 Pinter, Harold, *Mountain Language*, in *Plays Four*, p. 255. Subsequent references are in parentheses.

19 'Joe Dokes' or 'Doakes' is an idiomatic everyman name, now rarely used, employed to suggest everyone and no one in particular, or used as a placeholder name, like 'Fred Bloggs' or 'John Doe'. Pinter later invokes this no-man figure in his 2005 Nobel Lecture: 'The United States possesses 8,000 active and operational nuclear warheads [...] Who, I wonder, are they aiming at? Osama bin Laden? You? Me? Joe Dokes?' (Pinter, Harold, 'Art, Truth and Politics: The Nobel Lecture', in Harold Pinter, *Various Voices: Sixty Years of Prose, Poetry, Politics 1948–2008*, third edition. London: Faber and Faber, 2009, p. 298).

20 Pinter, Harold, *Party Time*, in *Plays Four*, p. 296. Subsequent references are in parentheses.

21 See p. 247 of Ann C. Hall's contribution to this volume.

22 Pinter, Harold, *Celebration*, in *Plays Four*, p. 480. Subsequent references are in parentheses.

Chapter 5: Politics and the Artist as Citizen

1 Wardle, Irving, 'Comedy of Menace', in Charles Marowitz, Tom Milne and Owen Hale (eds), *The Encore Reader: A Chronicle of the New Drama*, London: Methuen, 1965, pp. 90–1.

2 Rebellato, Dan *1956 and All That: The Making of Modern Drama*. London; New York: Routledge, 1999, p. 13 and p. 18.

3 Roberts, Philip, *The Royal Court Theatre and the Modern Stage*. Cambridge: Cambridge University Press, 1999, p. 57.

4 Pinter, Harold, 'Writing for the Theatre', in *Plays One*. London: Faber and Faber, 1991, p. ix.

5 Pinter, Harold, 'The Art of Theatre', interview with Lawrence M. Bensky, in Ian Smith, *Pinter in the Theatre*, London: Nick Hern Books, 2005, p. 59.

6 Pinter, Harold, 'Writing for Myself', in *Plays Two*. London: Faber and Faber, 1996, p. x.

7 The most notable document of the distinction between an engaged theatre and a poetic theatre from this period is the argument between Kenneth Tynan and Eugène

Ionesco that took place in the letters pages of *The Observer* in 1958 (Zarhy-Levo, Yael, *The Theatrical Critic as Cultural Agent: Constructing Pinter, Orton and Stoppard as Absurdist Playwrights*. Oxford and New York: Peter Lang, 2001, pp. 19–20).

8   Fraser, Antonia, *Must You Go? My Life with Harold Pinter*. London: Phoenix, 2011, p. 173.

9   Pinter, Harold, *The Hothouse*, in *Plays One*, p. 186.

10 The previous two British laureates were Vidiadhar Surajprasad Naipaul in 2001 and William Golding in 1983.

11 The BBC management were experiencing a difficult relationship with the British government at this time, in the aftermath of a programme broadcast of the *Today* programme on 29 May 2003 in which the government's use of intelligence in the lead up to the war in Iraq was heavily criticised (Bennett, Daniel, *Digital Media and Reporting Conflict: Blogging and the BBC's Coverage of War and Terrorism*. London: Routledge, 2013, pp. 45–6).

12 See p. 1 of the introduction to this volume.

13 Taylor-Batty, Mark, and Linda Renton, 'Report from Britain', in Francis Gillen (ed.), *Pinter Review: Nobel Prize/Europe Theatre Prize Volume*, Tampa: University of Florida Press, 2008, p. 227.

14 Pinter, Harold, 'House of Commons Speech', in *Various Voices: Sixty Years of Prose, Poetry, Politics 1948–2008*, third edition. London: Faber and Faber, 2009, p. 264.

15 Pinter, Harold, 'Art, Truth and Politics: The Nobel Lecture', in *Various Voices*, p. 285. All subsequent references to this edition are given in parentheses, except where source would be unclear.

16 Pinter, Harold, 'Writing for the Theatre', p. xi.

17 Pinter, Harold, interview with Nicholas Hern, 'A Play and its Politics, a conversation between Harold Pinter and Nicholas Hern', in Harold Pinter, *One for the Road*, London: Methuen, 1985, pp. 20–1.

18 Pinter, Harold, 'Arthur Miller's Socks', in *Various Voices*, p. 66.

19 Pinter, Harold, 'The Art of Theatre', interview with Lawrence M. Bensky, p. 59.

20 See p. 264 of Basil Chiasson's contribution to this volume.

21 Billington, Michael, *Harold Pinter*, second edition. London: Faber and Faber, 2007, p. 423.

22 The political spillage from the phone-hacking scandal of 2011 brought to public attention significant relationships between Rupert Murdoch, his family and members of his senior staff and the successive Prime Ministers Tony Blair, Gordon Brown and David Cameron.

23 Pinter, Harold, *Precisely*, in *Plays Four*. London: Faber and Faber, 2011, pp. 218–19. Subsequent references are in parentheses. Government papers that were declassified on 1 August 2013 revealed the degree to which the world was on the brink of nuclear aggression and that, in 1983, Thatcher's 'government rowed with the British Medical Association over its estimate that Britain would suffer 33 million casualties in a nuclear attack, with more than 1 million dying from the blasts in London alone'. Booth, Robert and Alan Travis, 'National archives, Whitehall prepared Queen's speech for third world war', *The Guardian*, 1 August 2013, p. 1.

24 Pinter, Harold, 'Wilfred Owen Award for Poetry', in *Various Voices*, p. 267.

25 Fraser, Antonia, *Must You Go? My Life with Harold Pinter*, p. 167.

26 Pinter, Harold, interview with Nick Hern, 'A Play and its Politics, a conversation between Harold Pinter and Nicholas Hern', p. 13.

27 Pinter, Harold, *One for the Road*, in *Plays Four*, p. 244.

28 Pinter, Harold, *The New World Order*, in *Plays Four*, p. 277.

29 Pinter, Harold, *Press Conference*. London: Faber and Faber, 2002, p. 10. Subsequent references are in parentheses.

30 See p. 242 of Ann C. Hall's contribution to this volume.

31 Pinter, Harold, *The Birthday Party*, in *Plays One*, p. 61. Subsequent references are in parentheses.

32 Pinter, Harold, *The Hothouse*, in *Plays One*, p. 272.

33 Pattie, David, 'Feeding Power: Pinter, Bakhtin and Inverted Carnival', in Mary Brewer (ed.), *Harold Pinter's 'The Dumb Waiter'*, Amsterdam and New York: Rodopi, 2009, pp. 57–8.

34 Gordon, Robert, *Harold Pinter*. Ann Arbor: University of Michigan Press, 2012, p. 177.

35 Pinter, Harold, *Party Time – A Screenplay*. London: Faber and Faber, 1991, p. 28. Page numbers for this play will usually be given from the *Plays Four* collection. Additional scenes from the screenplay shall refer to this publication.

36 Pinter, Harold, 'Order', in *Various Voices*, p. 189.

37 Pinter, Harold, 'After Lunch', in *Various Voices*, p. 275.

38 Pinter, Harold, *Celebration*, in *Plays Four*, p. 460. Subsequent references are in parentheses.

39 Pinter, Harold, *The Birthday Party*, p. 74.

40 Margaret Thatcher became Lady Thatcher in 1990. That Melissa is one of only two titled female characters in Pinter's works and the proximity of the composition of *Party Time* to the receipt of a title by Thatcher, facilitates speculation that she is one model for that character.

41 Pinter, Harold, *Party Time*, in *Plays Four*, p. 290. Subsequent references are in parentheses.

42 Pinter, Harold, 'American Football', in *Various Voices*, p. 280.

43 Pinter, Harold, 'The "Special Relationship"', in *Various Voices*, p. 281.

44 Grimes, Charles, *Harold Pinter's Politics: A Silence beyond Echo*. Madison, WIS and Teaneck, NJ: Fairleigh Dickinson University Press, 2005, pp. 41–2.

45 Pinter, Harold, interview with Mark Batty, in Mark Batty, *About Pinter: The Playwright and the Work*. London: Faber and Faber, 2005, p. 87.

46 Pinter had his name removed from the credits of *The Remains of the Day*, after his work had been radically revised by the production team.

47 Pinter, Harold, *Ashes to Ashes*, in *Plays Four*, p. 404. Subsequent references are in parentheses.

48 I consider the issues of prosthetic memories and the manifestations of the Holocaust in *Ashes to Ashes* in more detail in my work, 'What remains? Ashes to Ashes, popular culture, memory and atrocity', in Craig Owens (ed.), *Pinter etc.*, Newcastle: Cambridge Scholars Publishing, 2009, pp. 99–116.

49 If this film was indeed Pinter's source, it offers some thematic connections with the play, including eroticism, a man's attempts to know and control a woman and the liminal spaces between people, places and political history. That Rebecca recalls others in the cinema laughing at the film underscores her isolation in feeling dread and empathy.

50 Pinter, Harold, 'Art, Truth and Politics: The Nobel Lecture', p. 288.

Chapter 6: Some Concluding Remarks

1   It would be another five years before he publicly acknowledged his decision that there would be no more plays from his pen. Pinter, Harold, interviewed by Mark Lawson, *Front Row*, BBC Radio 4, 28 February 2005.

2   Pinter performed Krapp in a wheelchair. This was not out of place in a drama by Samuel Beckett, whose work is populated by the disabled and the infirm. The choice was made of necessity, to enable Pinter to manage the rehearsal process and the ten performances.

3   Beckett, Samuel, *Krapp's Last Tape*, in *The Complete Dramatic Works*, London: Faber and Faber, 1986, p. 223.

4   Hare, David, in Richard Eyre (ed.), *A Celebration: Harold Pinter*. London: Faber and Faber, 2000, p. 21.

5   Eyre, Richard, 'A fair cricketer, a good actor and a playwright of rare power and originality', *The Observer*, 28 December 2008, http://www.theguardian.com/culture/2008/dec/28/harold-pinter-theatre (accessed 19 September 2013).

6   'Et pour ne parler que du silence, n'attend-il pas toujours son musicien?', Beckett, Samuel, letter to Edouard Coester, 11 March 1954, in George Craig, Martha Dow Fehsenfeld, Dan Gunn and Lois More Overbeck (eds), *The Letters of Samuel Beckett, 1941–1956*, Cambridge: Cambridge University Press, 2011, pp. 475–6.

Chapter 7: The Curse of Pinter

1   Pinter, Harold, 'Writing for Myself', in *Plays Two*. London: Faber and Faber, 1996, p. ix.

2   Pinter, Harold, interview with Brian Johnston, 'A View from the Boundary', *Test Match Special*, BBC Radio 4, broadcast 25 August 1990.

3   Pinter, Harold, interview with Harry Burton, *Working With Pinter*, DVD, London: Illuminations, 2010.

4   Pinter, Harold, Personal Statement to Conscientious Objectors Tribunal, 1948. Public Records Office, Kew, London.

5   Billington, Michael, *Harold Pinter*, second edition. London: Faber and Faber, 2007, p. 59.

6   Pinter, Harold, 'On *The Birthday Party* I', in *Various Voices: Sixty Years of Prose, Poetry, Politics 1948-2008*, third edition. London: Faber and Faber, 2009, p. 24.

7   Judgement at Pinter's Conscientious Objectors Tribunal, 1948. Public Records Office, Kew, London.

8   Pinter, Harold, 'Hutton and the Past', in *Various Voices*, p. 47.

9   Pinter, Harold, 'Writing for the Theatre', in *Plays One*. London: Faber and Faber, 1991, p. xii.

10 Billington, Michael, *Harold Pinter*, p. 43.

11 Woolf, Henry, interview with Harry Burton, *Working With Pinter*, DVD, London: Illuminations, 2010.

12 Billington, Michael, *Harold Pinter*, p. 72.

13 Pinter, Harold, interview with John Sherwood, *The Rising Generation, No. 7. A Playwright – Harold Pinter*, BBC European Service, 3 March 1960.

14   Pinter, Harold, *The Birthday Party*, in *Plays One*, p. 43.
15   Pinter, Harold, *A Night Out*, in *Plays One*, p. 342.
16   Pinter, Harold, *The Dumb Waiter*, in *Plays One*, pp. 130–1.
17   Pinter, Harold, interview with Harry Burton, *Working With Pinter*, DVD, London: Illuminations, 2010.
18   Henry Woolf in conversation with the author.
19   Henry Woolf in conversation with the author.
20   Email from Antonia Fraser to the author.
21   Lahr, John, *Demolition Man: Harold Pinter*, December 2007, http://www.johnlahr. com/pinter.html (accessed 28 July 2013).

Chapter 7: 'Who the Hell's That?': Pinter's Memory Plays of the 1970s

1   Pinter, Harold, 'Writing for the Theatre', in *Plays One*. London: Faber and Faber, 1991, pp. ix–x.
2   Smith, Ian, *Pinter in the Theatre*, London: Nick Hern Books, 2005, p. 33.
3   Gussow, Mel, *Conversations with Harold Pinter*. London: Nick Hern Books, 1994, pp. 38-9.
4   The dates in parentheses refer to the year of first production. At the time of writing (early 2013), a major revival of *Old Times* is in production at the Harold Pinter Theatre in London, with Kristin Scott Thomas and Lia Williams alternating the roles of Anna and Kate, and Rufus Sewell as Deeley; the director is Ian Rickson. Rickson also directed Scott Thomas in *Betrayal* at the Comedy Theatre in 2011. Mike Nichols is directing Daniel Craig, Rachel Weisz and Rafe Spall in a Broadway revival of *Betrayal* at the Ethel Barrymore Theatre, due to open in October 2013; Ian McKellen and Patrick Stewart are also due to appear on Broadway in *No Man's Land*, in repertory with a revival of their West End production of *Waiting for Godot*, in late 2013, both directed by Sean Mathias.
5   See Quigley, Austin, 'Pinter, Politics and Postmodernism (1)', in Peter Raby (ed.), *The Cambridge Companion to Harold Pinter*, second edition. Cambridge: Cambridge University Press, 2009. p. 8.
6   Smith, Ian, *Pinter in the Theatre*, p. 34.
7   Ibid., p. 157.
8   Stokes, John, 'Pinter and the 1950s', in Peter Raby (ed.), *The Cambridge Companion to Harold Pinter*, p. 32.
9   Quigley, Austin, 'Pinter, politics and postmodernism (1)', ibid., p. 23.
10   Pinter, Harold, interview with John Sherwood, *The Rising Generation, No. 7. A Playwright – Harold Pinter*, BBC European Service, 3 March 1960. Quoted in Malcolm Page, *File on Pinter*. London: Methuen Drama, 1993, p. 102.
11   Pinter, Harold, *Landscape*, in *Plays Three*. London: Faber and Faber, 1997, p. 166. All subsequent references to this edition are given in parentheses.
12   Pinter, Harold, *Silence*, in *Plays Three*, p. 198. Subsequent references are in parentheses.
13   Barber, John, *Daily Telegraph*, 3 July 1969, quoted in Malcolm Page (ed.), *File on Pinter*, p. 80.

Notes

14 See p. 96.

15 See James Palmer and Michael Riley, *The Films of Joseph Losey*, Cambridge: Cambridge University Press, 1993, especially the analysis of *The Go-Between* in 'Chapter 6: The Annihilation of Time', pp. 90–116.

16 Pinter, Harold, *Old Times*, in *Plays Three*, p. 246. Subsequent references are in parentheses.

17 See p. 107.

18 Quoted in Ian Smith, *Pinter in the Theatre*, p. 147.

19 Raby, Peter, 'Tales of the City: Some Places and Voices in Pinter's Plays', in Peter Raby (ed.), *The Cambridge Companion to Harold Pinter*, p. 61.

20 Pinter, Harold, *No Man's Land*, in *Plays Three*, p. 317. Subsequent references are in parentheses.

21 John Bury designed the first productions of *Landscape, Silence, Old Times, No Man's Land* and *Betrayal* and deserves immense credit for creating a distinct visual style for Pinter in the 1970s.

22 Quoted in Ian Smith, *Pinter in the Theatre*, p. 164. Italics in original.

23 Lambert, J. W., *Drama*, No. 102 (Autumn 1971), pp. 15-7, quoted in Malcolm Page (ed.), *File on Pinter*, p. 42.

24 Quoted in Ian Smith, *Pinter in the Theatre*, p. 147.

25 Simon, John, *Hudson Review*, Spring 1972, in Malcolm Page (ed.), *File on Pinter*, p. 46.

26 Kalem, T. E., *Time*, 29 November 1971, in Malcolm Page (ed.), *File on Pinter*, p. 43.

27 Raine, Craig, *New Statesman*, 1 August 1975, in Malcolm Page (ed.), *File on Pinter*, p. 52.

28 Not all of the scenes in the play follow the reverse time-scale: scenes two, six and seven take place chronologically 'Later' than the preceding scene.

29 Roche, Anthony, 'Pinter and Ireland', in Peter Raby (ed.), *The Cambridge Companion to Harold Pinter*, p. 208.

30 Pinter, Harold, *Betrayal*, in *Plays Four*, p. 19. Subsequent references are in parentheses.

31 This speech can usefully be compared to A's impassioned monologue in Sarah Kane's *Crave* (1998) which also takes the form of a convulsive torrent of feeling. Kane's linguistic experimentation, especially in *Crave* and *4.48 Psychosis* (2000), carries Pinter's influence; Pinter admired Kane's work and publicly defended her controversial play *Blasted*. See *Crave* in Sarah Kane, *Complete Plays* (London: Methuen Drama, 2001), pp. 169–70.

32 Peter, John, *Sunday Times*, 27 January 1991, quoted in Malcolm Page (ed.), *File on Pinter*, p. 58.

33 Quoted in Ian Smith, *Pinter in the Theatre*, p. 153.

34 Richard Allen Cave, 'Body Language in Pinter's Plays', in Peter Raby (ed.), *The Cambridge Companion to Harold Pinter*, p. 125.

35 Grant, Steve *Time Out*, 8–14 August 1975, quoted in Malcolm Page (ed.), *File on Pinter*, p. 53.

36 Austin Quigley, 'Pinter, Politics and Postmodernism (1)', in Peter Raby (ed.), *The Cambridge Companion to Harold Pinter*, p. 25.

37 Pinter in interview in 1966, quoted in Ian Smith, *Pinter in the Theatre*, p. 52.

Chapter 7: Revisiting Pinter's Women

1   Gussow, Mel, *Conversations with Harold Pinter*. London: Nick Hern Books, 1994, pp. 151–2.

2   As he notes during his interview with Nicholas Hern in the preface to the 1985 edition of *One for the Road*, politics has always been a part of his work. Referencing *The Dumb Waiter* as an example, Pinter says, '[t]he political metaphor was very clear to the actors and the directors of the first production in 1960. It was not, however, clear to the critics of the time – Kenneth Tynan, for instance, discussed the play in terms of its supposed debt to T. S. Eliot [...] He was clearly considering the play for its formal properties. It never occurred to him that it was *about* anything' (Pinter, Harold, interview with Nicholas Hern, 'A Play and its Politics, a Conversation between Harold Pinter and Nicholas Hern', in Harold Pinter, *One for the Road*, London: Methuen, 1985, p. 7). Critics, however, continued to see his plays as distinct from the political drama of the London theatre of the 1960s and 1970s. As Drew Milne observes:

> Based principally on *The Birthday Party*, *The Caretaker*, and *The Homecoming*, Pinter's reputation was fostered in opposition to the forms of political theatre which emerged in the 1950s and persisted in the 1970s. Many British playwrights of this period were socialists, engaged in theatre as a political forum. Among Pinter's attractions for the critical establishment was the way his work appeared to scorn such approaches and could be seen as the continuation of dramatic art as something above and beyond politics. (Milne, Drew, 'Pinter's Sexual Politics', in Peter Raby (ed.), *The Cambridge Companion to Harold Pinter*, second edition. Cambridge: Cambridge University Press, 2009, p. 233)

3   Pinter, Harold, *The Dumb Waiter*, in *Plays One*. London: Faber and Faber, 1991, pp. 130–1.

4   Pinter, Harold, *The Homecoming*, in *Plays Three*. London: Faber and Faber, 1997, pp. 60–1.

5   Mark Taylor-Batty in Chapter 2 of this volume clearly illustrates the feminine difference in Pinter's plays, but for many critics, the representation of Pinter's women continues to confound. In a recent essay, Austin Quigley, for example, discusses the relationship between the personal and the political in postmodern terms, with no mention of the feminist contribution to the discussion.

6   Pinter, Harold, interview with Nicholas Hern, 'A Play and its Politics, a Conversation between Harold Pinter and Nicholas Hern', p. 8.

7   Ibid., p. 18.

8   Billington, Michael, *Harold Pinter*, second edition. London: Faber and Faber, 2007, p. 294. Subsequent references are in parentheses.

9   Pinter, Harold, interview with Nicholas Hern, 'A Play and its Politics, a Conversation between Harold Pinter and Nicholas Hern', p. 22.

10 Milne, Drew, 'Pinter's Sexual Politics', in Peter Raby (ed.), *The Cambridge Companion to Harold Pinter*, p. 239

11 Pinter, Harold, *One for the Road*, in *Plays Four*, London: Faber and Faber, 2011, p. 224. All subsequent references to this edition are given in parentheses.

12 Billington, Michael, *Harold Pinter*, p. 296.

13 Roche, Anthony, 'Pinter and Ireland', in Peter Raby (ed.), *The Cambridge Companion to Harold Pinter*, p. 209.

14 Pinter, Harold, *Mountain Language*, in *Plays Four*, p. 255. Subsequent references are in parentheses.

15 Billington, Michael, *Harold Pinter*, p. 311.

16 Billington notes that she has been defined as a prostitute, and now she behaves like one: 'In short, we take on the role society assigns to us' (Billington, Michael, *Harold Pinter*, p. 312). And while that is certainly true, the horror of this play is represented in the decline of the strong female character, the process of her descent into the patriarchal gulag.

17 Pinter, Harold, *Party Time*, in *Plays Four*, p. 286. Subsequent references are in parentheses.

18 Pinter, Harold, *Party Time – A Screenplay*. London: Faber and Faber, 1991, pp. 9–10. Page numbers for this play are from the *Plays Four* collection, except in cases such as this where some of the additional scenes from Pinter's screenplay version are being quoted.

19 Billington, Michael, *Harold Pinter*, p. 306.

20 Ibid., p. 307.

21 Ibid., p. 318.

22 Ibid., p. 351.

Chapter 7: Pinter's Political Dramas: Staging Neoliberal Discourse and Authoritarianism

1 Harvey, David, *A Brief History of Neoliberalism*. Oxford and New York: Oxford University Press, 2005, p. 23.

2 See Foucault, Michel, 2008; Brown, Wendy, 2005; Lemke, Thomas, 2001, 2002 and 2011; and Giroux, Henry A., 2008.

3 There have been few links between Pinter's dramas and Margaret Thatcher's politics. One exception is Mary Luckhurst, who claims that 'the Conservative party's regime, especially their economic and foreign policies under Margaret Thatcher from 1979–1990' was one the several factors important in determining Pinter on the path to politicization as both playwright and activist. Luckhurst, Mary, 'Torture in the Plays of Harold Pinter', in Mary Luckhurst (ed.), *Blackwell Companion to Modern British and Irish Drama 1880–2005*, Malden MA: Blackwell, 2006, p. 364.

4 Watt, Stephen, 'Things, Voices, Events: Harold Pinter's *Mountain Language* as Testamental Text', *Modern Drama*, Vol. 52, No. 1 (2009), p. 49.

5 Gordon, Robert, 'Pinter's Mise-en-Scène: *Party Time* as Television Drama', in Francis Gillen, with Steven H. Gale (eds), *The Pinter Review, Nobel Prize/European Theatre Prize Volume: 2005–2008*, Tampa: University of Tampa Press, 2008, p. 177.

6 Harvey, David, *A Brief History of Neoliberalism*, p. 37.

7 Klein, Naomi, *The Shock Doctrine: The Rise of Disaster Capitalism*. Toronto: Vintage, 2008, pp. 139–40.

8 Peck, Jamie, *Constructions of Neoliberal Reason*. Oxford: Oxford University Press, 2012, p. 25.

9   Pinter, Harold, *Precisely*, in *Plays Four*. London: Faber and Faber, 2011, pp. 215–16. All subsequent references to this edition are given in parentheses.

10 Grimes, Charles, *Harold Pinter's Politics: A Silence beyond Echo*. Madison, WIS and Teaneck, NJ: Fairleigh Dickinson University Press, 2005, pp. 209–10.

11 Klein, Naomi, *The Shock Doctrine*, p. 100.

12 Ibid., pp. 121–2.

13 Horkheimer, Max, *Critique of Instrumental Reason: Lectures and Essays since the End of World War II*. New York: Seabury Press, 1974.

14 Hall, Stuart, 'New Labour Has Picked Up where Thatcherism Left Off', the *Guardian*, 6 August 2003, http://www.guardian.co.uk/politics/2003/aug/06/society.labour (accessed 20 July 2013).

15 Quoted in Billington, Michael, *Harold Pinter*, second edition. London: Faber and Faber, 2007 p. 304.

16 Bull, John, *New British Political Dramatists: Howard Brenton, David Hare, Trevor Griffiths and David Edgar*. Pennsylvania: Macmillan, 1984, p. 219.

17 Pinter, Harold, 'Art, Truth and Politics: The Nobel Lecture', in *Various Voices: Sixty Years of Prose, Poetry, Politics 1948–2008*, third edition. London: Faber and Faber, 2009, p. 288. Subsequent references are in parentheses.

18 Pinter, Harold, *Mountain Language*, in *Plays Four*, pp. 253–4. Subsequent references are in parentheses.

19 Couldry, Nick, *Why Voice Matters: Culture and Politics after Neoliberalism*. London: Sage, 2010, p. 100.

20 Fraser, Antonia, *Must You Go? My Life with Harold Pinter*. London: Phoenix, 2011, pp. 167–8.

21 Couldry, Nick, *Why Voice Matters*, p. 98.

22 Billington, Michael, *Harold Pinter*, p. 329.

23 Pinter, Harold, *One for the Road*, in *Plays Four*, p. 224. Subsequent references are in parentheses.

24 Batty, Mark, *Harold Pinter*. Tavistock: Northcote House, 2001, pp. 112–13.

25 See, for example, Quigley, Austin 1975, p. 275, and 2001, pp. 14–17; Silverstein, Marc, 1993, p. 144; Batty, Mark, 2001, p. 91.

26 Hudgins, Christopher C., 'Harold Pinter's *The Handmaid's Tale*: Freedom, Prison, and a Hijacked Script', in Thomas Fahy and Kimball King (eds), *Captive Audience: Prison and Captivity in Contemporary Theatre*. New York and London: Routledge, 2003, pp. 82–3.

27 Luckhurst, Mary, 'Torture in the Plays of Harold Pinter', in Mary Luckhurst (ed.), *Blackwell Companion to Modern British and Irish Drama 1880–2005*, Malden MA: Blackwell, 2006, pp. 364–5. Luckhurst quotes Pinter, Harold, interview with Nicholas Hern, 'A Play and its Politics, a Conversation between Harold Pinter and Nicholas Hern', in Harold Pinter, *One for the Road*, London: Methuen, 1985, p. 17.

28 Sontag, Susan, *Regarding the Pain of Others*. London: Hamish Hamilton, 2003, p. 44.

29 Klein, Naomi, *The Shock Doctrine*, p. 18.

30 Harvey, David, *A Brief History of Neoliberalism*, p. 77.

31 Ibid., p. 64.

32 Fairclough, Norman, *New Labour, New Language?* London: Routledge, 2000, p. 7.

33 Deleuze, Gilles, *The Logic of Sense*, trans. Mark Lester with Charles Stivale,

Constantin V. Boundas (ed.), third edition. London and New York: Continuum, 2004, p. 165.

34 Pinter, Harold, *Party Time*, in *Plays Four*, pp. 292–3. Subsequent references are in parentheses.

35 Pinter, Harold, *The Homecoming*, in *Plays Three*. London, Faber and Faber: 1997, pp. 38–9.

36 Quigley, Austin, *The Pinter Problem*. Princeton and London: Princeton University Press, 1975, p. 227.

37 Foucault, Michel, *The Birth of Biopolitics: Lectures at the Collège de France 1978–1979*, trans. Graham Burchell, (ed.) Michael Senellart, (gen. eds) François Ewald and Alessandro Fontana, (series ed.) Arnold J. Davidson. Basingstoke and New York: Palgrave Macmillan, 2008, p. 35.

38 Couldry, Nick, *Why Voice Matters*, p. 86.

39 Batty, Mark, *About Pinter: The Playwright and the Work*. London: Faber and Faber, 2005, p. 75.

40 Massumi, Brian, *Parables for the Virtual: Movement, Affect, Sensation*. Durham and London: Duke University Press, 2002, p. 40.

41 Colebrook, Claire, 'Introduction', in Adrian Parr (ed.), *The Deleuze Dictionary*, Edinburgh: Edinburgh University Press, 2005, p. 4.

42 Peck, Jamie, *Constructions of Neoliberal Reason*, p. 33.

43 Ibid., pp. 33–4.

44 Couldry, Nick, *Why Voice Matters*, p. 14.

BIBLIOGRAPHY

Primary Sources

Pinter, Harold, *Collected Screenplays 1*. London: Faber and Faber, 2000.

—*Collected Screenplays 2*. London: Faber and Faber, 2000.

—*Collected Screenplays 3*. London: Faber and Faber, 2000.

—*The Dwarfs*. London: Faber and Faber, 1990.

—'Letters from Harold Pinter to Henry Miller', in Francis Gillen and Steven H. Gale (eds), *The Pinter Review, Collected Essays 2003 and 2004*, Tampa: University of Tampa Press, 2004, pp. 1–4.

—*Party Time – A Screenplay*, London: Faber and Faber, 1991.

—*Plays One*. London: Faber and Faber, 1991.

—*Plays Two*. London: Faber and Faber, 1996.

—*Plays Three*. London: Faber and Faber, 1997

—*Plays Four*. London: Faber and Faber, 2011.

—*Press Conference*. London: Faber and Faber, 2002.

—*Various Voices: Sixty Years of Prose, Poetry, Politics 1948–2008*, third edition. London: Faber and Faber, 2009.

Interviews with Harold Pinter

Bosworth, Patricia. 'Why Doesn't He Write More', *New York Times*, 27 October 1968, sec. V, p. 3.

Gussow, Mel, *Conversations with Harold Pinter*. London: Nick Hern Books, 1994.

Pinter, Harold, interview with Barry Davis, 'The 22 From Hackney to Chelsea: A Conversation with Harold Pinter', *Jewish Quarterly*, No. 144, Winter 1991/92, pp. 9–17.

—interview with Brian Glanville, 'I am a Jew who Writes', *Jewish Chronicle*, 11 March 1960, p. 8.

—interview with Brian Johnston, 'A View from the Boundary', *Test Match Special*, BBC Radio 4, broadcast 25 August 1990.

—interview with John Sherwood, *The Rising Generation, No. 7. A Playwright – Harold Pinter*, BBC European Service, 3 March 1960.

—interview with Harry Burton, *Working With Pinter*, DVD, London: Illuminations, 2010.

—interview with Mark Batty, in *About Pinter: The Playwright and the Work*. London: Faber and Faber, 2005, pp. 79–92.

—interview with Mark Lawson, *Front Row*, BBC Radio 4, 28 February 2005.

—interview with Mel Gussow, 'Pinter on Pinter: The Lincoln Center Interview', in

Francis Gillen and Steven H. Gale (eds), *The Pinter Review: Collected Essays 2001 and 2002*, Tampa: University of Tampa Press (2002), pp. 14–37.

—interview with Nicholas Hern, 'A Play and its Politics, a Conversation between Harold Pinter and Nicholas Hern', in Harold Pinter, *One for the Road*, London: Methuen, 1985, pp. 7–23.

Releases of films of Harold Pinter's screenplays or television plays

Anderson, Michael (dir.), *The Quiller Memorandum*, Carlton, 2003 (DVD).

Apted, Michael (dir.), *Laurence Olivier Presents Harold Pinter's 'The Collection'*, Network, 2009 (DVD).

Branagh, Kenneth (dir.), *Sleuth*, Paramount Home Entertainment, 2008 (DVD).

Clayton, Jack (dir.), *The Pumpkin Eater*, Sony Pictures, 2010 (DVD).

Donner, Clive (dir.), *The Caretaker*, BFI, 2002 (DVD).

Friedkin, William (dir.), *The Birthday Party*, Fremantle, 2001 (DVD).

Hall, Peter (dir.), *The Homecoming*, Ind DVD, 2004 (DVD).

Jones, David (dir.), *Betrayal*, Universal, 1998 (VHS).

—*The Trial*, Synergy, 2002 (DVD).

Losey, Joseph (dir.), *Accident*, Warner, 2003 (DVD).

—*The Go-Between*, Optimum Releasing, 2007 (DVD).

—*The Servant*, Optimum Releasing, 2008 (DVD).

Pinter, Harold (dir.), *Simon Gray's Butley*, Ind DVD, 2004 (DVD).

Reisz, Karel (dir.), *The French Lieutenant's Woman*, Twentieth Century Fox, 2002 (DVD).

Schrader, Paul (dir.), *The Comfort of Strangers*, Twentieth Century Fox, 2004 (DVD).

Secondary Sources

Almansi, Guido and Simon Henderson, *Harold Pinter*. London and New York: Methuen, 1983.

Batty, Mark, *Harold Pinter*. Tavistock: Northcote House, 2001.

—*About Pinter: The Playwright and the Work*. London: Faber and Faber, 2005.

Beckett, Samuel, *The Complete Dramatic Works*, London: Faber and Faber, 1986.

—George Craig, Martha Dow Fehsenfeld, Dan Gunn and Lois More Overbeck (eds), *The Letters of Samuel Beckett, 1941–1956*, Cambridge: Cambridge University Press, 2011.

Bennett, Daniel, *Digital Media and Reporting Conflict: Blogging and the BBC's Coverage of War and Terrorism*. London: Routledge, 2013.

Billington, Michael, *Harold Pinter*, second edition. London: Faber and Faber, 2007.

Bourne, Stephen, *Black in the British Frame: The Black Experience in British Film and Television*. London: Continuum, 2001.

Bull, John, *New British Political Dramatists: Howard Brenton, David Hare, Trevor Griffiths and David Edgar*. Pennsylvania: Macmillan, 1984.

Burkman, Katherine, *The Dramatic World of Harold Pinter: Its Basis in Ritual*. Columbus: Ohio State University Press, 1971.

Brown, Wendy, *Edgework: Critical Essays on Knowledge and Politics*. Princeton and Oxford: Princeton University Press, 2005.

Colebrook, Claire, 'Introduction', in Adrian Parr (ed.), *The Deleuze Dictionary*, Edinburgh: Edinburgh University Press, 2005, pp. 1–6.

Couldry, Nick, *Why Voice Matters: Culture and Politics after Neoliberalism*. London: Sage, 2010.

Curtis, Nick, 'The Madness of Patrick Marber', *London Evening Standard*, 7 November 2000, p. 23.

Deleuze, Gilles, *The Logic of Sense*, trans. Mark Lester with Charles Stivale, (ed.) Constantin V. Boundas, third edition. London and New York: Continuum, 2004.

Dorfman, Ariel, 'The World That Harold Pinter Unlocked', *Washington Post*, 27 December 2008, p. 15.

Esslin, Martin, *Pinter the Playwright*. London: Methuen, 1982.

—*The Theatre of the Absurd*. London: Penguin, 1991.

Eyre, Richard (ed.), *A Celebration: Harold Pinter*. London: Faber and Faber, 2000.

—'A Fair Cricketer, a Good Actor and a Playwright of Rare Power and Originality', *The Observer*, 28 December 2008, http://www.theguardian.com/culture/2008/dec/28/harold-pinter-theatre (accessed 19 September 2013).

Fairclough, Norman, *New Labour, New Language?* London: Routledge, 2000.

Foucault, Michel, *The Archaeology of Knowledge*, trans. A. M. Sheridan Smith, second edition. London and New York: Routledge, 2002.

—*The Birth of Biopolitics: Lectures at the Collège de France 1978–1979*, trans. Graham Burchell, (ed.) Michael Senellart, (gen. eds) François Ewald and Alessandro Fontana, (series ed.) Arnold J. Davidson. Basingstoke; New York: Palgrave Macmillan, 2008.

—'The Order of Discourse', in Robert Young (ed.), *Untying the Text: A Post-structuralist Reader*. London and New York: Routledge, 1981, pp. 52–64.

Fraser, Antonia, *Must You Go? My Life with Harold Pinter*. London: Phoenix, 2011.

Gale, Steven H. (ed.), *The Films of Harold Pinter*. New York: Albany, 2001.

Gale, Steven H., *Sharp Cut: Harold Pinter's Screenplays and the Artistic Process*. Lexington: University of Kentucky Press, 2003.

Giroux, Henry A. *Against the Terror of Neoliberalism: Politics beyond the Age of Greed*. Boulder, CO and London: Paradigm, 2008.

Gordon, Lois, *Stratagems to Uncover Nakedness: The Dramas of Harold Pinter*. Columbia: University of Missouri Press, 1969.

Gordon, Robert, *Harold Pinter*. Ann Arbor: University of Michigan Press, 2012.

—'Pinter's Mise-en-Scène: *Party Time* as Television Drama', in Francis Gillen, with Steven H. Gale (eds), *The Pinter Review, Nobel Prize/European Theatre Prize Volume: 2005-2008*, Tampa: University of Tampa Press, 2008, pp. 168–79.

Grimes, Charles, *Harold Pinter's Politics: A Silence beyond Echo*. Madison, WIS and Teaneck, NJ: Fairleigh Dickinson University Press, 2005.

Hare, David, 'In Pinter You Find Expressed the Great Struggle of the 20th Century', *The Guardian*, 14 October 2005, G2, p. 8.

Bibliography

Harwood, Ronald, *Sir Donald Wolfit: His Life and Work in the Unfashionable Theatre*. New York: St Martin's Press, 1971.

Hall, Stuart, 'New Labour Has Picked Up where Thatcherism Left Off', *The Guardian*, 6 August 2003, http://www.guardian.co.uk/politics/2003/aug/06/society.labour (accessed 20 July 2013).

Harvey, David, *A Brief History of Neoliberalism*. Oxford and New York: Oxford University Press, 2005.

Horkheimer, Max, *Critique of Instrumental Reason: Lectures and Essays since the End of World War II*. New York: Seabury Press, 1974.

Hudgins, Christopher C., 'Harold Pinter's *The Handmaid's Tale*: Freedom, Prison, and A Hijacked Script', in Thomas Fahy and Kimball King (eds), *Captive Audience: Prison and Captivity in Contemporary Theatre*. New York and London: Routledge, 2003, pp. 81–108.

Joyce, James, *Exiles*. London: Four Square, 1962.

Kane, Leslie (ed.), *David Mamet in Conversation*. Michigan: University of Michigan Press, 2001.

Klein, Naomi, *The Shock Doctrine: The Rise of Disaster Capitalism*. Toronto: Vintage, 2008.

Knowles, Ronald, 'Joyce and Pinter: Exiles and Betrayal', *Barcelona English Language and Literature Studies*, No. 9 (1998), pp. 183–91.

—*Understanding Harold Pinter*. Columbia: University of South Carolina, 1995.

Lahr, John, *Demolition Man: Harold Pinter*, December 2007, http://www.johnlahr.com/pinter.html (accessed 28 July 2013).

Lemke, Thomas, *Biopolitics: An Advanced Introduction*. New York: New York University Press, 2001.

—'"The Birth of Bio-Politics": Michel Foucault's Lecture at the Collège de France on Neo-liberal Governmentality', *Economy and Society*, Vol. 30, No. 2 (2001), pp. 190–207.

—'Foucault, Governmentality, and Critique', *Rethinking Marxism*, Vol. 14, No. 3 (2002), pp. 1–17.

Luckhurst, Mary, 'Torture in the Plays of Harold Pinter', in Mary Luckhurst (ed.), *Blackwell Companion to Modern British and Irish Drama 1880–2005*, Malden, MA: Blackwell, 2006, pp. 358–70.

Massumi, Brian, *Parables for the Virtual: Movement, Affect, Sensation*. Durham and London: Duke University Press, 2002.

Merritt, Susan Hollis, *Pinter in Play: Critical Strategies and the Plays of Harold Pinter*. Durham and London: Duke University Press, 1995.

—'Talking About Pinter', in Francis Gillen and Steven H. Gale, (eds), *The Pinter Review: Collected Essays 2001 and 2002*, Tampa: University of Tampa Press (2002), pp. 144–67.

Page, Malcolm, *File on Pinter*. London: Methuen Drama, 1993.

Pattie, David, 'Feeding Power: Pinter, Bakhtin and Inverted Carnival', in Mary Brewer (ed.), *Harold Pinter's 'The Dumb Waiter'*, Amsterdam and New York: Rodopi, 2009, pp. 55–69.

Peacock, D. Keith, *Harold Pinter and the New British Theatre*. London: Greenwood, 1997.

Peck, Jamie, *Constructions of Neoliberal Reason*. Oxford: Oxford University Press, 2012.

Pinter, Harold, 'Butley', The American Film Theatre/Cinebill, January 1974, p. 33.

Quigley, Austin E., 'Pinter, Politics and Postmodernism (Pt. 1)', in Peter Raby (ed.), *The Cambridge Companion to Harold Pinter*, second edition. Cambridge: Cambridge University Press, 2009, pp. 7–26.

—*The Pinter Problem*. Princeton and London: Princeton University Press, 1975.

Raby, Peter (ed.), *The Cambridge Companion to Harold Pinter*, second edition. Cambridge: Cambridge University Press, 2009.

Rebellato, Dan, *1956 and All That: The Making of Modern Drama*. London; New York: Routledge, 1999.

Roberts, Philip, *The Royal Court Theatre and the Modern Stage*. Cambridge: Cambridge University Press, 1999.

Sakellaridou, Elizabeth, *Pinter's Female Portraits: A Study of Female Characters in the Plays of Harold Pinter*. London: Macmillan, 1988.

Sierz, Aleks, *In-Yer-Face Theatre: British Drama Today*. London: Faber and Faber, 2001.

Silverstein, Marc, *The Language of Cultural Power*. Lewisburg, London and Cranbury, NJ: Associated University Presses, 1993.

Smith, Ian, *Pinter in the Theatre*, London: Nick Hern Books, 2005.

Sontag, Susan, *Regarding the Pain of Others*. London: Hamish Hamilton, 2003.

Taylor-Batty, Mark, 'Joyce's Bridge to Late Twentieth-Century British Theater: Harold Pinter's Dialogue with Exiles', in Richard Brown (ed.), *A Companion to James Joyce*, London: Blackwell, 2008, pp. 300–17.

—and Linda Renton, 'Report from Britain', in Francis Gillen (ed.), *Pinter Review: Nobel Prize/Europe Theatre Prize Volume*, Tampa: University of Florida Press (2008), pp. 223–35.

—'What Remains? Ashes to Ashes, Popular Culture, Memory and Atrocity', in Craig Owens (ed.), *Pinter etc.*, Newcastle: Cambridge Scholars Publishing, 2009, pp. 99–116.

Trussler, Simon, *The Plays of Harold Pinter*, London: Victor Gollancz, 1973.

Wardle, Irving, 'Comedy of Menace', in Charles Marowitz, Tom Milne and Owen Hale (eds), *The Encore Reader: A Chronicle of the New Drama*, London: Methuen, 1965, pp. 86–91.

Watt, Stephen, 'Things, Voices, Events: Harold Pinter's *Mountain Language* as Testamental Text', *Modern Drama*, Vol. 52, No. 1 (2009), pp. 38–56.

Woolf, Henry, interview with Harry Burton, *Working With Pinter*, DVD, London: Illuminations, 2010.

Wylie, Andrew, *Sex on Stage: Gender and Sexuality in Post-War British Theatre*. Bristol: Intellect, 2009.

Zarhy-Levo, Yael, *The Theatrical Critic as Cultural Agent: Constructing Pinter, Orton and Stoppard as Absurdist Playwrights*. Oxford and New York: Peter Lang, 2001.

NOTES ON CONTRIBUTORS

Harry Burton is an actor and director. His professional association with Harold Pinter began in 1991 when he acted in a double bill of *Mountain Language* and *Party Time* at The Almeida Theatre, directed by the author. He appeared in the feature film of Pinter's screenplay of Franz Kafka's *The Trial*, played Jerry in *Betrayal*, acted alongside Pinter (as father and son) in BBC Radio's production of Pinter's *Moonlight*, and played in BBC Radio 3's *Voices*, commissioned for Pinter's 75th birthday. He leads Pinter workshops and classes around the world. His directing credits include Harold Pinter's *The Lover* (Bridewell, 2006) and *The Dumb Waiter* (Trafalgar Studios, 2007). He has directed two films, both for Channel Four: the documentary *Working With Pinter* (2007) and *Thinspiration* (2008) starring Karen Gillan.

Basil Chiasson is Assistant Professor at Grenfell Campus, Memorial University of Newfoundland, Canada. He writes on twentieth and twenty-first-century drama, and particularly on post-war British theatre. He is foremost interested in the relationships and possible intersections between aesthetics and politics as expressed in writing for the theatre. Currently, he is working on a project which traces changes in dramatic and performance aesthetics in Britain since the 1980s and their connection to the ascendancy of 'neoliberal' rationalities in that nation.

Ann C. Hall has published widely on drama, theatre, performance, and women's studies. Her books include *Phantom Variations: The Adaptations of Gaston Leroux's Phantom of the Opera, 1925 to Present* (McFarland, 2009); *Mommy Angst: Motherhood in American Popular Culture* (Praeger, 2009); *Delights, Dilemmas, and Desires: Essays on*

Women and the Media (Greenwood, 1998) and *Making the Stage: Essays on the Changing concept of Theater, Drama, and Performance* (Cambridge Scholars, 2008). She also has written a number of plays, short stories, and monologues. She has served as president of the Midwest Modern Language Association, and is president of the Harold Pinter Society. She is writing a book about Ronald Harwood and a collection of short stories.

Chris Megson is Senior Lecturer in Drama and Theatre at Royal Holloway, University of London. He has taught and published widely in the field of modern drama, and is editor of *The Methuen Drama Book of Naturalist Plays* (Methuen Drama, 2010). Other works include: *Get Real: Documentary Theatre Past and Present* (with Alison Forsyth; Palgrave MacMillan, 2009) and *Decades of Modern British Playwriting: the 1970s – Voices, Documents, New Interpretations* (Methuen Drama, 2012).

INDEX